Legend

D0174477

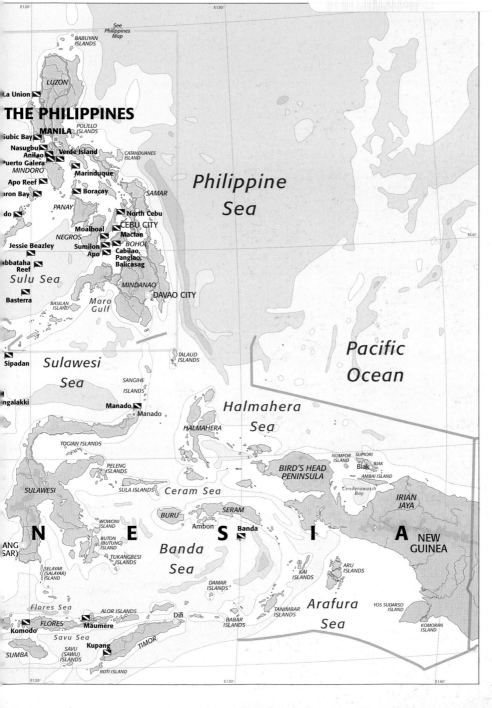

See Philippines Map

BABUYAN ISLANDS

LUZON

La Union ◩

THE PHILIPPINES

POLILLO ISLANDS

Subic Bay ◩ **MANILA**

Nasugbu ◩
Anilao ◩ **Verde Island** ◩   CATANDUANES ISLAND
MINDORO
Puerto Galera ◩

Apo Reef ◩   **Marinduque**

Coron Bay ◩   **Boracay** ◩   SAMAR

PANAY

do ◩   **North Cebu** ◩
              CEBU CITY
Moalboal ◩   **Mactan**
NEGROS   BOHOL
Jessie Beazley ◩ Sumilon ◩ Cabilao,
               Apo ◩ Panglao,
Tubbataha ◩   Balicasag

Sulu Sea   MINDANAO

Basterra ◩   BASILAN Moro □ DAVAO CITY
               ISLAND Gulf

Sipadan ◩   Sulawesi   TALAUD
               Sea   ISLANDS

ngalakki ◩   SANGIHE
                 ISLANDS

       Manado ◉ Manado

                 Halmahera
          HALMAHERA   Sea

TOGIAN ISLANDS

                    NUMFOR SUPIORI
                    ISLAND
PELENG   Biak BIAK
ISLANDS   BIRD'S HEAD AMBAI ISLAND
          PENINSULA
SULAWESI SULA ISLANDS Ceram Sea   Cenderawasih
                        Bay
           BURU   SERAM   IRIAN
N   WOWONI Ambon ◩ Banda ◩   **E** **S** **I** JAYA **A**
           ISLAND   NEW
ANG   BUTON   GUINEA
(SAR)   (BUTUNG) Banda
         ISLAND
       TUKANGBESI
SELAYAR ISLANDS   Sea   ARU
(SALAYAR)   KAI   ISLANDS
ISLAND   DAMAR   ISLANDS
           ISLANDS   YOS SUDARSO
Flores Sea   ISLAND
     ALOR ISLANDS Difi Arafura   KOMORAN
FLORES ◩ Maumere ◩   BABAR Sea   ISLAND
Komodo ◩   TANIMBAR ISLANDS
   Savu Sea Kupang ◩ ISLANDS
SUMBA   SAVU   TIMOR
       (SAWU)
       ISLANDS
       ROTI ISLAND

Philippine Sea

Pacific Ocean

Diving
Southeast Asia

A Guide to the
Best Dive Sites
in Indonesia,
Malaysia,
the Philippines
and Thailand

Text by Kal Muller,
Fiona Nichols,
Heneage Mitchell and
John Williams

Edited by Fiona Nichols
and Michael Stachels

PERIPLUS

Published by Periplus Editions (HK) Ltd.

Copyright © 1999 Periplus Editions (HK) Ltd.
ALL RIGHTS RESERVED

ISBN 962-593-312-3
Printed in Singapore

Publisher: Eric Oey
Editors: Fiona Nichols, Michael Stachels
Production: Mary Chia
Cartography: David Pickell, Violet Wong
Design: William Atyeo

Distributors

Asia-Pacific   Berkeley Books Pte. Ltd.
                      5 Little Road, #08-01
                      Singapore 536983
                      Tel: (65) 280-3320
                      Fax: (65) 280-6290

Indonesia   PT Wira Mandala Pustaka
                      (Java Books—Indonesia)
                      Jl. Kelapa Gading Kirana
                      Blok A-14 No. 17, Jakarta 14240
                      Tel: (62-21) 451-5351
                      Fax: (62-21) 453-4987

Japan   Tuttle Shokai Ltd.
                      1-21-13, Seki
                      Tama-ku, Kawasaki-shi
                      Kanagawa-ken 214-0022
                      Tel: (044) 833-0225
                      Fax: (044) 822-0413

United States   Tuttle Publishing
                      Distribution Center
                      Airport Industrial Park
                      364 Innovation Drive
                      North Clarendon, VT 05759-9436
                      Tel: (802) 773-8930, (800) 526-2778

Cover The green sea turtle *(Chelonia mydas)*, which can weigh up to 200 kilos, is commonly encountered by divers in Southeast Asia. Photo by Mark Strickland.

Pages 4–5 Protected inner reef flats, like this one off Madang, Papua New Guinea, provide the ideal environment for communities of finely branching acroporid corals. Photo by Roger Steene.

Frontispiece The profusion of soft corals and gorgonians make Southeast Asian sites like this one, in Thailand's Similan Islands, such favorites with divers. Photo by Mark Strickland.

Contents

Photo by Mark Strickland

DIVING SOUTHEAST ASIA

The Philippines

See page 96

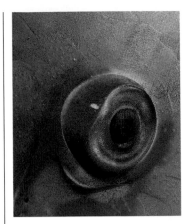

See page 171

Thailand

Practicalities

Appendix

Contributors

Gerald R. Allen is one of the leading ichthyologists working today on Indo-Pacific reef fishes. He is the author of dozens of books, including Periplus Editions' *Marine Life*. He received his PhD from the University of Hawaii in 1971, and has been with the Western Australian Museum since 1974.

Charles Anderson is British-born marine biologist who has been working in the Maldives since 1983. He authored a series of guidebooks to the marine life of the Maldives, and contributed to Periplus Editions' *Diving Indonesia*.

Michael Aw is a Singaporean photojournalist based in Sydney. He manages the environmental group Ocean Discoverers.

Gary Bell is an underwater photographer based in New South Wales. With his wife Meri he runs the photo agency Ocean Wide Images, specializing in marine natural history photography. His work has been published worldwide, and he has received many awards including, for three years running, the Australasian Underwater Photography prize.

Ashley Boyd is an underwater photographer based in Thailand. He has co-authored a number of publications on diving in Thailand. With thousands of dives under his weight belt, Boyd has built up an impressive body of photographic work. He continues to dive frequently, and now teaches underwater photography.

Clay Bryce has spent thousands of hours below water, photographing the marine life of the Indo-Pacific. He has co-authored five books, including *Sea Slugs of Western Australia,* and his photography and writing have appeared in magazines such as *Aqua Geographica* and *Ocean Realm*.

Lynn Funkhouser is a Chicago-based photographer, author, and environmentalist. In 1994 she received the Seaspace/PADI Environmental Awareness Award for actively promoting reef preservation.

Jack Jackson is a British underwater photographer who has photographed underwater from the Red Sea to the Philippines. Jackson managed a dive operation in the Red Sea for more than 12 years, and his photography has been published in a number of international publications. His work has also been featured in several well-reviewed exhibitions in Britain.

Ingo Jezierski is a Singapore-based travel photographer. He contributed to the photo editing of this book.

Burt Jones and **Maurine Shimlock** are a Texas-based underwater photographic team who have worked extensively in Indonesia, Malaysia, and the Philippines. They run the photo agency Secret Sea Visions, and their work regularly appears in *Ocean Realm* and other magazines, as well as the monograph *Secret Sea*.

Heneage Mitchell is a British writer and editor now based in the Philippines. Mitchell first visited the Philippines in 1980 while on leave from his job as a hydrographic surveyor. When he discovered how good the diving was, he quit his job, began exploring the islands in earnest, and in 1983 set up a dive center in San Fernando, La Union. He is now a publisher as well, and his Samon Publishing Inc. produces *Philippine Diver* magazine.

Kal Muller is a photographer and writer who for the last two decades has specialized in Indonesia. He is the author of at least a dozen books, including the Periplus guides to the eastern Indonesian provinces and the ground-breaking *Diving Indonesia*. His photography and writing appear regularly in travel and dive publications.

Fiona Nichols is a freelance editor, writer, and photographer who was based in Southeast Asia for a decade, regularly diving these waters. Her published works include two travel guides (one on Phuket, Thailand), photo features for travel and lifestyle magazines, and contributions to a number of guidebooks. She now works as a freelance writer in Europe.

Mike Severns is a Hawai'i-based photographer whose work has appeared in *Natural History, Islands, Aqua,* and many other magazines. Two monographs of his work have been published: the acclaimed *Sulawesi Seas,* distributed by Periplus, and *Molokini,* both co-authored by Pauline Fiene-Severns, a biologist specializing in opisthobranchs.

Michael Stachels is an editor who has been stationed in Singapore for ten years.

Roger Steene is an Australia-based underwater photographer who is one of the pioneers of the field. He regularly teams with Gerald Allen, and his work has appeared in dozens of books, including several large-format monographs.

Mark Strickland is an American underwater photographer who now lives and works in Phuket, Thailand. Stickland, who is also a divemaster, has written and photographed for a number of books and magazines worldwide.

Takamasa Tonozuka is a Tokyo-born underwater photographer now based in Bali. He has been diving since age 18, and has worked as a dive instructor. Tonozuka has traveled extensively through Indonesia, and is the owner of the dive operation Dive & Dive's on Bali. His photography has appeared in magazines and books in Japan, Hong Kong, and Singapore.

John Williams is a California-born writer and dive instructor now based in Thailand. He has been diving for two decades. Williams spent four years traveling and diving in the Bahamas, Mexico, Fiji, Hawaii, New Zealand and Australia before settling on Phuket in 1987. He now runs the diving operation Siam Dive n' Sail on Kata Beach.

Additional acknowledgements

The authors and editors would also like to thank the following people who provided invaluable assistance and information during the research and production of this book:

Ron Holland and **Graham** and **Donna Taylor** of Borneo Divers.

Dr. Hanny and **Inneka Batuna** of Manado Murex Resort.

Anton Saksono of Pulau Putri Resort.

Michael Lee, recreation manager of Berjaya Beach Resort.

Henrik Nimb, PADI course director and director of Master Divers, Singapore.

Diving Southeast Asia

A Bounty of Reefs, Wrecks, and Coral Gardens

Access

Visibility

Current

Coral

Reef type

Fish

Highlights

In subsequent chapters, the above symbols will provide at-a-glance information about dive locations.

Whatever extraordinary notion possesses us, that first time, to strap on our backs a metal tank full of compressed air, fit fins to our feet, stuff an uncomfortable contraption in the mouth and a tight-fitting piece of glass across our eyes? Uncomfortable and inept, struggling and sweating, we lurch in our new uniform, wondering whether the effort is worthwhile. But our gracelessness soon vanishes as we tumble below the surface and move weightless through the water, drift with currents and have the chance to observe, often at close quarters, creatures large and small that we would never otherwise have imagined. It is quite simply a magic world and one which invariably seduces the novice diver. He is hooked on scuba diving.

Ten years ago, while snorkeling from a dive boat in the gin-clear waters of the Similan Islands, a divemaster friend suggested I don a tank and reg, and drop below the water to see what diving was all about. With little more comment, he told me to stick by his side, ascend slowly and remember to breathe out. Within minutes of descending, I was amidst a school of sweetlips, then visited by Moorish idols, and was enthralled by the pink soft corals sprouting from the reef like some exotic cotton wool. For some, that might have been enough, but when I caught sight of a blacktip shark (shark!), admittedly at the edge of the 20-meter visibility, I, too, was hooked. Within two months I had crawled the length of a public swimming pool where second-hand Band

Aids were the only novelty to spot, had learned to control buoyancy somewhere under the diving board and was rewarded with a PADI open water certificate. Armed with this little plastic card, the real diving experience was about to begin.

For many a novice diver, education takes place after work in public swimming pools in the cold northern latitudes. Dive tables seem like just another bit of school maths and the idea of search and rescue, in a swimming pool, appears totally absurd. The promise of warm water and subtropical species is a lure but rarely a reality.

In Asia, one of the most species-rich areas in the world, diving is a whole different ball game. Water that hovers around the 25°C mark, a tropical climate that is tempered by sea breezes, more species than most books cover, and a wealth of different marine environments—not to mention idyllic sandy shores for surface interval picnics—make diving a special pleasure. Imagine learning in this particular environment!

Pioneer Divers

The sport has evolved quite radically in the last 20 years and this has something to do with both the Vietnam War and the oil industry. The former brought Americans who were used to recreational diving in the New World and who sought to enjoy their hobby when on R&R, notably in Pattaya, while the latter brought expatriates from

Opposite: Giant barrel sponge *(Xestospongia testudinaria)*; Togian Islands, North Sulawesi. *Photo by Gary Bell.*

the United States, Europe and Australia to work in the fast developing oil business. Amid the personnel who came to work in the industry—in Thailand, Indonesia and Malaysia—there were plenty of professional divers and, often benefitting from periods of long leave and a fat salary, many of these people explored the region diving recreationally.

Today, you'll come across dozens of divemasters whose first experience of diving in Asia was at the bottom of the Gulf of Thailand, off platforms in the South China Sea, or from some deserted island in Indonesia. Working at depths that were measured more often in fathoms than feet, diving was not always a pleasure. But armed with the skills to withstand the most taxing conditions, recreational diving in more shallow waters, on reefs that were in pristine condition, was

a real pleasure even if the infrastructure for diving was largely missing. These pioneers of sports diving lugged their tanks from far-flung compressors, bartered with local fishermen and *bêche-de-mer* and pearl divers for a boat ride, and picked the brains of local mariners for reefs and shoals in a bid to find good diving. The rest was easy; life on shore in Southeast Asia was (and still is to some extent) inexpensive and they had no need of fancy hotels. Nipa thatched huts and simple meals in the local cafes were good enough.

But what about their buddies who were envious of their travels and fun? In the early seventies there were precious few places to learn to dive in Asia (Pattaya was one of them), and it was not until the last few years of the decade, with easier air travel and greater awareness of the sport, that the bulk of dive shops and operators began to open their doors to novices.

It was then that a number of saturated professional divers took a look at the area they had grown to love and decided to turn their skills to teaching recreational diving. All it took was a little capital and some formal qualification from one of the professional dive associations.

Growing Professionalism

The debate as to which of the professional dive associations is the best, is one which continues without respite. Despite the conflict of opinion, it is PADI which has the greatest foothold in Asia and is constantly upgrading its services and instruction. You'll find that the majority of dive operators are PADI qualified and adhere to the standards set out by this American association. NAUI instructors also work in Southeast Asia, and so do BSAC, CMAS (and the local Indonesian equivalent, POSSI) dive instructors.

Today there are a dozen or so PADI 5-star operations in Southeast

Below: Striped triplefin (*Helcogramma striata*) resting on ball tunicates and soft corals. Tulamben, Bali. *Photo by Gary Bell.*

Asia, and more waiting for certification. But there are also too many fly-by-night operations run by locals who employ a dive instructor for a season and advertise themselves as professionals. It is advisable to check out the qualifications and facilities of the dive operator before parting with money! Borrowed boats may be okay, but borrowed BCs and regs are definitely to be avoided.

In the popular resorts of Southeast Asia, dive operators lure prospective divers with very inexpensive introductory and resort courses. These are fine, up to a point, but they really only qualify you to dive that resort. There is a lot more to diving than a resort course.

Furthering your dive education in Asia is, however, also an interesting option. Learning in a tropical environment is fun but perhaps a second, and deciding factor is the relatively inexpensive cost of upgrading skills. The major training centers in Pattaya, Phuket, Samui, Hong Kong, Singapore, Kuala Lumpur, Manila, Anilao and Jakarta offer courses right up to instructor level at prices that compare very

favorably to courses in the Caribbean or Australia. Most popular courses are the Advanced Open Water and specialty courses— Wreck Diving, Photography, Night Diving, Navigation and Search and Rescue—which can be put to good use on a diving holiday. Indeed, a course need not interfere at all with a dive trip but can enhance it.

Eco-sensitivity

Another improvement in the dive scene over the last two decades is the growing awareness of environmental concerns which touch not only the requirements of recreational divers but the lives of locals and the flora and fauna. Finally, deforestation, discharge of sewage, oil and refuse in the sea, destructive fishing methods, as well as coral and shell collection, have all come under the environmental spotlight in Asia.

While lifestyles have not radically changed, some of the destructive practices have been curtailed and local governments have begun to set up marine reserves to encourage the regeneration of the marine

Above: Gorgonian fan (*Melithaea*) in the waters around Sumbawa, Indonesia. *Photo by Takamasa Tonozuka.*

environment. Of course, mangrove swamps that have been suffocated by silt do not recover overnight, nor do coral reefs that have been blasted by dynamite or repeatedly broken up by anchors and fins. But recover they do, albeit more slowly than from the blanket damage inflicted by natural disasters, and the results are encouraging. The marine environment rarely returns to what it was before damage, but it does recover and proliferate.

Where to Dive

So where do divers head for, and what can they expect to find in Southeast Asia?

Most diving has been centered on the Gulf of Thailand and from Phuket, in the Philippines from Batangas and the Visayas, in Malaysia from the East Coast and Sabah, and in Indonesia from Bali, Manado, and Flores.

Thailand In the search for pristine locations and big pelagics, Phuket - based operators have pushed out into the Andaman Sea as far as the Andaman Islands themselves, which are in Indian waters, and to the Burma Banks, which are in international waters. They have also forged southward, toward the Malaysian border, where they have discovered, like their pioneering colleagues from Pattaya, untouched coral reefs and forgotten wrecks.

Philippines The diving fraternity in the Philippines has benefited from a burgeoning infrastructure in the smaller island destinations, and a proliferation of live-aboard boats which explore the Sulu Sea. The retreat of the United States military has opened once off-limits areas to the public.

Malaysia In Malaysia, the development of an infrastructure on a number of East Coast islands has made it easy for dive enthusiasts to enjoy some of the best coral reefs, while the country's premier dive spot in the deep waters off Sabah has developed into a real dive destination. Off Sabah too, the oceanic reef, Layang-Layang, has developed into a world-class destination for dive enthusiasts.

Indonesia A country with far-flung islands, Indonesia has developed resorts in tandem with the establishment of regular air connections, and in many of these diving and snorkeling are given priority. Outside flights to Manado have further opened up this fine dive site, and Live-aboard boats have also made their debut, offering divers the chance to explore really remote areas like the Banda Sea.

Dive Topography

Most Southeast Asian reefs are fringing reefs, and most diving will be along the outer reef edge, often quite close to shore. The profile is sometimes gently sloping, and sometimes full of bommies and coral heads. But the region is perhaps most famous for its steep dropoffs, particularly in Indonesia and the Philippines. The wall at Bunaken near Manado is world-famous, and Menjangan, Komodo, Kupang, the Bandas, and Sangalaki also feature steep dropoffs.

The Philippines offers plenty of good walls—at Verde, Anilao, Nasugbu, Apo as well as a dozen more places. Malaysia offers fabulous walls at Sipadan and Layang-Layang, and even tiny Tenggol off peninsular Malaysia offers a good one.

And while not particularly widespread, Southeast Asia also has its fair share of wrecks. There are numerous war graves and vessels lost during World War II off Pattaya in Thailand, in the bay at Coron in the Philippines, and there are easily dived wrecks off Manado and Bali in Indonesia. Then there are fishing vessels that met an untimely end and even the odd dive boat or two.

In some places, artificial wrecks (tires, old buses and broken boats) have been sunk to encourage regeneration of reefs and their associated fauna. Singapore has done this outside its harbor waters; the Philippines and Thailand too have adopted this method.

You'll find that diving in Southeast Asia is generally on the continental shelf, but oceanic diving is possible too. This inevitably entails a trip on a live-aboard.

sophisticated but less costly, dive courses are becoming more competitively priced and the cost of diving itself is getting more expensive—mainly because today's diver is a more sophisticated animal and not the hardy aficionado of yesteryear. In the Practicalities section at the end of this book you will be able to see how the cost of diving compares through the region.

But best of all, there are still

Below: Juvenile round-faced batfish (*Platax orbicularis*). *Photo by Lynn Funkhouser.*

Live-aboard Diving

Live-aboard dive boats have made a big impact on the scope and range of diving. In Indonesia, live-aboard operations take divers to the Banda Sea, the islands north of Manado, and Komodo and other islands in the Nusa Tenggara provinces. Yacht chartering is becoming popular in Bali with holidaymakers who also enjoy diving. In the Philippines the fabulous reefs at Apo and those of Tubbha-taha, Jessie Beazley and Basterra are only accessible by live-aboards while other live-aboards and chartered yachts ply the small islands of the Visayas and Palawan. So do yachts and dive vessels in Sabah, Malaysia, that offer diving in remote offshore areas, while yachts and small motor boats (often converted fishing vessels) offer diving trips in Malaysian and the northern Indonesian waters from Singapore. Phuket too, has developed this industry, building new marinas to accommodate charter yachts and dive vessels. And, if you want to, you can dive on the Burma Banks from Thailand, discover the reefs off the southeast coast by the Cambodian border in the Gulf of Thailand, or head for the absolutely virgin territory in the Andaman Sea. Well-equipped live-aboards are the only answer to reaching these remote areas.

When diving first started in the region, it was a cheap hobby once you had bought a regulator and basic gear. Today, the relationship between learning to dive, buying the gear and getting going has changed. The gear is getting more

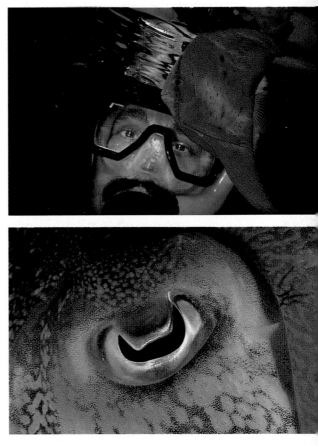

many areas in Asia to be charted, let alone developed as dive destinations. Areas that have, up to now, discouraged tourism and development, places that were off limits for political or commercial reasons and spots where transport was almost non-existent. But it is only a matter of time before these virgin areas open up their world to the enthusiastic scuba diver.

— *Fiona Nichols*

Above: The eye of the cuttlefish (*Sepia latimanus*), is functially very advanced for a mollusk. *Photo by Mark Strickland.*

Diving in Indonesia

A Vast and Largely Unexplored Archipelago for Divers

An archipelago of over 17,000 islands, stretching more than 5,000 km from west to east, with a coastline of more than 80,000 km, washed by tropical waters, Indonesia has the potential for fabulous diving. Indeed, the world's fourth largest country contains 10–20 percent of the world's coral reefs.

Indonesia is the least known of the world's best dive locations, but things are changing fairly fast. The introduction of scuba gear and the beginnings of dive operations in the country go back 15 years or so now, and each year more new, exciting locations are opening their doors.

It will be many years before diving in Indonesia reaches its full potential because it has both great advantages and serious drawbacks. The advantages of diving the clear, rich waters of an uncrowded site or, better still, the virgin waters of an unexplored corner of the archipelago, need hardly be mentioned. Ask anyone who has dived in Indonesia. But the country's advantage is also its drawback—distances and remoteness conspire against all but the most adventurous or well-heeled diver. For those whose pockets are deep, a number of charter vessels and dive boats operate in the more remote areas of the country, offering keen divers a chance to really sample some of the most exciting diving in the world.

Interestingly, the country's most popular tourist destination—Bali—also has some excellent diving, including a superb wreck, and is the area of the country where the standard and number of dive operations is the highest. But good diving is not exactly located in your hotel lobby! You have to be prepared to travel an hour or so away from the urban areas to really experience some of the best the island has to offer.

Fishing with Fire

An island nation, many Indonesians rely on fishing as their sole income. While many of their fishing practices are traditional and inadvertently eco-sensitive, some are far from suitable for the environment. Since the turn of the century, explosives have been used to fish the seas. Fish bombing is an easy process and requires little more than a small amount of explosive powder, a beer bottle and often a papaya to sink the bomb and muffle the sound. The result is fairly disastrous for both reef and fish.

Cyanide poisoning, too, has dire effects. Used as a method of collecting aquarium fish and high-value food fish, it has the effect of killing coral where it is used. However, in areas where diving has a foothold, villagers are beginning to see the economic benefits of joining this new, lucrative industry and catering to tourists who want to see reefs with healthy, live fish, rather than destroying the source of this excellent livelihood.

In the Back of Beyond

As more and more dive operations open their doors, professionalism is certainly increasing. However,

Overleaf:
Indonesian reefs are so rich that on a single fist-sized chunk one can find soft corals, sponges, hydroids, four species of algae, and five species of tunicates. Tulamben, Bali.
Photo by Gary Bell.

Opposite:
Snorkeling on the reef flat off Bunaken Island. The common, and distinctive, blue sea stars are *Linkia laevigata*.
Photo by Mike Severns.

Above: Leather corals, like these dead man's fingers (*Sinularia*), are common on shallow, and current-exposed reefs in Southeast Asia. *Photo by Takamasa Tonozuka.*

some stumbling blocks continue to thwart divers. The country's international airline will bring divers to the country with little hassle, but things slow down rather considerably from there onwards.

But it is worth noting, that there is some excellent diving that is accessible in Indonesia with direct overseas flights. Kupang, in West Timor, has frequent flights to and from Australia. Manado is now directly connected with Singapore, making access to the offshore sites around Bunaken very simple, and Bali is linked directly to a score of international destinations.

National connections are the domain of the country's second airline, Merpati, and however much this airline has improved in the last few years, it's reliability still leaves much to be desired. The further you travel from the tourist centers, the greater the problems. The biggest problems are delayed or cancelled flights. Also, the aircraft serving some of the smaller islands are modest Twin Otters and Cessnas, and a diver may find himself stymied by 20 kilogram baggage limits.

That is not to say that everything falls foul—but just to warn travelers that things do not always run as smoothly as one would like and some margin of time should be allowed for travel to and from the more remote parts of the archipelago. Patience, tolerance and a strong sense of humor are indispensable for travel in this country.

Once at the dive destination, there will be more innovative ways of travel. You can forget flashy cruisers—journeys to and from dive sites are often on local outriggers and simple fishing boats.

Diving Operations

The caliber of dive guides is certainly improving. However, despite the fact that your guide may have dived the spot hundreds of times, don't expect quite the same service as you'd get in the Maldives or Caribbean.

What they lack in knowledge and organization, they make up for in charm. And a few have the rare combination of both, which makes a dive with such a character thoroughly memorable. Lack of professionalism is not usually a problem for well-trained and experienced divers, but beginners should take great care. It is far better to take a certification course before coming to Indonesia, although the larger operations do offer resort courses. But it is better to avoid those that are not recognized by CMAS, NAUI, PADI, SSI or one of the other large organizations.

Generally, gear available in Indonesia is fairly basic, and is not always in tip-top condition. We recommend that divers take as much of their own gear and spare parts as possible, and rely as little as possible on rentals. If you do choose to rent, make careful equipment checks regularly.

Indonesia is not a place, either, to push the dive tables or argue with dive computers. There is a decompression chamber at the Sanglah hospital in Denpasar, the capital of Bali, but many of the dive sites are a long way from Bali.

The best practice is to dive conservatively (even to the point of extreme caution) and safely, and always to make a decompression stop on the ascent. The reefs are rich enough that you will never be bored spending a few extra minutes at the end of a dive exploring the shallows.

When and Where to Visit

Because of the size of the country, there is no recommended best season—indeed diving is possible year round. The main seasons for tourists are July and August, and the Christmas and New Year holidays.

The areas included in this dive guide all have compressors, equipment and other professional facilities for diving. Some areas offer the visitor a great place to holiday and have the added bonus of well-organized diving as a diversion. Others have great diving, but only modest accommodations. As mentioned earlier, there are a number of boats, luxury and otherwise, that ply the Indonesian waters, and these are generally fairly well equipped.

El Niño, which brought the widely reported drought to Indonesia in 1997–1998, also created a wave of coral bleaching in Bali and other areas of Indonesia in the spring of 1998. The effect was heaviest in the shallow, protected reefs, which will require some time to recover. In this update we have noted the areas where the damage can be seen.

— *Fiona Nichols*

Below: Loading the dive boats at the Nusantara Diving Club, Manado. *Photo by Charles Anderson.*

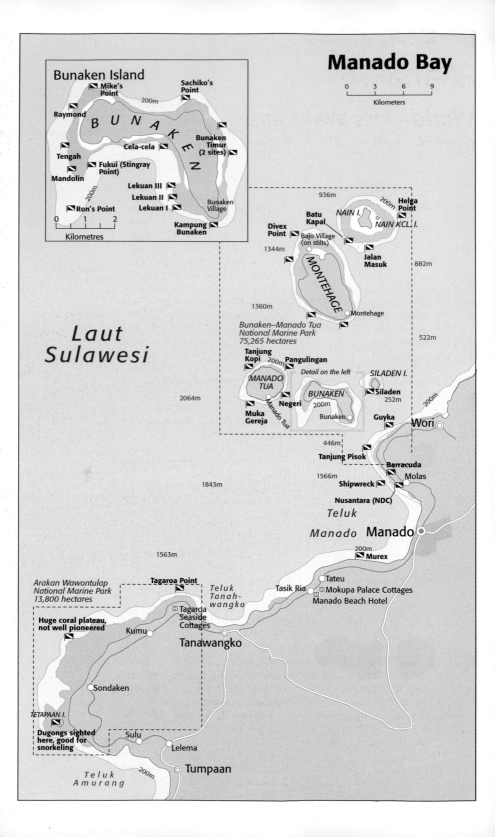

Manado

World-class Walls and Outstanding Fish Life

45 min to 1.5 hrs
by boat

Fair to very good,
12–25 m

Usually gentle; at
some sites to 2
knots or more

Excellent condition
and variety, partic-
ularly soft corals

Steep coral walls

Good numbers and
excellent variety

Pristine walls; sheer
number of species;
interesting wreck

Divers have nothing but praise for the reefs surrounding the small islands in Manado Bay. These are very steep, pristine coral walls, covered with an incredible amount and variety of soft coral. Visibility here is usually only 12–25 meters due to plankton, which sustains the area's rich fish and invertebrate life.

The reefs here are relatively untouched, with little damage by fishermen or divers. In 1989, thanks to the efforts of Loky Herlambang, founder of Nusantara Diving Club and the pioneering dive operator here, 75,265 hectares of underwater area around Bunaken, Manado Tua, Siladen, Montehage and Nain islands became a national marine reserve: Taman Nasional Laut Bunaken–Manado Tua.

North Sulawesi and the islands in the Bunaken group face the Sulawesi Sea, which plummets down to more than 6,000 meters. Nutrient-rich water from these depths sweeps across the reefs.

The variety of marine life here is excellent; the surfaces of the walls are crowded with hard and soft corals, whip corals, sponges and clinging filter-feeders like crinoids and basket stars.

Huge schools of pyramid butterflyfish, black triggerfish and clouds of anthias swarm around the reef edge and the upper part of the wall. Sharks, schools of barracuda, rays, moray eels, and sea snakes—particularly the black-and-grey-banded colubrine sea snake—are relatively common here.

Beginners like the ease of the conditions. There is usually very little current, and the boats anchor right on the edge of the walls. Groups are kept small: 4–7 persons.

The Bunaken–Manado Tua reserve features some 18 dive sites. Most are concentrated off the south and west coasts of Bunaken, a low, crescent-shaped coral island surrounded by a steep fringing reef. Adjacent Manado Tua—Old Manado—is a volcano, a well-shaped cone reaching 822 meters. Three other islands complete the group: tiny Siladen, a stone's throw northeast of Bunaken; Montehage, the largest of the islands, north of Bunaken; and Nain, a tiny island north of Montehage surrounded by a large barrier reef.

Bunaken Island

The reef is good all the way around Bunaken, and the 6-km-long island features no less than 13 dive sites. Bunaken is the centerpiece of the reserve and, with careful observation on this island, you could probably see the majority of coral reef fishes in Indonesia.

All the sites are similar in that they feature steep walls of coral with small caves, buzzing with reef fish. Good coral growth usually extends down to 40–50 meters, and in the deeper parts of the wall one can see sharks, large rays and Napoleon wrasses.

Lekuan I, II and III: The most popular site on Bunaken is this three-pronged coral wall in front of **Lekuan Beach**. Check out the turtles, Napoleon wrasses and sleepy whitetips. **Bunaken Timur** offers similar sights as Lekuan.

Sachiko's Point has particularly good soft coral growth and caves around 30 meters—watch out for currents. **Mike's Point** offers excellent coral growth with large, showy gorgonians. The point is sometimes swept by strong currents, and one can occasionally see sharks and large schools of jack. At **Raymond** non-aggressive colubrine sea snakes are particularly common, both on the reef flats and in the reef itself. **Mandolin** is a good spot for schooling yellowtail fusiliers and good coral growth. **Fukui Point**, also called **Stingray Point**, is known for its rays, of course, as well as for turtles, barracuda and a couple of Tridacna clams. **Siladen** offers steep walls down to about 35 meters, and features good soft corals. This is a place to see big pelagic fish and the largest stingrays in the reserve.

Below: *Acropora hyacinthus* is one of the most common corals seen on the upper edge of outer reef slopes or on reef flats.
Photo by Gary Bell.

Manado Tua

"Old Manado" is a dormant volcano jutting up just west of Bunaken. The two best sites are wall dives on the west coast: **Muka Gereja** features sharks, barracuda and Napoleon wrasses as well as a cave; and **Tanjung Kopi**, also a wall, offers sharks—usually reef whitetips, but with an occasional hammerhead—and barracuda. *Gorango* means "shark," and these can usually be seen here. The reef profile is a steep wall to about 40 meters. **Barracuda Point**, known for its schools of barracuda is also a good spot for sharks, Napoleon wrasses and bumphead parrotfishes. **Batu Kapal** with a deep canyon is where we saw sharks, big tuna, groups of parrotfish and Napoleon wrasses. Tanjung Pisok is some 15 minutes motoring from **Molas Beach**, on

the mainland. The profile begins with a gentle slope, and then becomes a wall. It is known for the shy blue ribbon eels.

Montehage and Nain

Montehage is a large, flat island north of Bunaken. The dive sites are off the west and south, fringed by a wide shallow reef flat. The fish and coral life are much the same as those of Bunaken.

Nain is a tiny island, surrounded by a wide lagoon filled with patches of reef and a barrier reef.

The Manado Wreck

A steel-hulled merchant ship lies in the mud just five minutes from Molas beach, and makes a fine

break from wall diving. Loky Herlambang of NDC found the wreck in 1980. It is assumed to be Dutch because of a few porcelain plates found on board. The ship probably sank during World War II.

Once the wreck is located—it lies on a sandy slope, at 25–40 meters—the crew drops anchor and you follow the line down, as visibility is usually lousy here.

The twin screws of the 60-meter ship are still intact while the hull is largely undamaged. You can enter the wreck through several openings on the deck. Bring good underwater lights! Most of the cargo space is easily accessible, but the engine room is tricky. The engines and pistons are in good shape, as is one of the two electrical gauges, but you must move very slowly. A few careless strokes of your fins and you won't be able to see your hand for silt.

Because of the depth and the generally murky water (8–10 meters at best), there is little hard coral growth here. But there are plenty of giant black coral bushes, and some gorgonians and feather stars. Fish are not normally abundant. Our favorites were a beautiful and shy juvenile pinnate batfish, and an adult roundfaced batfish that seemed to be living in the wheelhouse. If you ask your guides ahead of time, they might find and point out to you two unusual species in the wreck: banded pipefish and the longsnout flathead.

Conservation Efforts

North Sulawesi's reefs are becoming famous thanks to Loky Herlambang, who founded the Nusantara Diving Club (NDC) in 1975. His efforts led to the creation of the national marine reserve in 1989.

A new dive operator, Novotel, plans to install 40 buoys in the Bunaken Marine Park in order to reduce damage to coral as a result of anchor dropping.

— *Kal Muller*

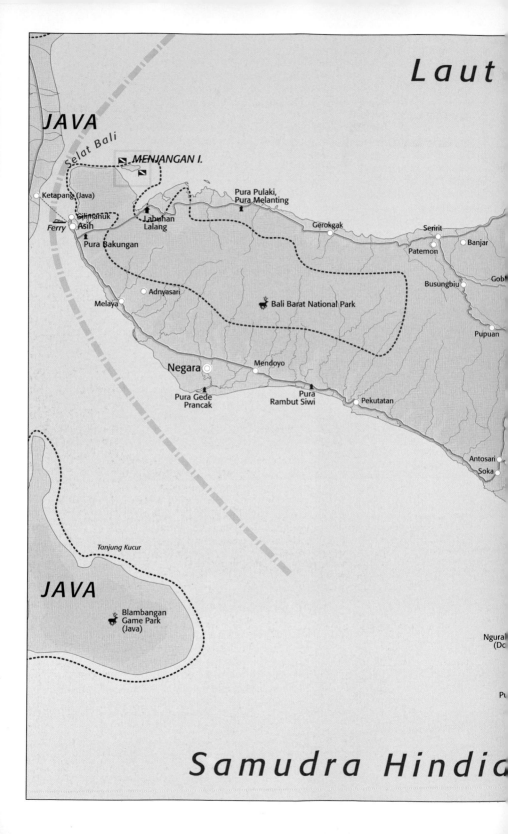

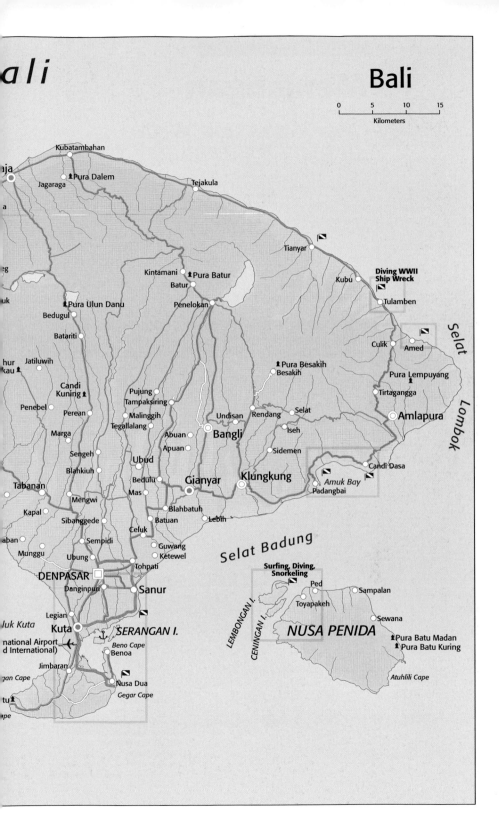

ali

Bali

0 5 10 15
Kilometers

Kubatambahan
Pura Dalem
Jagaraga
Tejakula
Tianyar
Kintamani ♦Pura Batur
Batur
Kubu
Diving WWII
Ship Wreck
♦Pura Ulun Danu
Penelokan
Tulamben
Bedugul
Batariti
Culik
Amed
Jatiluwih
♦Pura Besakih
Besakih
Pura Lempuyang
Candi
Kuning
Pujung
Tampaksiring
Tirtagangga
Penebel
Perean
Malinggih
Undisan Rendang
Selat
Amlapura
Tegallalang
Iseh
Marga
Abuan Bangli
Sengeh
Apuan
Sidemen
Blahkiuh
Ubud
Candi Dasa
Tabanan
Bedulu
Mas
Gianyar Klungkung
Amuk Bay
Padangbai
Mengwi
Kapal
Blahbatuh
Sibanggede
Batuan Lebih
Celuk
Selat Badung
Sempidi
Guwang
Ketewel
Munggu
Ubung
Tohpati
DENPASAR
Danginpuri
Sanur
Surfing, Diving,
Snorkeling
Ped
Sampalan
Toyapakeh
Legian
Sewana
Juk Kuta Kuta
SERANGAN I.
NUSA PENIDA
national Airport
d International)
Beno Cape
Benoa
♦Pura Batu Madan
♦Pura Batu Kuring
Jimbaran
gan Cape
Nusa Dua
Atuhlili Cape
Gegar Cape
tu
pe

Selat
Lombok

LEMBONGAN I.
CENINGAN I.

30 min by boat from Labuan Lalang post

Very good to superb, 25–50 m

Very slight

Very good numbers and variety; abundant soft corals

Walls, particularly rugged; wreck

Good number, only average variety

"Anker" wreck

Menjangan

Clear Water and Walls off Bali's Westernmost Tip

Menjangan Island hangs just offshore from the mountainous point in far northwestern Bali. Because the island is in a protected position, currents and wind-generated waves are rarely a bother, and the reefs here offer fine, easy diving.

The reef flats of Menjangan, once famous for their sheer, uninterrupted growth of coral, were reduced to rubble by a crown-of-thorns starfish outbreak in 1997 and the El Niño warming of 1998. The reef wall is still rich, however, and the flats are coming back—with more variety, particularly in soft corals and gorgonians, than before.

The island is part of Bali Barat National Park, a protected reserve area that encompasses much of Bali's sparsely populated western end, some three hours from the popular resorts.

Craggy Vertical Walls

The coral walls around Menjangan are vertical down to 30–60 meters, and then slope outward. The reef surface is particularly rugged: caves, grottoes, crevices and funnel-like splits break up the coral wall. Gorgonians reach large sizes here,

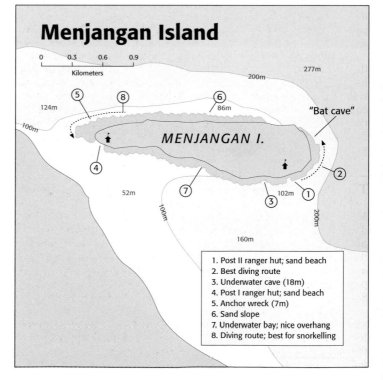

Menjangan Island

0   0.3   0.6   0.9

Kilometers

277m

200m

124m

⑤   ⑧   ⑥

86m

"Bat cave"

100m

MENJANGAN I.

④

②

52m   ⑦

102m ①

③

100m

200m

160m

1. Post II ranger hut; sand beach
2. Best diving route
3. Underwater cave (18m)
4. Post I ranger hut; sand beach
5. Anchor wreck (7m)
6. Sand slope
7. Underwater bay; nice overhang
8. Diving route; best for snorkelling

and huge barrel sponges are very common.

The variety of fish here is somewhat inferior to Bali's other dive sites—although there are plenty of them. Large batfish accompany divers, and an old barracuda occupies a large crevasse on the south side of the island.

Small boats ferry divers from the Nature Reserve dock at Labuhan Lalang to the dive sites, and a surface interval is spent onshore at either of the two posts. The edge of the reef terrace is between one and five meters, and a V-shaped delta of sand points the way out to the edge.

The Anchor Wreck

Menjangan's western tip holds a deeper, more interesting dive on an old wreck. The wreck lies just off the reef edge, and is very close to one of the small docks and guard posts maintained by the Park Service.

The wreck itself lies on a deep sand slope, about 40–50 meters, and few guides like to take their clients this deep. Most stop at the beautifully encrusted anchor, at five meters, and head along the reef wall to the east or west.

We decided to have a look at the wreck, and dropped over the reef edge, following a fairly steep slope with bits and pieces of wreckage and anchor chain down to where the 25-meter-long ship was resting. Along the way, we saw a reef whitetip shark and lizardfishes.

Flat rectangular sheets of copper sheathing material lay in what had been the hold. On the wreck we saw several snappers, sweetlips, goatfishes, wrasses and Moorish idols. Large gorgonians grow on the wreck.

We decided to ascend a bit after less than ten minutes, partially because of the depth, but mostly to get a better look at the reef. Following the wall we quickly encountered a green turtle, and then decided to take a closer look at the corals growing back on the reef flat. On one dead *Acropora* table about the size of a serving platter, we counted twelve different species of sponges, gorgonians, hard corals, and tunicates now growing. In its recovery, Menjangan may even be a better site.

— *Kal Muller*

Above: Gorgonian (*Ctenocella*) and batfish. Menjangan, Bali.
Photo by Takamasa Tonozuka.

Beach; ship is 30 m offshore. Avoid midday—often crowds

Fair to good, 15 m

None

Good growth on ship, fine growth on wall

Liberty shipwreck; wall

Excellent variety, prolific

Full moon night dive

Tulamben

Fine Wreck Diving and a Treasure-trove of Fish Species

At first sight, the little village of Tulamben is rather uninviting. Its beach is a rough spread of black sand, small boulders, and rubble cast here by nearby Gunung Agung's 1963 eruption. But its attraction lies below water. People come to dive the *Liberty* shipwreck.

Divers simply walk out from the beach and go. The volcanic rock is a bit hard on the feet and the waves can be a bit rough, but this is very definitely a worthwhile dive. As you descend, you'll see something that at first looks like a bed of seagrass. It turns out to be spotted garden eels, heads and bodies swaying in the current like plants in a breeze. You look up and see the welcoming committee: several species of snubnose chubs, sweetlips, parrotfishes and a small army of fearless sergeant-majors. Electric blue neon damsels stand out vividly against the black sand and rocks. We watched a hawkfish inhale an unsuspecting damselfish and then resume his motionless stance as he awaited the next careless live morsel. Small groupers, cornetfish and trumpetfishes, the odd parrotfish and a few morays inhabited patches of coral along our route. Photographers should show some restraint at this point for there is still a lot more to capture on film.

On to the Wreck

Just 30 meters from the beach at Tulamben is the wreck of the *Liberty,* broken up but impressively large, stretching along more than 100 meters of steeply sloping sand. The top of the wreck is just three meters underwater; the bottom is at 29 meters.

On 11 January, 1942, this ship was hit by torpedoes from a Japanese submarine while crossing the Lombok Strait. After attempts to save her she was finally beached at Tulamben. There she stayed until 1963. Local entrepreneurs stripped the boat of its cargo—one source says raw rubber and railroad parts—and were in the process of

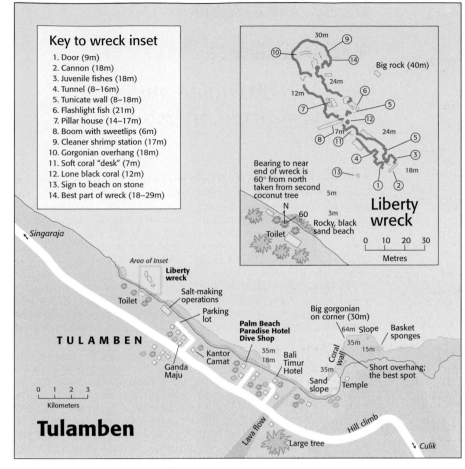

Key to wreck inset

1. Door (9m)
2. Cannon (18m)
3. Juvenile fishes (18m)
4. Tunnel (8–16m)
5. Tunicate wall (8–18m)
6. Flashlight fish (21m)
7. Pillar house (14–17m)
8. Boom with sweetlips (6m)
9. Cleaner shrimp station (17m)
10. Gorgonian overhang (18m)
11. Soft coral "desk" (7m)
12. Lone black coral (12m)
13. Sign to beach on stone
14. Best part of wreck (18–29m)

30m
9
10
14
Big rock (40m)
24m
12m
6
7
5
12
7m
24m
8
11
5
4
3
Bearing to near
end of wreck is
60° from north
taken from second
coconut tree
13
18m
1
2
5m
N
60
3m
Rocky, black
sand beach
Liberty wreck
Toilet
0   10   20   30
Metres

Singaraja

Area of Inset

Liberty
wreck

Toilet
Salt-making
operations
Parking
lot
Big gorgonian
on corner (30m)
64m Slope
Basket
sponges

TULAMBEN

Kantor
Camat
**Palm Beach
Paradise Hotel
Dive Shop**
35m
18m
Bali
Timur
Hotel
35m
Coral wall
35m
15m
Short overhang;
the best spot
Ganda
Maju
Sand
slope
Temple

0   1   2   3
Kilometers

Tulamben

Lava flow
Large tree
Hill climb
Culik

cutting her up for scrap when Gunung Agung exploded. The eruption, which killed more than 1,000 people, pushed the ship off the beach and to its present location.

The wreck lies approximately parallel to the shore and part of the superstructure is within snorkeling distance of the surface. The hull is broken into large chunks and laced by big holes, making it easy to explore the vessel's innards. But don't expect any glittering bounty. The treasures of Tulamben are swimming in and around the wreck: hundreds of species of fish in quantity, most having become semi-tame and used to divers. We saw several fairly large specimens, but it is the huge numbers of medium-sized fish—30–80 cm—that make the wreck such an interesting dive. Author Rudie Kuiter estimates that some

400 species of reef fish live on the wreck, which is also visited by perhaps 100 species of pelagics.

Although we never sighted any sharks or other really large fish, we saw a few good-sized bonito, tuna, emperors and jacks, Napoleon wrasses and a large scribbled filefish. Rays, barracuda, and even oceanic sunfish (*Mola mola*) have been sighted here, the latter on the deep slope behind the wreck proper.

Apart from the prolific fish, the encrusted wreck is mostly a community of opportunists: soft corals, sponges, gorgonians, hydroids, bryozoans, tunicates, bivalves and crinoids. Daytime dives are extraordinary, but a night dive, especially around full moon, is particularly memorable for the bioluminescence, fish and bright coral polyps.
— *Kal Muller*

Opposite:
Tulamben is famous for the wreck of the *Liberty,* the top of which lies just three meters underwater.
Photo by Takamasa Tonozuka.

TULAMBEN

INDONESIA

35

Beach; 5 min by
small boat

Fair to good,
10–20 m

Mild

Excellent; best hard
coral variety in Bali

Coastal reef; flats,
slope and wall

Excellent numbers,
superb variety

Density of fish on
the deep wall; coral
species just off the
beach

CEMELUK

INDONESIA

36

Cemeluk (Amed)

An Outstanding Variety of Fishes and Corals

The little bay at Cemeluk has one of the richest reefs in Bali. The site is just off Bali's main east coast highway, about 10 km before the village of Tulamben. The turnoff from the main road is at the village of Amed, which the site is also sometimes called.

Divers on a tight schedule could dive Cemeluk in the morning, followed by the Tulamben wreck in the afternoon. But these are both excellent dive spots, each deserving more time.

Diving Cemeluk

Below: A gorgonian fan, swarming with basslets. Amed. *Photo by Takamasa Tonozuka.*

The reef curves around a rock outcropping on the east side of the bay. We were lucky enough to dive with leading dive professional, Wally Siagian, on this trip. We took a *jukung* out into the bay, and dropped into a very slight current pushing us southeast along the reef. At about eight meters, we came down on an extensive spread of staghorn coral teeming with damselfishes and cardinalfishes. A short slope led to a coral wall, where we dropped to 43 meters, hanging there about 8–10 meters above the sandy bottom. The wall was magic.

Schools of fish cascaded down the wall: the numbers were staggering. The schools included black triggerfish, lots of bannerfishes, black snappers, humpback snappers, pyramid butterflies and countless others. Further off from the wall, the usual school of yellowtail fusiliers kept a watchful eye.

Towards the end of the dive, the

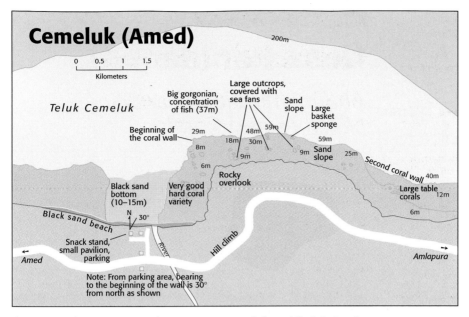

Cemeluk (Amed)

Teluk Cemeluk

Big gorgonian, concentration of fish (37m)

Large outcrops, covered with sea fans

Sand slope

Large basket sponge

Beginning of the coral wall — 29m

48m

59m

18m / 30m

8m

9m

6m

9m Sand slope

25m

59m

Second coral wall 40m

Large table corals 12m

6m

Black sand bottom (10–15m)

Very good hard coral variety

Rocky overlook

Black sand beach

N / 30°

Snack stand, small pavilion, parking

← Amed

River

Hill climb

Amlapura →

Note: From parking area, bearing to the beginning of the wall is 30° from north as shown

0   0.5   1   1.5
Kilometers

200m

---

dense growth of sponges and gorgonians created a tunnel between two of the outcrops. Inside, it was wall-to-wall with life. Large barrel sponges poked out from clearings in this forest.

The larger fishes included a longnose emperor, a patrolling giant trevally and several blue-fin trevallies. Two very large tuna, both over a meter, shot by quickly. As we finished the dive, we saw a mismatched pair of Napoleon wrasses: a very large adult and a very small juvenile. Our visibility was around 10 meters, but it can double under the right conditions. The area is calm year-round with only very occasional surge and high current conditions.

A Dive from the Beach

A dive directly from the black sand and pebble beach at Cemeluk gave a very different perspective: smaller fishes, but a great number and variety of corals. We had barely donned our fins, and dropped to a depth of a couple of meters when we saw a scattered group of orangeband surgeonfish with their distinctive orange marks.

Neon blue devils darted around, two parrotfish paddled furiously, and a graceful pair of Moorish idols swam into view. A dozen striped convict tangs, which we had not seen in Bali before, swam across our path.

Further north all life stopped, and the slopping grey sand offered nothing until we came across an area where a number of crate-like enclosures segregated bits of coral as part of an experiment to determine coral growth in this environment. There was not much more to see except a few isolated outcrops.

Finally we came to the reef wall, which follows the coast from this point. About 10 meters from the surface, the irregular wall started sprouting fan gorgonians and pastel trees of *dendronephthya*. Tube sponges were numerous. The reef here is topped by quite a flat area, just 2–5 meters deep and 30 or more meters from the rocky shore.

Unfortunately, Cemeluk was heavily hit by the El Niño warming of 1998. The reef is recovering, but the coral in the shallowest part of the reef suffered severe damage. The famous gorgonians in the deeper areas are still fine, however, and the shallow areas, like Menjangan, will surely come back.

— *Kal Muller*

45 min to 1.5 hrs
by boat

Good, 15 m

Moderate to very
strong. Currents are
unpredictable, often
fierce. Cold water

Very good variety of
hard corals; excel-
lent stand of
Dendronephthya

Drop-offs, steep
slopes

Excellent variety;
many pelagics

Large schools of
sweetlips; very large
hawksbill turtle. Site
also hosts sharks,
mantas and even
oceanic sunfish

Nusa Penida

Abundant Pelagics and Some Fierce Currents

Nusa Penida, across the Badung Strait from Bali's southern tip, offers some of the best diving to be found anywhere. But conditions around Penida and its two small sister islands—Nusa Lembongan and Nusa Ceningan—can sometimes be difficult, with cold waters and unpredictable currents reaching four or more knots. This is not a place for beginning divers or inexperienced boatmen.

Coral Walls and Pelagics

Most of the dive spots are around the channel between Nusa Penida and Nusa Ceningan. The standard reef profile here has a terrace at 8–12 meters, then a wall or steep slope to 25–30 meters sloping gently to the seabed at 600 meters. Pinnacles and caves are often encountered. At 35–40 meters, long antipatharian wire corals are common, spiraling outward more than 8 meters. Pelagics are the main attraction and you have a good chance to see jacks, mackerel and tunas. Reef sharks are so common that after a while you stop noticing them. Mantas are frequently sighted. The most unusual pelagic visi-

Nusa Penida & Lembongan

tor to Nusa Penida is probably the weird 2-meter-long *Mola mola,* or oceanic sunfish, a mysterious, large, flattened fish with elongated dorsal and ventral fins, and a lumpy growth instead of a tail fin.

The most common dive spots are just south of the dock at Toyapakeh, or a bit further east, at Ped and "SD," named for the *sekolah dasar,* or primary school, there. There are other dive spots down the northeast and southwest coasts of Penida, but these areas, swept by tricky currents, require an experienced dive guide and more time than is available in a day trip to reach.

Our first dive was off Ped. From an initial 7-meter depth, we followed the slope of 45 degrees down to a depth of 37 meters. There was good hard coral cover, and an occasional pinnacle reared up. We crossed a big school of black triggerfish mixed with a few sleek unicornfishes.

A small cave in one of the coral knolls held a densely packed school of pygmy sweeps. Early in the dive we crossed paths with a large blackspotted stingray, at close quarters. A huge hawksbill turtle, several groupers and even more sweetlips, schools of yellow-tailed and lunar fusiliers, and occasional schools of longfin bannerfish can all be sighted on an average dive.

Toyopakeh

We motored a bit further west along the coast of Nusa Penida, and dropped anchor a few hundred meters from the dock at Toyapakeh. We descended through a slight current into veritable clouds of peach fairy basslets and firefishes.

A long stretch of our dive route—this at 25–30 meters—consisted of an almost unbroken thicket of pastel-tinted soft corals. A school of two dozen or more greater amberjacks swam several lazy circles around our group, mixing sometimes with a larger school

of bigeye jacks. As we started upwards, we saw a huge blackspotted moray, with about 1 meter of its snaky body sticking out of its lair.

But conditions in the same dive spot are never the same. On another occasion, we drift dived in a 2- to 3-knot current and encountered some 40 sweetlips, divided into four groups, all facing the current. The sight of these attrac-

Below: Dive boat off Nusa Penida. *Photo by Kal Muller.*

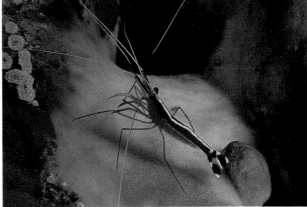

tively patterned fish was too much to just pass by, so we carefully grabbed onto some hard corals and crawled along the bottom for a closer look at the sweetlips show which was taking place just 2 meters away. Later, we met up with a turtle, a blotchy grouper and a whitetip shark, but the sweetlips were certainly the climax of the dive.

— *Kal Muller*

Above: The cleaner shrimp *(Lysmata amboinensis)* removes parasites from fish. *Photo by Mark Strickland.*

20–30 min by small outboard

Variable; poor to very good; 6–20 m

Can be extremely strong—more than 5 knots and very tricky. Cold water

Excellent coverage and variety

Steep coral walls; underwater canyon

Literally teeming with fish

Tepekong's Canyon, good chance to see pelagics

Below: Fishermen with outrigger canoe, Bali. *Photo by Gary Bell.*

Candi Dasa

Spectacular, Bone-chilling Dives in Tepekong's Canyon

Just offshore from Candi Dasa in eastern Bali is tiny Tepekong, a little outcrop that offers some spectacular diving. The coral walls are steep, the water is cold, and the current can be strong. But for an experienced diver, drifting with a 3-knot current through The Canyon offers an outstanding underwater experience.

There are actually three dive sites here: Tepekong Island (sometimes called Kambing—"Goat"—Island); Gili Mimpang (three mini-islands, sometimes called Batu Tiga, "Three Rocks"); and Biaha Island, sometimes called Likuan Island. Your ride to the dive site is by a fishing boat or *jukung*, fitted with a tiny outboard. Two or three divers, at most, will fit in a *jukung*.

Tiny Tepekong has the best diving. It is also the coldest—occasionally a bone-chilling 19° C—and

most difficult. Tepekong is just 100 meters long with no beaches. The sides of the island plunge straight into the sea.

This is not easy diving. Our first two attempts were thwarted, but the third time we were lucky. We dropped in about halfway along the western side of Tepekong, descending in a slight current to a sloping bottom at 9 meters, near the vertical underwater continuation of Tepekong's above-water cliff. Roundface batfish and Napoleon wrasses can sometimes be spotted here. We followed the slope, dotted with coral knolls, to 24 meters, then dropped down into a canyon. The Canyon is lined with huge boulders and bottoms out at 32 meters. Here, visibility increases to close to 20 meters and the amount of fish life increases considerably. But so does the current.

As soon as we entered The Canyon we saw a huge aggregation of sweetlips, 50 or 60 of them, hovering next to a pinnacle: Goldmann's sweetlips, oriental sweetlips, and yellow ribbon sweetlips. Then we saw a very healthy-looking grouper—possibly an Australian potato cod—over a meter in length. Because of the gusting currents, we were forced to hang on to outcrops but were still able to watch schools of rainbow runners, big-eyes, sleek unicornfishes and little packs of Moorish idols. At one outcrop, we woke a resting whitetip.

Each coral-covered pinnacle hosted firefishes, which flicked their long dorsal spines in the current, and clouds of lyretail coralfish (*Pseudanthias squammipinnis*).

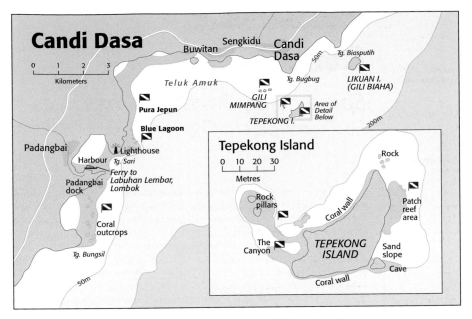

These were all at our 5-meter decompression stop. The teeming fish life makes it well worth any effort it takes, however, to make this dive. It is particularly easy here to get very close to normally wary fish. You might even see an oceanic sunfish, the strange *Mola mola*. All in all, it can be one of the best dives in Indonesia.

East Tepekong

After one of our aborted attempts on The Canyon, we moved to the far east of the island and dropped into surging, cold water, and shivered as we descended. Visibility was restricted by the water movement to around 8 meters. The surge was too strong to allow us to peer into the many caves—between 16 and 32 meters—as well as a 10-meter-long passage between several huge boulders that appear to have fallen from the topside cliff.

The coral cover is good, including both stony corals and soft corals, and several blunt pinnacles sheltered reef fish in shallow pockets. Fish huddle between overlapping layers of table coral, each irregular shelf holding several species. It is not ideal and the surge, poor visibility and cold generally gets to you.

Gili Mimpang

These same conditions plague diving on Gili Mimpang, a cluster of three little exposed rocks between Tepekong and the coast of Bali. Despite wet suits, you are often cold and this puts a real damper on the dive. However, there are thermoclines. Around 18 meters we hit a thermocline, and life took a very definite turn for the better. Almost instantaneously, the water temperature increased 6°C. Fish life improved considerably, beginning with a docile star puffer, three whitetip sharks and a blue-finned trevally. A school of blue-lined snapper buzzed us from above.

As we stopped on top of a pinnacle at around 7 meters, a school of bignose unicornfish parted just enough to afford us a glimpse of a Napoleon wrasse on one side and several bumphead parrotfish on the other. Longfin bannerfish also ·accompanied us. There are also plenty of large pelagics here—for those who can stand the cool water temperatures.

— *Kal Muller*

Nusa Dua

Convenient, Undemanding Diving near Bali's Resorts

5 min by small boat

Low, 6–8 m (can reach 15 m on occasion)

Very gentle

Limited coverage, few species. Nusa Dua has a slightly better coral cover

Drop-off to moderate depth

Surprisingly good variety

Feeding frenzy on a fresh spawn

Opposite: *Photo by Takamasa Tonozuka.*

The dives just beyond the reef line east of the northern part of Tanjung Benoa peninsula, or in front of Sanur, are not the best in Bali. But the sites are easy to get to, and there is quite a good variety of reef fish to see. These dives serve perfectly as a quick refresher if you haven't dived in a while, or as your first dive if you have just completed a dive course.

An outboard-powered outrigger canoe takes you the few hundred meters from the beach to the dive location, just beyond where the waves break. The only way out is over very shallow reef flat at low tide. Be prepared for a bit of spray during the ride out or back and when crossing the (usually low) breaking waves.

On the reef face off Tanjung Benoa, we dropped down to 8–9 meters on a slightly sloping bottom with scattered coral formations. Visibility was just 6–8 meters, but we were told that it is usually twice this. The majority of the fish were at 8–10 meters. We made a couple of quick dips to 14 meters, and saw nothing.

Good Variety of Fish

The coral cover here is not fantastic, but the few mini-pinnacles drew plentiful fish life with a good variety of species. We saw several 50–75-cm fish glide by, but visibility was too restricted to make an identification. Our guide found a giant moray and pointed him out to us. This big fellow lives in a coral cave with several openings, and for a while he played hide and seek, popping his head out of three different holes. Groupers were common, especially the white-lined grouper, which we saw in both white and brown-green. On the smaller end of the scale, fusiliers, snappers, damsels, and fairy basslets were plentiful, while parrotfishes were present in good variety. The only species we noticed more than once was the blue-barred parrotfish. The only

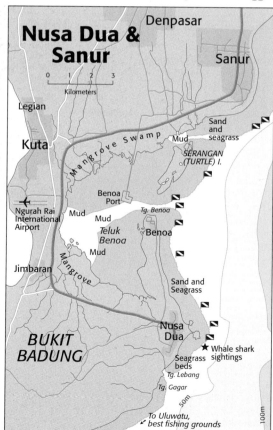

Nusa Dua & Sanur

Denpasar

Sanur

0 1 2 3
Kilometers

Legian

Kuta

Mangrove Swamp

Mud

Sand and seagrass

SERANGAN (TURTLE) I.

Benoa Port

Tg. Benoa

Ngurah Rai International Airport

Mud

Mud

Teluk Benoa

Benoa

Mud

Jimbaran

Mangrove

Sand and Seagrass

BUKIT BADUNG

Nusa Dua

★ Whale shark sightings

Seagrass beds

Tg. Lebang

Tg. Gagar

50m

To Uluwatu, best fishing grounds

100m

angelfishes we saw were the dwarf bicolor angel and several big emperor angels. Surgeonfishes were common, particularly the spotted unicornfish. We saw pairs of rabbitfishes of at least three species, and a single pair of titan triggerfish.

A Feeding Frenzy

The highlight of the dive came when we saw a furious cloud of several dozen fishes of various species

Photo by Jones/Shimlock

whirling around what looked like a bare patch of dark, reddish coral. Caught up in a feeding frenzy, the small fishes allowed us to approach as close as we wished. We could even touch them, they were so intent on their meal. We never did identify what it was they were eating, although it is likely it was a fresh spawn of some kind.

Dives off Nusa Dua will probably not offer such a show very often, but are still worth making for the variety of fish here and the proximity to the tourist centers. The reef to the north, off the Sanur coast, is similar—wide tidal flats behind the reef front, and inaccessible at low tide.

The variety of fishes is quite good in Sanur, but there is even less coral cover than at Nusa Dua. If you are a serious diver, these dives will just whet your appetite for the numerous more challenging locations that the region has to offer.

— *Kal Muller*

Komodo

Dragons and Pioneer Diving

Up to 2.5 hrs from Labuhanbajo by boat

Variable, 2–50 m

Can be extremely strong, up to 8 knots

Quite good generally

Sloping reef and some walls

Very variable

Pioneer diving in many places. Encounters with a variety of large pelagics

Komodo, and the islands scattered around it between Sumbawa and Flores, seems to belong to another time and place. Rugged, dry and covered by a thin layer of coarse grass, it is an anomaly located just a few degrees south of the equator, in the middle of the generally lush Indonesian archipelago. Komodo island is most famous as the habitat of the Komodo dragon.

Biological Riches

The wild Komodo area offers just about every imaginable type of diving, from current-swept sea mounds patrolled by groups of sharks, tuna and other big fish to plunging walls, covered in impressive corals, to calm reefs alive with invertebrates and hundreds of colorful reef fishes. The water temperature varies from a chilly 22°C to 30°C bath water. Visibility ranges from a clear 25–30 meters to a dismal 3 meters, when clouds of tiny fish and plankton allow only macrophotography.

The variety of marine life in the Komodo area rivals the world's best. There are deep seas both north and south of the narrow straits running between the little islands, and strong currents and upwellings bring nutrients and plankton, keeping all the marine creatures well-fed.

The Komodo area is not well explored—most of our dives were true exploration dives. Although this is exciting, and the kind of diving we like the best, it means that you have to take the bad with the

good. In general, there are two seasons to diving Komodo—the winter for the southern sites, and the summer for the northern sites.

Diving the South

Conventional wisdom has it that December is the wrong time to visit Komodo, but in our experience this is not so. Although the rainy season is well on its torrential way in the western part of Indonesia, around Komodo the skies are usually blue and the tanning sun beats down. The seas are calm, and there is enough of a breeze to cool sunburnt bodies. Between November and January visibility is as good as it can get in such plankton-rich seas, 10–15 meters, and the coral growth and fish life in the south are nothing short of excellent.

The best visibility, however, is afforded in the dry season, between April and October.

Tala Island Tala, a tiny, angular island in Langkoi Bay, just south of the southernmost part of Komodo Island, offers several excellent sites. The inner passage between Tala and Komodo proper is shallow, and ripping with current, but the southern point of the island has two adjacent sites.

On our first dive off Tala, the current at the point broke east, so we dropped in and went that way. We descended along a steep slope, full of coral-encrusted chunks of black rock, ending up in a strange forest of spiral whip coral on a sand bottom at 40 meters. We were

Opposite: Fishing boats anchoring at dawn; Komodo Island. *Photo by Clay Bryce.*

KOMODO

INDONESIA

45

immediately greeted by a group of whitetip reef sharks, including one large and friendly individual who acted as if he had never seen a diver before. We also encountered a turtle, met a large school of boldly patterned sweetlips, passed snappers and several schools of surgeonfish.

West of the point is a sheer wall of rock where we saw sharks, rays, morays and rich coral growth in the cuts and shelves. The flat areas of the wall are covered with vast fields of orange cup corals, a beautiful effect against the dark rock.

Pillarsteen This site is identified by a tiny pinnacle, just off the southern tip of a small island east of Padar's southern point. The structure off the southernmost point is wonderful, with huge chunks of rock broken up by caves and channels, canyons and chimneys. The rugged underwater topography continues to 50–60 meters. There are good caves at about 40 meters, and at 16 meters. Visibility in the winter averaged about 10–12 meters here. The fish life is first rate, with large groups of schooling fish such as fusiliers, sweetlips and surgeonfish, as well as sharks, and schools of *Mobula* rays. In areas, wire corals grow out horizontally 4–5 meters from the rock, and the variety of soft corals and gorgonians here is excellent. This is definitely a world-class site.

Nusa Kode Off Kode, we followed the coral-covered ridges down to 50 meters. The water was cold, a result of the upwelling of deep water that also gives the area its biological richness, but visibility was 15 meters. The shallows were very rich in fish life, particularly plankton feeders. Fork-tailed fairy basslets swarmed around the dropoffs in great orange and purple schools. Pairs of colorful butterflyfish foraged in the reef crannies. Clown triggerfish, staked out their territory along the face of the reef.

In the deeper waters a couple of whitetip reef sharks swung around to give us a closer look. Then we encountered a huge grouper. Red snappers, with bright yellow eyes, kept a wary distance while a green turtle rowed by, followed by a huge school of narrow banded batfish—a rare sight. At 20 meters, a fabulous encounter with a whale shark made it one of the more memorable dives.

Gili Motang The south face of Gili Motang, which sits between Flores and southern Rinca, offers sites with good coral growth, nice bommies and seasonal pelagics like whale sharks and mantas. But our favorite site is in the north: "Apple Orchard." This spot is literally covered with the colorful filter-feeding sea cucumbers called sea apples. These beautiful animals—deep blood-red or purple, and with contrasting white or yellow radial stripes—are rarely seen.

Diving the North

The first dive we made some years ago was off Komodo Island's Pantai Merah. This site is near the old dragon feeding station, and snorkeling and lunch here was a regular stop on tour operators' schedules. The snorkeling is excellent, over a healthy, shallow reef. Where we decided to dive, however, was at the reef edge, where the bottom drops down to 20 meters or so, but because of the raging currents on the surface only a few of us managed to get down and enjoy the fabulous fish and corals.

Banta Island Perhaps the best site in the north Komodo area, and dive guide Wally Siagian's personal favorite, is "GPS Point," a small bank reef just off the point of the easternmost of Banta Island's two north-facing peninsulas.

This is one of the very best sites to see sharks, and five species can be identified in a single dive. GPS Point is also often swarming with jacks, dogtooth tuna and big schools of barracuda, and surgeonfish. Unfortunately, this site seems to have been discovered by shark fin

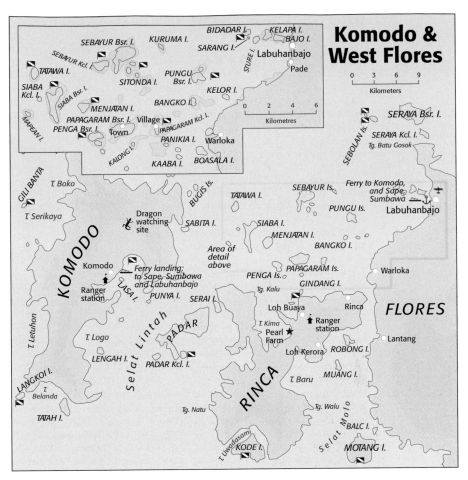

Komodo & West Flores

hunters who kill the creatures for their fins and leave the rest. The soft coral growth at GPS Point is excellent, and the entire surface of the sea mound is richly overgrown with sessile invertebrates.

Strong currents often sweep the shallows but things settle down around 25 meters or so. However, this is not a beginners dive. Visibility here is variable, and can drop below 10 meters because of plankton in the water. It is usually clearer at depth.

Sabolan Kecil Sabolan Kecil and its partner island, Sabolan Besar, are north of Labuhanbajo, just a bit west of the large island of Seraya Besar. Just east of Sabolan Kecil, heading toward Sabolan Besar, are two sea mounds—a site called "Wally's Shark Bank."

Hard coral cover here is minimal, but there are lots of soft corals and some very large gorgonians. The reason to dive here, however, is for the fish life, particularly sharks. Work your way down to the valley between the two mounds and pause for a while to watch the whitetips, silvertips and blacktips.

Sebayur Kecil Another great dive off the north coast of Sebayur Kecil Island. Our entry point was 25 meters off a white sand beach onto a reef sitting just 4–5 meters from the surface which dropped to a sandy bottom at 25–30 meters.

Visibility was excellent, more than 25 meters. As we began our descent, we met Napoleon wrasse, schools of bristletooth tangs, and a giant grouper.

— *Kal Muller*

Up to 2 hrs
by boat

Good to very good,
10–20 m

Gentle on coastal
sites; can be strong
around isles

Good at some
sites

Mostly steep walls

Good numbers of
large fish at best
sites

Sharks, dogtooth
tuna

Maumere

Regeneration After a Devastating Earthquake

Maumere was universally considered one of Indonesia's best dive spots until December 1992 when disaster struck: a strong earthquake which was followed by *tsunami* waves and a cyclone.

Opinions today are divided on the diving from Maumere. Author, biologist and underwater photographer Rudie Kuiter writes: "Little has changed and in a way it is even more interesting." Kuiter, who has dived here more than just about anyone else, continues: "I would say that perhaps 10 percent of the outer drop-offs have suffered bad damage, but little on the coastal reefs." Yet, contrary opinions abound. After a relatively short series of dives there in early September 1993, our own opinion is, at best, divided. A year after the disaster, there was little evidence of damage on land. But what about underwater? According to one of the most experienced local divers, eleven of of the previous 45-odd dive sites are still worth diving.

Where's the Top Diving?

Is it still worthwhile to travel to Maumere just for the diving? The answer depends on your interests, level of experience, time available in Indonesia, and a host of other factors. With other Indonesian dive sites in mind, we would give good marks to only three locations: Pamana Kecil, with its many sharks and tuna which, according to Marcos, are almost always there; Maragajong, which despite the restricted visibility and gusting cur-

rent, we still recommend for its teeming fish life; and Pangahbatang, with its huge soft coral trees, sharks and stingrays.

Pamana Kecil Our first dive, off the Pamana Kecil, was the best for big fellows. Even before beginning our descent, just as I peered below, two large dogtooth tuna cruised by some 10 meters beneath me. We descended in very good 15–20-meter horizontal visibility, down a sheer vertical wall which bottoms out around 60 meters. Several whitetip sharks checked us out from a respectful distance and a couple of grey sharks looked us over from a bit closer, and we saw some hammerheads in the distance. While the big fish were exciting enough for anyone, the wall was disappointing: little coral growth and few reef fishes. Much of it was covered with a sandy layer, a condition we saw at other dive sites here.

Two dives off the south side of the islands blocking northeast Maumere Bay showed Maumere diving like its old, glorious, pre-earthquake days.

Maragajong At Maragajong we anchored on the reef flat and swam against a fairly strong current over dead coral rubble to reach a vertical, 40-meter wall with good invertebrate cover, especially small soft coral trees and sponges, overhangs and small, shallow caves. Visibility was none too good, fluctuating from 6 to 10 meters. The current gusted to 2 knots, but most of the time it was manageable, at less than a

Maumere Bay

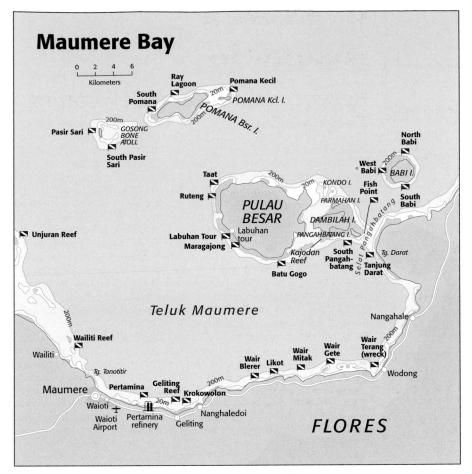

knot.

The good growth lasted but about 100 meters before an underwater landslide marked our turnaround point. On the way back, rounding an outcrop, we were greeted with strong gusts of current and a plethora of fish: large, colorful parrotfish, a huge cloud of sergeant-majors, an unusual school of emperors and the usual fusiliers. The mass of fish life was impressive but the current forced us to hang on to rocks to watch the show.

South Pangahbatang Another dive to the east, off south Pangahbatang also started in a strong current. But here the reeftop was in top shape, the growth dominated by large leather corals. Visibility was not great (less than 10 meters) and the current gusted to 1.5 knots as we dropped along a slope to sand bottom at 27 meters, the maximum for this dive. A good-sized whitetip shark was curious enough to come in fairly close, but there were too many of us (six) for its careful nature. Other whitetips hovered in the current further off along with a couple of 2-meter greys and a blacktip. While the shark aggregation was impressive, so were the soft coral trees, among the largest, most colorful and splendid we have ever seen.

We crossed a white sand trough, spotting a couple of good-sized tuna, a crocodilefish, several blue-spotted rays, a Napoleon and a lumbering bumphead parrotfish, at the very edge of visibility. At one edge of the sand, a mini-forest of garden eels disappeared during our approach, cautiously slithering out heads and part of their bodies after our passage.

One rocky area was speckled with many small bright yellow sea cucumbers. This was the only place we have seen them in a concentration outside of Kupang. A splendid dive indeed, despite the strong finning required by the current.

Wailiti Reef On the far west side of Maumere Bay, where the full force of the *tsunamis* hit, diving was said to be good only below the 20-meter level, to where the slope stops at around 30 meters and blends into an almost flat sand bottom. We found the contrary to be true. Except for a couple of blue-spotted stingrays, fish life was better further up: fairly good numbers and variety, but nothing outstanding by Indonesian standards. We noticed the common yellow-eyed black snappers, several Phyllidia nudibranchs covered with yellow-tipped bumps, as well as a couple of nudibranchs. The invertebrate scene was dominated by several fairly large gorgonians decorated with crinoids. The dive's highlight was a friendly cuttlefish, which allowed a very close encounter for several minutes before drifting off backwards, gently undulating. The reeftop was in very good condition at snorkeling depths.

Other Sites

We did not try three of the 11 spots which Marcos said still offered good diving. These were Ray Lagoon/Shark Point where, Marcos says, the coral is all gone and there is strong current, but big fish are often encountered. At Pamana Selatan, the topside coral is gone, but the lower levels are worthwhile. This site also often has a strong current and choppy seas.

Wair Terang At Wair Terang, where a sunken Japanese freighter from World War II lies close to the beach, the coral growth on the

wreck is unaffected, according to Marcos. Some parts of the wreck collapsed, but the fish life is the same as pre-*tsunami* days.

On a previous dive, it proved to be a difficult, but excellent, spot. Nowhere else have we seen so many lionfish, in groups of four, six and even up to a dozen, including some huge old fellas. The wreck lies on its side, almost completely turned over, on a slope. Although depths range from 12 to 24 meters there is more than enough to see near the top. The ship is less than 100 meters from the beach. The substrate here is a fine, grey sand that produces an instant smoke screen as soon as someone gets a fin within 2 meters of its surface—this is not a dive on which one wants to invite neophytes still struggling with their buoyancy control.

The silty bottom restricts coral growth, so there is none around the wreck. On the hull itself, however, we found small clumps of branching hard coral protecting tiny fish. A few sponges and lots of clams cling to the side of the hull, along with bunches of grassy whip coral. Several sea cucumbers crawled along the ship. Although far from overwhelming, we found the fish life here quite adequate. In addition to the remarkable number of lionfish, a small cloud of anthias decorated the top of the lower hull and fat goatfish rooted in the silt.

Postscript

Rudie Kuiter's opinion is that by 1998 a lot of soft coral will be back and life on the reefs will be the same as before. Scientists have noticed elsewhere that reef recovery from natural disasters seems to take place much more quickly than recovery from damage caused by man. In fact, storm damage in some areas seems to have a positive relationship to diversity or coral regeneration.

— *Kal Muller*

Opposite:
Acropora, one of the most important of the reef-building corals, takes a number of growth forms. Seen here are a plate or table form (maybe *A. cytherea*) and a branching, or cae-spitose form (maybe *A. nobilis*). *Photo by Jack Jackson.*

45 min by boat
from Kupang

Variable, 5–15 m

Light or none

Generally good

Slopes and walls,
some pocked with
caves

Generally good
numbers of big fish
at best sites

Night dive at
Donovan's Delight

Kupang

Big Fish and a Great Dive Operation

Kupang, located on the southwest tip of Timor Island, has started to acquire a well-deserved reputation in diving circles the world over. In Kupang one of the best diving outfits in Indonesia is well-run by two Australians, the Whitfords, who have thoroughly explored the area.

The best time to visit is September to December and late March to May. Visibility is never very good, but the suspended planktonic matter sustains a great diversity of both invertebrates and fishes.

For a variety of practical reasons, dives from Kupang are restricted to the area around the harbor, the northeast coast of Semau Island and Kera Island, a low-lying, sand-fringed island north of Kupang.

Pulau Kera ("Monkey Island"), circled by a brilliant white sand beach, lies at the entrance of Kupang Bay. "The Aquarium," a shallow site off Kera's south coast, offers good diving, particularly for beginners. Visibility varies considerably, but there are fair numbers and varieties of reef fish here.

"PTR," is a site on the far side of Kera featuring turtles and rays. With the boat anchored offshore, we dropped some 20 meters and as soon as I neared the bottom, a startled blue-spotted stingray flew off, the first of at least a half dozen we spotted during the dive. We also discovered a very large black-spotted stingray. Some four or five turtles shot out of our way as we worked along at 20 meters. Then we caught a napping turtle, with two striped remoras firmly attached to its back, while a school of perhaps a dozen bumphead parrotfish passed at the very edge of visibility.

Semau Island

"Graeme's Groupers" lies about 100 meters off the beach at Semau. We identified a half-dozen species of groupers: blotchy, coral, flagtail, polkadot, saddleback and white-lined. Cleaner wrasses worked their stations along the wall, servicing the groupers as well as longnose

Kupang Bay

0   5   10   15
Kilometers

Pitoby's Turtles and ⬛
Rays (PTR) ⬛   ○ KERA I.
20m ⬛

Tg. Kurong

The Aquarium

Teluk Kupang

Tg. Bolong

Graeme's
Groupers ⬛   ⬛ Ray Review

Namasan ⬛

Tulong

Namasan

S E M A U

Karangbesar

Cave City ⬛

Donovan's
Delight ⬛   KUPANG

Hamburger ⬛

Teluk
Pelikaan   Tg. Kataba

Bolok ⬛

Pitoby's Pipefishes
(Pertamina Dock) ⬛

Baun

Tg. Upeoh

Batakte

KAMBANG I.

Selat Semau

W E S T
T I M O R

Tg. Lelat

Batubau

20m

Selat Roti

Tg. Oisina

emperors, black-and-white snappers, sweetlips, dogface puffers and roundfaced batfish. We saw several large emperor and six-banded angelfish.

"Cave City" is on the east coast of Semau, around the northeast tip and past the skeleton of the Japanese pier. The site is a coral wall more than a kilometer long, with at least a dozen good sites. The caves are the distinguishing feature here, some reaching back more than 5 meters. Hard coral growth is good, and we saw lots of large gorgonians. Soft corals grew in white tufts like wind-blown snow. On the very deepest sections of the wall, we encountered bushy growths of antipatharian black corals.

Donovan's Delight

This is fine, fascinating diving indeed—with the usual caveat of poor to fair visibility. A fair variety and number of hard corals cover the top of the dome (there is some fish bomb damage, but it is not extensive) and soft corals are plentiful. The wall features several shallow caves. During several dives here we saw sharks, both reef whitetip and reef blacktip, a number of large hawksbill turtles and groupers. Blue-spotted lagoon rays hid under table coral in the shallows or in the sandy bottom. Towards the ragged bottom of the wall, we saw clusters of sweetlips, emperor fish and puffers.

Groups of 10–20 roundfaced batfish patrolled the walls, and pairs of very large six-banded and bluegirdled angelfish wandered the reef face. Lionfish hovered near the top of the wall.

A night dive at Donovan's Delight was one of the most fascinating hours of my life. Among the highlights were three Spanish dancer nudibranchs, a lengthy trumpetfish, sea urchins on the move, a hawksbill turtle, creeping basket stars, several cuttlefishes, lionfishes in force and a squid in a playful mood.

— *Kal Muller*

Opposite:
Exploring the wall at Donovan's Delight.
Photo by Ashley Boyd.

5 min to 1.5 hrs by
speedboat

Fair to excellent,
10–20 m in off-sea-
son, 40 m at best

None to 1.5 knots

Excellent undam-
aged reefs

Vertical walls,
slopes

Excellent numbers
and superb variety

Pristine sheer walls;
number of species
off Hatta and Ai

BANDA ISLANDS

INDONESIA

54

INDONESIA

Banda Islands
Pristine Reefs and Many Pelagics

In the midst of the Banda Sea, rising from a depth of over 4,000 meters are the Banda Islands, one of Indonesia's top destinations for divers. Both experts and beginners will enjoy diving here as there is a choice of a shallow lagoon between Banda Neira and Gunung Api, or the vertical walls of Hatta Island.

The variety and numbers of fish are both excellent; the chances here are always good to see several big animals. The reefs are pristine, with no signs of fish bombing damage. Currents were negligible at the sites and times we dove.

There is some good diving near the hotels, at Sonegat and Pulau Keraka, then slightly further away at Lontar and the two isles to its north, Batu Kapal and Sjahrir. Locally, Keraka is a good spot to combine a dive and picnic. We enjoyed the plentiful tunicates on a small wall here and swam amidst plenty of reef fish.

Notable at Batu Kapal were the profusion of barrel sponges, fan corals and a good variety of soft corals. There are also some huge coral pinnacles reaching to around 10 meters of the surface. From 30-meter depth, the bottom dropped down out of our range of vision. The variety and number of fish swimming around or lurking in the caves in these towers of coral was overwhelming. A superb dive, marred only by the visibility, 10–12 meters.

At Sjahrir, we dropped down a steep coral slope, met a black-spotted stingray, a spotted eagle ray, and an unusual number of trigger-fishes and butterflyfishes. Other

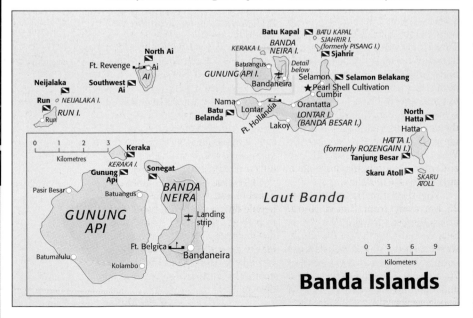

Banda Islands

divers have reported reef sharks.

It is interesting to see that after Gunung Api's last major explosion in 1988, many sponges were spared damage. Not so the corals, but they are beginning slowly to regenerate. We found plenty of bright reef fish.

Hatta Island (formerly Rosengain) is a great area, some 50 minutes away by speedboat. We made several dives here and encountered a variety of fish in excellent numbers. One highlight was near Tanjung Besar. The wall was sheer here and ended in white sand at 40 meters. Its surface was honeycombed with small grottos and overhangs—at times we felt ourselves in a hanging garden, due to the unusual variety of soft coral dangling from the roof of the grottos. We saw an abundance of moray eels and more gorgonians here than anywhere else in Banda.

Together with Hatta, Ai, some 25 km away from Banda Neira, offers the best diving in the Banda Sea. Both the north and the southwest coasts are ringed with flawless coral walls, dropping in one place to 70 meters. The walls are rugged and full of caves harboring plenty of fish. Some of the gorgonians are the biggest we have ever seen.

The southwest features perhaps the best wall in all of Banda with good growth to 70 meters. Tube and barrel sponges and great quantities of soft coral of all hues were growing on a wide terrace on the west coast. The richness of fish life, the sheer drop-off, the caves and fissures in the rock, and the overwhelming richness of life here compares only to the very best sites in south Komodo and a few sites on the isolated islands of the Banda Sea, reachable only by live-aboard.

Banda has two dive seasons—one in April, the other in October. The months immediately before and after these are usually quite good also. Visibility, however, remains restricted to 10–20 meters off season, reaching 30–40 meters only around the ideal months.

The cost of diving is quite reasonable and if there are just two people diving, there are good spots near Banda Neira to keep boat costs down. For trips further out, it's easier on the wallet to form groups of 4–6 divers. Bring your own equipment. The boatmen know the good dive spots.

— *Kal Muller*

Above: Balled anemone with a pair of anemonefish. *Photo by Jones/Shimlock.*

10–60 min by boat, depending on location

5–25 m

Variable, 0–2 knots

Mostly very good

Walls and coral slopes

Fairly good variety

Mantas; diving in saline lake

Sangalaki

Mantas, Turtles and a Mysterious Lake

Since Sangalaki opened for sports diving in April 1993, under the careful development of Borneo Divers, the pioneering dive operation based in Malaysia's Kota Kinabalu, practically every client has seen some mantas. One group reported seeing over 100 mantas on one dive! As mantas tend to feed near the surface in light currents, divers have only to descend to 5 meters or so to enjoy the spectacular show. During the local rainy season (November to March), the visibility is sometimes restricted to 5 or 8 meters, but with a few days of sunshine it soon improves. Even in restricted visibility, there's plenty to see, thanks in part to the keen-eyed, experienced divemasters.

Every dive at Sangalaki is worthwhile, revealing something unusual. Over 40 species of nudibranchs along with at least six colorful flatworms have been identified here. During one of our night dives, over three species of barracuda were seen along with sleeping flounders, a nesting titan triggerfish and lots more. One day a dive brings a huge grouper into view, another comes up with a pair of unusual pink leaf-fish. Friendly cuttlefish abound, allowing close encounters. Polka-dot groupers (barramundi cod, *Chromileptes altivelis*) are common, as are scorpionfishes. Sleeper or crab-eyed gobies are also frequently seen around here.

Green turtles live, breed and lay eggs on several of the small islands off the northeast coast

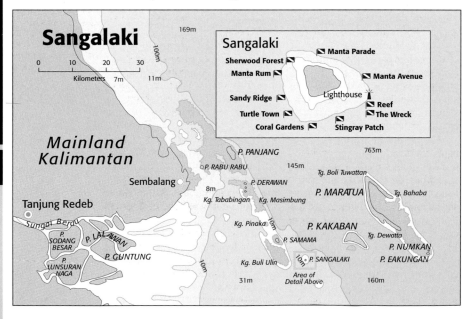

of Kalimantan. Sangalaki is their island-of-choice, a genetically imprinted home ground, programmed when the baby turtles hatch and make a mad dash for the sea before birds and other predators gobble the helpless young.

Kakaban Island

Less than half an hour away in one of the dive boats, Kakaban Island offers an excellent wall dive with a vertical, cave-pocketed drop to some 50 meters. There could be a current here to fin against, but it is quite easy for experienced divers. Fish tend to like currents and we saw many schooling surgeons and snappers, along with barrel sponges and, at depth, great gorgonian fans. Other divers here have spotted reef whitetip sharks, greys and a bone-chilling, 5-meter hammerhead. The topside decompression stop alone is worth the dive with excellent wall-to-wall coral cover swarming with colorful fairy basslets.

But Kakaban lays claim to a much more extraordinary fame. A lake fills much of the central part of the island, slightly above sea level, with a salt concentration only about two-thirds that of the ocean. The lake holds many species of marine life, some very probably new to science. There are, for instance, hundreds of stingless jellyfishes of four different species, pulsating along on the surface; over a half dozen fish species, generally shaped like gobies, cardinals, halfbeaks and heartyheads.

Other marine life observed includes tunicates, small, colonial bivalves, nudibranchs, a land snake, pure white anemone-like animals, at least three species of holothurian sea cucumbers, sponges of two distinct growth forms and two kinds of crabs. Scientific exploration of the lake has just begun.

The lake is ringed by thickly encrusted mangrove roots, and the slopes at the lake edge are covered in lush vegetation. It's an easy, 10-minute walk to the lake along a wide trail.

Derawan

Derawan Island, which can be reached from Sangalaki, also offers diving and tourist facilities. While the diving is not as good on Derawan or as nearby as at Sangalaki, the scuba facilities are well-run by two PADI-trained divemasters from Bali. The compressor and rental equipment seem well maintained. The nearby dive spots are interesting, but Sangalaki is without a doubt still the best spot in the area.

There are two inexpensive losmen on the island, the possibility of home stays, and a resort with cottage-style rooms facing the white-sand beach.

— *Kal Muller*

Above: The ribbon eel *(Rhinomuraena quaesita)* is one of the most beautiful, and unusual, of the moray eels. *Photo by Michael Aw.*

45 min to 2 hrs by boat, depending on location and type of vessel

Poor to fair, 8–15 m

Quite gentle

Can be very good

Coral slopes

Good varieties and numbers

Wooden shipwreck at Pulau Piniki; excellent coral at Pulau Kotok and Pulau Gosonglaga

Pulau Seribu

Diving from Java's "Thousand Islands"

While not noted for Indonesia's best diving, Pulau Seribu—the Thousand Islands—is very convenient because of its proximity to Jakarta. The islands are scattered in a vertical group north from the Indonesian capital in the shallow Java Sea.

The dive possibilities here are countless. The reefs around many of the 110 islands are excellent in terms of coral growth and fish life. What makes the diving here just fair by Indonesian standards is the generally poor visibility. With few exceptions, the marine life at most Pulau Seribu locations will include an abundant variety of hard and soft corals, a good variety of reef fishes and some pelagics, turtles and an occasional shark. Unfortunately, at some sites the deterioration of marine life is increasingly noticeable due to human presence. Pollution, and in some cases, mismanagement, is killing off the coral.

Pulau Piniki This is an oblong island oriented along a north-south axis. There is an interesting reef off the western side of Piniki starting at a depth of 5 meters, but it has its best coral growth and fish life at around 20 meters. At the southwest point is the wreck of a

Right: A school of big-eyed jacks, *Caranx sexfasciatus.* The jacks belong to a large family of silvery, fast swimming fishes found on both temperate and tropical reefs.
Photo by Jones/Shimlock.

20-meter wooden cargo ship. The ship's cargo of cement has solidified, but the weakened wooden structure is not safe to enter. Schools of barracuda, batfishes, large parrotfishes and moray eels have made the wreck their home.

Pulau Papa Theo This island, formerly called Pulau Tondan Timur, was renamed when the *Papa Theo*, a cargo vessel, sank here in 1982. The 20-meter vessel rests now with its port side facing the reef and its bow in 20 meters. Until April 1991, the ship stood almost upright, but then its stern collapsed, spilling its until then intact cargo of paper products and pharmaceuticals, including condoms. This rates as a simple wreck dive, with lots of marine life and an occasional shark in the deeper waters at the stern end. Look out for parrotfishes, some resident groupers, many morays and a particular abundance of stingrays. The north reef is often chosen for night dives.

Kuburan Cina This very small island is among the best diving sites in Pulau Seribu. The good reef begins due west of the island, continues around the south, then east. There is a small bit of reef at the north tip. Excellent coral growth provides the backdrop for a good drift dive in 8–20-meter depths. In some areas off the coral is good to 30 meters and you'll find there is a difference in the size of the island at high and low tide.

Pulau Kotok This island sits on the western edge of the Pulau Seribu group and thus offers some of the best coral growth. The undamaged reef here is particularly good for snorkeling as well as diving. Because it faces the open sea, Kotok is the place to see schools of sweetlips, turtles and sharks. Small manta rays have been spotted here. The area is abundant in gorgonians and soft corals.

Pulau Malinjo A very good reef extends from the west around to

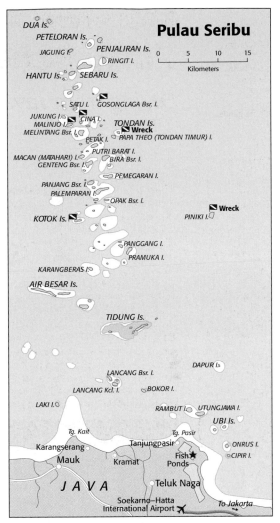

Pulau Seribu

the north, and along the southwest edge of the island and the best diving is around 10 meters. You can find lobsters here up to 30 cm long. The reef is also home to a great number of moray eels.

Pulau Gosonglaga This island is basically a small sandbank surrounded by an immense reef. The entire circumference of the reef is good, and in areas good coral growth extends down to more than 20 meters. Since the island is on the fringe of the Pulau Seribu group, it is one of the best places to see larger reef fish and occasional pelagics.

— *Janet Boileau*

Live-aboard: The Pindito

Diving in the Remotest Locations

10 min
from *Pindito*

Good to very good,
15–25 m

Variable;
nil to strong

Generally excellent

Walls, coral gardens

Excellent numbers

Excellent vessel.
Exciting encounters
with grouper,
sharks. Sheer
number of species

Built in south Kalimantan, part of Indonesian Borneo, the 40-meter *Pindito*, a 230-ton ship, is the pride and joy of its Swiss designer and general manager, Edi Frommenwiler, who has been operating the *Pindito* as a dive vessel since 1992.

The *Pindito* takes divers to sites in the Banda Sea, and when the weather shifts, to the Raja Empat Islands off Irian Jaya's Bird's Head Peninsula. We accompanied the ship during a Banda Sea run.

Cruises to Raja Empat take divers to sunken World War II Japanese fighter aircraft in the Sorong area, some excellent dives off tall offshore pinnacles, and— from April to September—some lucky clients are taken to one of the very few known nesting beaches of the giant leatherback sea turtles.

Koon Island

During our 10-day dive cruise on the *Pindito*, we checked out a couple of dozen locations pioneered by Peter, the on-board dive instructor, and Frommenwiler. Visibility was generally good—ranging from 15 to 25 meters—but not really excellent due to the plankton in the water. Most of the reefs were drop-offs and steep slopes around isolated islands. All were top spots, but the best of the best was, without doubt, Koon Island.

Giant groupers are really something to see, but it was a combination of underwater spectacles that made our dives on Koon among the very best in Indonesia. Never have we seen so many huge schools and

aggregations of various fish species.

In addition to the bigeye jacks, we saw large groups of batfish, bright yellow sailfin snappers and yellow-eyed midnight snappers, barracuda, longnose emperors, bannerfish, blue-fin jacks, unicornfish, painted sweetlips, and blue triggerfish. While on other dives I have seen one or two of these species in schools or large, loose groups— except for the sailfin snappers and the painted sweetlips—at Koon the diversity and numbers were overwhelming.

Reef sharks were conspicuous by their absence—except for a string of five large whitetips, swimming by in single file, heads and tails almost touching, a formation I had never before witnessed. Other unusual marine life included many large groupers of a half-dozen species, all in the 60–100-cm range. And, of course, plenty of reef fishes of various kinds and an occasional turtle and sea snake.

Our next plunge was one of those once-in-a-lifetime experiences. We dropped in near the edge of the sloping reef and quickly made our way to where the vertical wall began. Right then we froze: one of the giant groupers decided to check us out. Slowly finning back and forth just out of decent photo range, the big fella must have decided that we were a harmless curiosity and drifted in for a closer look, stopping just a couple meters away. This was one big, big fish.

While we frantically photographed, our giant grouper seemed happy enough to pose until we had our visual fill. By then, we had spot-

Opposite:
Snorkeling in Southeast Asian waters is a special treat.
Photo by Jones/Shimlock.

ted a huge school of batfish below and dropped a bit to take a closer look. We needn't have bothered—apparently we piqued their curiosity, too, and they came up to check us out.

With our computers ready to edge into decompression mode, which is strongly discouraged by the *Pindito*'s divemaster, we slowly ascended to around 15 meters. From this vantage point, we watched schools of at least seven species, plus small groups of individuals of a dozen more species—a combined mass of fish that was truly breathtaking.

Night Diving The walls turn into night-time fish hotels, many species sleeping off their daytime labors. Species that would never allow a close-up at daytime look blissfully asleep with open eyes, unaware of divers being far inside their private

Below: Anthias swarm around a gorgonian fan. *Photo by Ashley Boyd.*

territory. One of these, a high-bodied grouper close to a meter in length, defied identification in any of the fish books on board.

Our lights also brought out the bright yellow and orange polyps of the cup corals, and the strong colors of soft coral trees. And crustaceans, seldom seen in daytime—a slipper lobster, hermit crabs—unconcerned by our bright lights.

Diving Manuk

Our first dive, off north Manuk, was good but not really spectacular. We saw lots of sea snakes, many of them coming to within a few centimeters of us, then losing interest. Lots of large barrel-sponges dotted the seascape, but we only saw one large school of fish. This was the only hint of the tremendous second dive which is definitely one of the best single dives of my career. A fearless whitetip shark, angelfishes, jacks and more species than we could count were sighted—all blessed with a curiosity which made photography a dream.

The highlights of the night dive were the still foraging sea snakes, and several interesting gastropods, including a rare cowry and a large, tun shell.

Karang Pekelo

The fish show at Karang Pekelo, a site off south-central Seram Island, was almost overwhelming. Even as we were descending we were greeted by a couple dozen long, sleek rainbow runners, a lone torpedo mackerel and several good-sized tuna.

At about 12 meters, just above the reeftop, we were mobbed by a huge school of bigeye jacks in a visibility of 20–25 meters. The school vanished quickly, but returned several times during the course of the dive. We dropped down the reef face to sand at 30–35 meters, with a few scattered coral outcrops on the flat substrate. Upon arrival, a school of unicorn filefish, a species we had never seen before, suddenly finned past us.

Then, some 20 meters away, we distinguished a familiar species, the yellow-eyed puffer—but instead of just one we were looking at a most unusual school of about 50 individuals.

Warned by our computers that bottom time was up, we rose to the 20-meter level and settled in for a ringside seat at the fish parade: big-nosed unicornfish, surgeonfish, yellow- and blue-streak fusiliers and red snappers. We never identified the fish in the biggest school, which kept parading back and forth. They were snappers of some kind, but with dirty-looking, mottled gray-brown bodies in need of a good scrubbing.

A couple of very obvious, and big, black jacks finned by, but our attention was riveted on a giant grouper, 2 meters long. Other big boys included several very large Napoleon wrasses, and a couple of bumphead parrotfish.

Schooling fishes of many species enliven all of Indonesia's better dive locations. During a typical dive, two or three schools put in a brief appearance, and quickly vanish. Only a very few dive locations literally swarm with masses of fish. Karang Pekelo, discovered only in late 1993, is one of these fantastic places.

Other Sites

While we have seen the highlights of a single *Pindito* cruise, other routes also feature exceptional diving. This includes a small group smack in the middle of the Banda Sea and well over 200 km away from the Banda Islands.

These "lost" mini islands are divided into two small groups, and are so little known they go under various names, either the Lucipara Islands or Pulau Tujuh.

Underwater in Lucipara, there are fine drop-offs with excellent hard corals and black corals. There is nothing unusual in the fish life there, except that common species grow much larger than normal, close to or surpassing record lengths.

Life On Board the Pindito

The *Pindito* operates most efficiently, but the dive schedule is flexible in the face of unforeseen circumstances: unseasonal weather, lost baggage, etcetera. The normal routine calls for two daytime dives, plus one at night.

Suiting-up has been well thought out and there's plenty of space for it. The crew brings filled tanks from the compressor area in the stern of the boat to the wide front deck where large open baskets hold the clients' dive gear. Everyone puts on his or her own BC and regulator, then the crew carries the tanks down wide ladders—one on the port side, the other on starboard—to the three waiting Zodiacs. After a briefing by the divemaster, the clients step down the ladders for the short ride (usually 5–10 minutes) to the dive site. Two safety rules apply: no diving deeper than 40 meters, and a maximum of 60 minutes' bottom time. The ship always anchors far enough away from the reefs to prevent damage.

Our cruise on the *Pindito* was one of the most exciting and enjoyable ones we have ever taken. The

all-wooden ship looks and feels great. Solid, top-quality ironwood below the waterline, meranti for the deck, and fine wood paneling elsewhere.

The crew of 15, while speaking little English, is as cheerful and efficient as any we had sailed with in Indonesia. The ever-varied meals were healthy and delicious and the atmosphere in the dining-room and lounge area was always cordial. With the main engine well muffled, and electric motors on the compressors, noise was never a problem.

— *Kal Muller*

Above: The impressive 40-meter *Pindito* has been operated as a dive vessel since 1992. *Photo by Kal Muller.*

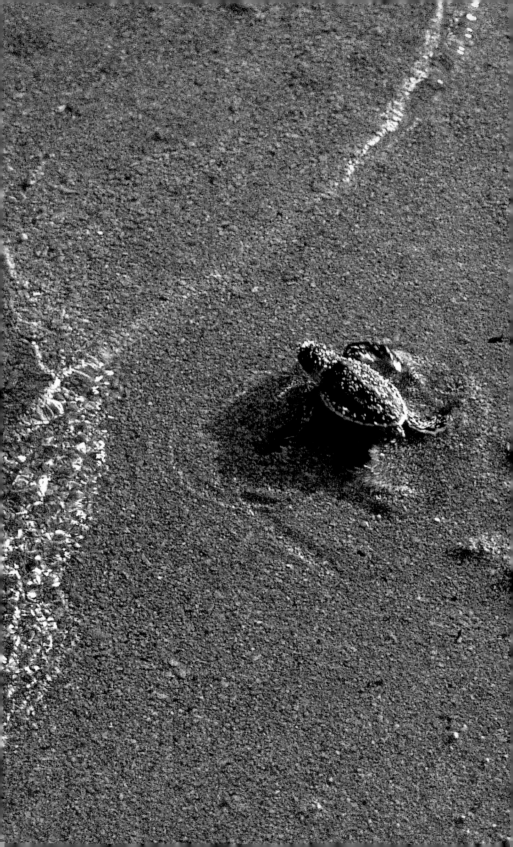

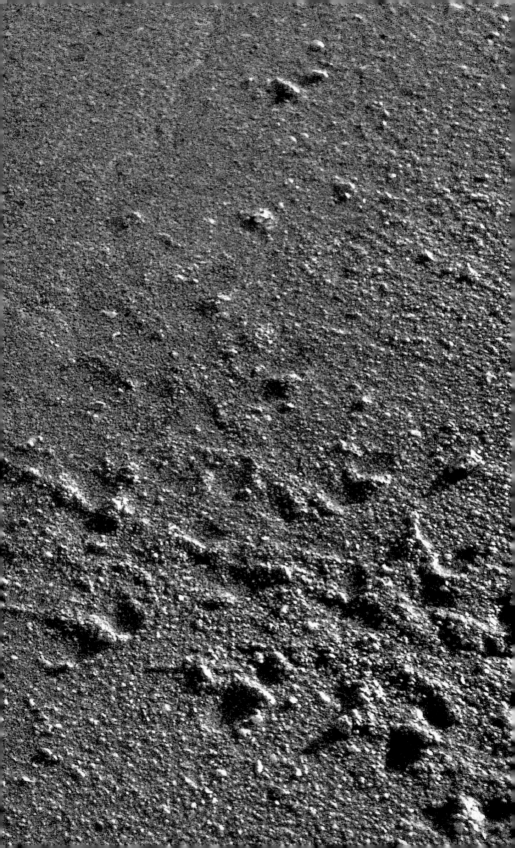

Diving in Malaysia
Where Rainforest Meets Reef

Fifteen years ago, those adventurous travelers who made their way to Malaysia were rewarded with a rich culture and a lifestyle that had changed little over the centuries. Occasionally they snorkeled the island coral reefs and even more occasionally they dived the offshore waters. The attractions that the country advertised overseas were, however, largely on *terra firma*. But much of that has changed, especially in the last 5 years. Scuba professionals have set up operations in a number of places in the country, and now offer a good variety of services and dive options. With the help of some individuals in the private sector, the tourism arm of the government has made a very conscious effort to attract overseas visitors to Malaysia's marine attractions. With considerable success.

Malaysia lies entirely within the tropics and is divided into two main geographical areas. Peninsular Malaysia joins, on its northern boundary, Thailand and on its southern shore, the Republic of Singapore through a causeway linking the two countries. Some 650 km away, on the huge island of Borneo, lie two more Malaysian states, the vast states of Sabah and Sarawak, separated by the independently ruled Sultanate of Brunei. The two states on Borneo complete the 13 states of Malaysia, ruled under a federal system from Kuala Lumpur on the Malay peninsula.

Like many of its Asian neighbors, Malaysia has made tremendous economic progress in the last decade resulting in a large growth in population and a huge increase in urban development, both on a commercial and domestic level.

The capital, Kuala Lumpur, has expanded both laterally and skyward, while Johor Bahru, the country's second largest town and Singapore's nearest neighbor, has similarly grown in size and population. Shopping malls, office buildings and international class hotels now decorate these skylines that once carried a silhouette of palm trees and thatched roofs.

Malaysia has two distinctive seasons, dividing the country climatically, though the temperatures at sea level do not vary radically with either season. You can expect a high that rarely exceeds 31°C on the coast, and a low that rarely drops below 22°C. Of course, in the highland areas temperatures are quite different. While the northeast monsoon lashes the eastern shores, dumping heavy rain from November to late February, the western parts of the country—and that includes the dive sites around Langkawi—enjoy drier, sunny tropical weather. Conversely, when the southwest monsoon picks up from May to October, it is time for the East Coast dive sites, and those in Borneo, to enjoy sunny dry days—and the western shores get their torrential downpours.

Of the 18.6 million inhabitants in the 13 states comprising Malaysia, 8 percent are ethnically Indian, 31 percent are of Chinese origin while the majority, approximately 60 percent, are pure Malays and aborigines.

The Malays, a Muslim population, have always been fishermen

Overleaf: A green turtle hatchling reaches the surf, still to face many predators. The best places in Malaysia for sea turtle watchers are Sipadan Island and Terengganu. *Photo by Jones/Shimlock.*

Opposite: Nazri's Beach on idyllic Tioman—often regarded as one of the ten most beautiful islands in the world. *Photo by Jack Jackson.*

though perhaps not sailors. They know their coastal waters and have fished them for centuries. Unfortunately with a growing population to feed, an active tourism industry and a worldwide interest in tropical fish for aquaria, their fishing techniques became more radical in the sixties and seventies. Dynamite and cyanide might bring more fish into their nets, but it also killed and maimed many more, and did irreparable damage to the coral reefs.

Creation of Marine Parks

In the mid-seventies, Sabah gazetted one of the first marine parks in the country, the Tunku Abdul Rahman Park. Then in the eighties, answering a call from concerned environmentalists and divers, four further marine reserves were gazetted to protect the fauna and flora off Peninsular Malaysia's coasts. These included Pulau Payar in Kedah and the three areas off the East Coast of Malaysia. These last three marine parks together cover thousands of square kilometers of water and embrace some of the most picturesque islands and coral reefs anywhere, among them Redang, Tenggol, Kapas, Rawa and Tioman. It was no accident that Tioman was chosen as one of the sites for filming part of the movie, *South Pacific*—an island that breathed the ingredients of a tropical paradise.

All the East Coast islands are reefed with coral and host a marine ecology which enthralls snorkelers and provides plenty of interest for divers. In addition, outer islands are sufficiently far away from the effects of the mainland and deep enough into the South China Sea to boast a variety of large pelagics.

These islands and the shores of the East Coast generally are also, interestingly, one of the main breeding grounds for leatherback, green and hawksbill turtles. Traditionally turtle eggs have been collected in Malaysia as they are believed, in some instances, to have aphrodisiacal qualities. This, and the killing of turtles for their flesh, has lead to a huge decline in numbers. In an effort to conserve these harmless creatures, wardens and volunteers search nightly during the summer laying season for nests containing turtle eggs, incubating them in the safety of government hatcheries and releasing the young turtles into the sea. Similar schemes to ensure turtle survival operate on the three islands comprising Turtle Island Park off Sandakan, on the tiny isle of Sipadan, Sabah, and on Pulau Besar, near Malacca, off the West Coast of Peninsular Malaysia.

Locating Malaysia's Coral Reefs

On Peninsular Malaysia's East Coast, the best coral reefs are to be

Below: If you see a cloud of juvenile fish or small cardinalfish like this one, look closely as there will probably be a frogfish lurking somewhere on the outcrop.
Photo by Jones/Shimlock.

found in the nine islands that comprise Pulau Rendang, until recently inhabited only by a number of fisherfolk. Its beauty has inevitably caught the eye of developers who have created a golf course on the island and will soon open hotel facilities where scuba diving will be one of the main attractions. Fine corals too, are to be found at fairly shallow depths around the two Perhentian islands and at Lang Tengah.

To the south, Pulau Tenggol has good coral formations in excellent condition and the only real wall diving in Peninsular Malaysia, while Kapas, with its exquisite white sandy beaches, offers shallow and pretty coral reefs.

Tioman, despite its beauty, is not the best place for corals; overfishing, dynamite fishing and human influence have done much to destroy the nearby corals. Offshore, and on submerged reefs, the conditions are better. However, because it is served by a small airport with daily flights to and from Kuala Lumpur and Singapore, and excellent sea connections, it proves a very popular resort for holidaymakers and divers, particularly over weekends. In the southern waters of the East Coast lies the small island of Aur, which boasts good corals and some fine diving. With its proximity to Singapore, it too attracts plenty of weekend divers from the republic.

Although the formation of marine parks has helped limit the damage caused by illegal fishing, it can do nothing to prevent the run-off from the peninsula itself (deforestation has not been kind to the rivers and offshore waters)—which has disastrous effects on the mangrove swamps as well as on inshore corals.

The best areas for coral on the west side of the country are around the three islands that form the Pulau Payar Marine Park, just south of Langkawi. With the creation of a new Australian-style platform in the Park, snorkelers and divers now have easy access to the reef. And although the visibility is not as good as that on the East Coast, divers report good coral and marine life.

In Borneo, the situation is far better. With the gazetting of Tunku Abdul Rahman Park over 20 years ago, the reefs around the five small islands off Kota Kinabalu's shore have benefited enormously from protection. Visibility is not the best, but the shallow reefs are a major attraction to holidaymakers in the area. Snorkeling and diving facilities are available to visitors.

But the best reefs lie, without a doubt, at Sipadan, a small mushroom-shaped island rising from the ocean floor, situated some 25 km off the coast from Tawau. The reefs are in excellent condition, with a rating amongst the best in Asia and when the waters are not filled with plankton, the visibility can be good. There are, however, now three dive operations on the island, a figure which some conservationists fear will be the island's downfall.

New to the diving fraternity as a dive destination is Layang-Layang, some 240 km north of Kota Kinabalu. Because of its remoteness, the reefs are in fine condition and provide divers with some fabulous encounters not only with reef life but with large pelagics.

Live-aboards

In the last few years, divers have found that live-aboard dive boats offer an excellent alternative to land-based diving in Malaysia. Divers at Pulau Layang-Layang invariably dive from a live-aboard boat. Divers can also enjoy Sipadan and the Kunak group of islands, north of Sipadan, from the comfort of a live-aboard dive boat. Lastly, many dive trips to Malaysia, in particular those to the islands off the East Coast, can also be organized from neighboring Singapore.
— *Fiona Nichols*

Photo by Roger Steene

Sipadan

Memorable Diving from an Oceanic Isle East of Borneo

2–15 min by boat

Variable, 10–22 m

Light, occasionally more

Generally good variety

Slopes and walls, cave

Generally good numbers of big fish at best sites

Hammerheads; Turtle Cavern; turtles galore

The diving is always good at Sipadan and, sometimes, superb. Good-sized pelagics generally represent Sipadan's main attraction to divers. While nothing is guaranteed, it's likely that a week's diving will be highlighted by one or more of the following: a hoard of 50 hammerheads, leopard sharks, barracudas in shoals of several hundred, a rumbling herd of many bumphead parrotfish, a manta or two and a half-dozen whitetip sharks.

Reef fish are present in fair numbers and variety and perhaps most impressive are the quantities of medium-sized fish—between 25 and 40 cm—in relatively shallow waters. This is especially the case for groups of up to a dozen harlequin sweetlips, but also snappers, emperors, triggerfishes, longfin batfish and a couple of species of unicornfishes.

Macro-lens wielders and those with acute powers of observation could spot an unusual crinoid, shrimp and tiny fish combination, all matching the host's coloration. Or a golden-spotted shrimp on a very flattened carpet anemone. Some divers have found a patch of relatively tame spotted garden eels, elsewhere requiring the patience of Job to photograph outside of their burrow. Sharp eyes can also reveal a pink sailfin leaf-fish or a scorpionfish, and nudibranchs.

It has been said that the reefs of Sipadan are less colorful than elsewhere in Southeast Asia. This is possibly due to the restricted visibility in the shallows (often of pea-soup quality) but also to far less aggregations of fairy basslets and other small fry. However, sponges are there in various shapes, especially enormous barrel sponges.

We find the dive spots live up to their names: White Tip Avenue, Turtle Patch, Staghorn Crest, Lobster Lair, Hanging Gardens (for soft corals).

But Sipadan also has problems; visibility is seldom great—our dives averaged 10–15 meters. There are also too many divers for the ecosystem. Three spartan but adequate resorts can put up 100 people, three times the number generally agreed as the optimum. The numbers swell on weekends.

South Point On one trip we saw a school of 50 hammerhead sharks at South Point; a solid wall of barracudas stretching over 10 meters high, almost motionless in the current and relatively undisturbed by the gazes of fellow divers, and several dozen bumphead parrotfish in a herd, lazing just under the surface in dappled sunlight. These highlights require a touch of luck. But on every one of our 18 dives we saw green turtles—up to a dozen in a single dive—along with reef whitetip sharks and, always, a fair variety of reef fishes.

Barracuda Point There is one good reason to dive this spot—barracuda. Time after time they turn up in their hundreds, a shoal that turns the water into a glinting wall of fish. There are also sharks, accompanying every dive along with a shoal of bumphead parrotfish.

Hanging Gardens Coral lovers

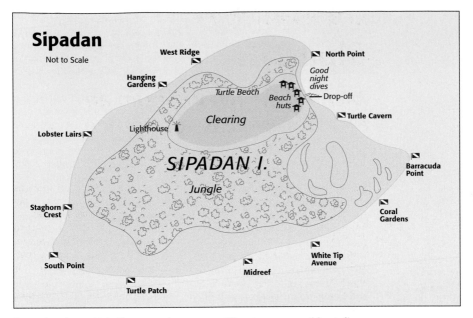

Sipadan

Not to Scale

West Ridge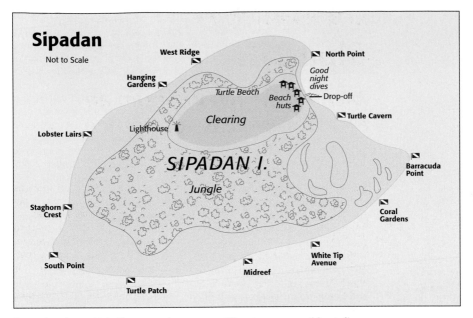

North Point

Hanging Gardens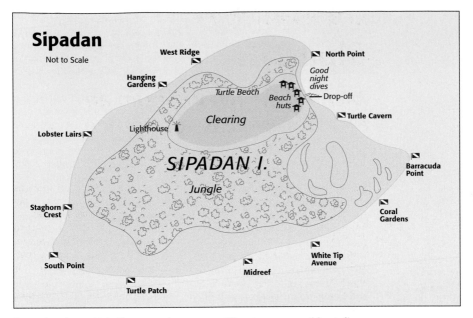

Good night dives

Turtle Beach

Beach huts

Drop-off

Clearing

Turtle Cavern

Lobster Lairs

Lighthouse

SIPADAN I.

Barracuda Point

Jungle

Staghorn Crest

Coral Gardens

South Point

White Tip Avenue

Midreef

Turtle Patch

love this beautiful dive spot just minutes from the resort. The soft corals hang like dripping wax from candles in a profusion of colors that can hardly be matched elsewhere. We have rarely had good visibility here (diving in the morning without sunlight is not the best) but the beauty of the sights compensates.

Turtles While you tend to become blasé about green turtles, this is the one guaranteed highlight on Sipadan. It is claimed that the waters off the island hold the largest turtle population found anywhere. And most of the gentle giants, used to humans, even allow physical contact, but this is rightly discouraged. Just swimming slowly close to one is thrilling enough. Or watching them tearing and chewing a chunk of soft coral. And almost nothing disturbs a mating pair, not even other males climbing on top, hoping to get in on the action.

Turtle Cavern offers the unusual, if macabre. This cavern, which turns into a cave, holds lots of turtle skeletons along with that of a dolphin. Just so you don't join the skeletons, cavern-diver certification is required. Borneo Divers offers the PADI speciality course on Sipadan. (This takes 4 days but you

can still get one normal boat dive a day while the course lasts.)

Entrance to the cavern passes through a wide opening: buoyancy control has to be strict or clouds of sediment get stirred up, taking hours to settle. Heading back towards the entrance, schooling fish often make a good parting shot, framed by the cavern entrance.

Turtle Facts

A large population of green turtles (*Chelonia mydas*) call Sipadan home. Their name comes not so much from their overall color, an olive-brown, as from their greenish fat. We saw some of these turtles on every dive, with an occasional individual close to the species' maximum size: 140 kg and a carapace length of over 1 meter. Indeed turtles are one of the main reasons for Sipadan's popularity.

The animals are almost exclusively vegetarian, feeding on sea grasses, algae, occasionally sponges and soft corals. While they are protected on Sipadan, elsewhere the green turtles are killed for their meat, hide and oil. Here their eggs are collected for local sale. Of course, egg collecting leads to a decrease in the numbers of the species as it has been calculated that it takes between 500 and 5,000 eggs to produce a single surviving adult.

But it's a lucrative business. The three families with traditional turtle egg gathering rights on Sipadan have earned a handsome living. Sea turtle eggs sell for 20 cents each in Sabah. Turtles take their time copulating and because of this, some believe the eggs increase male potency, especially if the first three of any batch are eaten raw.

Aside from the big chaps, schooling fish are below average, with only two species of fusiliers relatively abundant. An exception to this general rule is at Barracuda and South Point, where we sometimes drifted down through four good-sized schools. Anemones and their guest-fish can be spotted on almost every dive, along with hefty-size, solitary barracuda (usually in the shallows), and an occasional imperturbable crocodilefish, alias longsnout flathead. Moorish idols, often in pairs, usually accompany every dive.

Diving Basics

Sipadan diving is not for everyone. Currents are often present and shift during the course of a dive. At Barracuda Point, in particular, there is often 2 knots of current, heading away from the reef and downward. There are relatively easy dive spots, but we found the most interesting were also the ones with the strongest current: Barracuda and South Point.

All the resorts offer unlimited beach diving. The north wall drop-off next to the pier is only a few meters in front of the Borneo Divers' resort. Only night diving is allowed here.

Sipadan is largely boat diving. Suiting up on the resorts' premises, divers get on their boats in full gear for the two or three daily dives. It's a short ride to the various spots,

usually 10 minutes or less, but the surface can be choppy to or from the entry point. To avoid reef damage, the boats do not anchor but the boatmen will follow the divers conscientiously.

Sipadan Island lies not far, but in splendid isolation, from the continental shelf. While it's only some 12 km to Mabul Island on the edge of the shallow Sigitan reefs, the ocean plunges to almost 1,000 meters before rising abruptly.

The 15-hectare island, with its lush vegetation and white sand beaches, is but the tip of a marine outcrop. To walk the surrounding beach takes around 30 minutes, and there is much nature to observe along the shore and on land.

Three resorts are currently crowded on the island's northwest shore, spread behind a wooden pier. Just a few meters to the west of the jetty, where the reeftop extends less than 10 meters from the shore, the turquoise waters abruptly turn dark blue at the edge of a vertical wall. Elsewhere the shallow reef extends as an irregular fringe, over 500 meters off South Point. A dozen-odd dive spots dot the edge of the reef, all above vertical walls.

The discovery of Sipadan only goes back to 1984. While on a commercial job on a nearby grounded ship, Borneo Divers checked out the island, and liked very much what they saw. After obtaining all the necessary permits, the outfit started bringing clients here in 1985. Divers were initially put up in tents. Now the accommodation has been upgraded to a very comfortable dive resort, and two competing resorts have recently been established on Sipadan.

The island received a boost at international level when Jacques Cousteau spent several weeks here to shoot his film, *Ghost of the Sea Turtles*. While Cousteau claimed the discovery of Turtle Cavern, he and his team were allegedly taken there by Borneo Divers, who had already surveyed the site.

— *Kal Muller*

Opposite: The Borneo Divers' longhouse—accommodation for divers on Sipadan Island. *Photo by Jones/Shimlock.*

Layang-Layang and Kota Kinabalu

Diving off Sabah's Northwest Coast

Two world-class possibilities exist for diving from the East Malaysian state of Sabah on the island of Borneo. About 300 km northwest of Kota Kinabalu (KK), in the midst of the South China Sea, lies the Layang-Layang Atoll, part of the group of atolls that make up the controversial Borneo Banks. A small man-made island supports a military base, a 17-room resort, and the air-strip used to get visitors to and from the island. The remainder of the atoll lies under water, with the exception of rocks that are exposed at low tide. The reefs drop in walls on all sides to depths of up to 2,000 meters. However, there are some good, shallow reefs for repeat dives.

Below: Sea fans *(Melithaea sp.)* feed on plankton and thrive in exposed locations where the currents supply them with food. *Photo by Jones/Shimlock.*

A Gathering of Pelagics

Layang-Layang's diving season is from March until September. It is, above all, famous for schooling hammerhead sharks, and they are there in abundance until July, but as the water warms up the sharks go deeper. The best diving is around the northeastern end of the atoll, followed closely by the southwestern end.

The eastern point of the atoll is called Dog Tooth Lair, and in addition to the tuna that the site is named after, this seems to be the spot for hammerheads. Normally swimming at depths of 40 meters or more, we once encountered a school of sharks in the 10-meter-deep waters of the coral gardens. Schools of barracuda populate the reef and wall; a huge school of jacks hang out at 10–15 meters, and manta rays are also frequent visitors here.

The Gorgonian Forest is a continuation of the wall at Dog Tooth Lair, so it is not uncommon to see schooling hammerheads on this dive either. But this site is famous for its sea fans. From 20 meters down, the wall is covered in multicolored sea fans of impressive size—great for wide angle photography. Navigator Lane is next along the wall, and here the sea fans give way to an impressive display of soft corals. The site was visited by hammerheads during our dives, and invariably there were grey and whitetip sharks circling around off the wall. Tuna cruise up and down the drop-off in search of an unwary

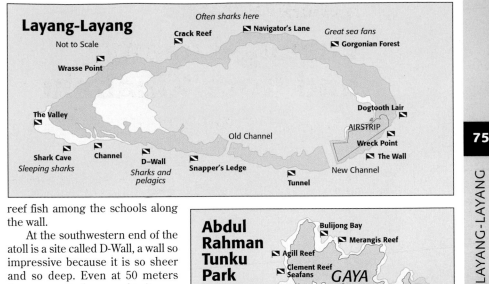

Layang-Layang

Not to Scale

Wrasse Point

The Valley

Shark Cave
Sleeping sharks

Channel

D–Wall
Sharks and
pelagics

Snapper's Ledge

Crack Reef

Often sharks here

Navigator's Lane

Old Channel

Tunnel

Great sea fans

Gorgonian Forest

Dogtooth Lair

AIRSTRIP

Wreck Point

The Wall

New Channel

reef fish among the schools along the wall.

At the southwestern end of the atoll is a site called D-Wall, a wall so impressive because it is so sheer and so deep. Even at 50 meters there seems to be no end to its vertical drop. The wall is festooned with colorful soft corals that entice the diver deeper. On one dive, while photographing soft corals at some 35 meters, a school of 40 hammerheads swam by. Although not sighted as often in this area, they are here! Whitetips, tuna and clouds of reef fishes populate the wall to make a great dive site.

At the end of D-Wall is a site aptly named Shark Cave, for at 20–25 meters there is a deep cave extending under the reef where a group of whitetips can often be found sleeping. Here we found 10 sharks piled up like logs on the left side of the cave and a school of about 50 snappers hanging around the entrance on the right side of the cave. Down current, the reef is flatter with rolling terrain. This area is generally swept by currents, and consequently is often favored by large fishes.

Abdul Rahman Tunku

If sharks are not your idea of fun diving, KK has an alternative. Twenty minutes by boat from the center of KK, capital of Sabah, lie five islands that make up the Tunku Abdul Rahman Park, offering secluded beaches and reefs just off-

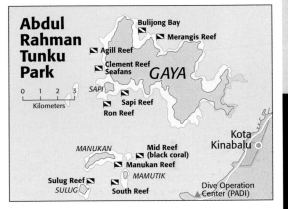

Abdul Rahman Tunku Park

0 1 2 3
Kilometers

Bulijong Bay

Merangis Reef

Agill Reef

Clement Reef
Seafans

GAYA

SAPI

Sapi Reef

Ron Reef

MANUKAN

Mid Reef
(black coral)

Manukan Reef

Kota
Kinabalu

MAMUTIK

Sulug Reef
SULUG

South Reef

Dive Operation
Center (PADI)

shore, perfect for snorkeling and diving.

Mid Reef near Manukan Island is a good site. The reef is generally round and slopes off on all sides from 5 to 20 meters. The top of the reef has good hard corals. Dropping down to 15–29 meters you encounter a garden of black coral trees. A small school of yellow-finned barracuda are present on most dives. Juvenile leopard sharks are often seen here on night dives.

Clement Reef, closer to Sapi Island, is also a sloping reef that ranges from 12 to 18 meters, with the exception of a small finger that juts out from the reef and reaches 25 meters in depth. This finger is covered with sea fans, sponges and soft coral, attracting schools of snappers and abundant reef fish. In February and March whale sharks migrate through the area and are sometimes seen by divers.

— *Bob Bowdey*

5–15 min by boat

Good, 10–25 m

Light to moderate

Excellent condition

Walls and reef crests

Good numbers and variety of big pelagics

Hammerhead sharks, dogtooth tuna, mantas, turtles

Terengganu

The Best Diving from Peninsular Malaysia

From its northern borders near the small coastal town of Besut to the sandy shores of Kemaman in the south, the East Coast state of Terengganu boasts some 225 km of nearly uninterrupted coastline and a score or so offshore islands, many of which offer excellent coral reefs that form part of a marine park.

The state of Terengganu is a traditional Muslim one with a pretty capital town, Kuala Terengganu, at the mouth of the river. Fishing, palm oil and agriculture were the mainstay of the economy. When oil was discovered offshore, the fortunes of this state changed radically, and it has become one of the wealthiest in the federation. And now tourism is beginning to play a major role in the state's economy, for its beaches and offshore islands have been discovered by sun lovers and divers. Indeed, a fabulous new golf club and hotel has taken shape on Rendang, while a hotel has recently been built on Lang Tengah, and among the marine recreational options, snorkeling and diving are being given priority.

Access to these tropical isles is from the capital, Terengganu, or alternatively from the small coastal towns of Kuala Besut, Marang and Dungun.

The Perhentian Islands

The two islands of Perhentian lie at the furthest extremity of Terengganu, some 14 nautical miles offshore, and are accessible by bumboat from Kuala Besut. Perhentian Kecil (the smaller island) has few facilities for tourists, so most stay on the larger island, Perhentian Besar, with its beautiful white sandy beaches, which has accommodation in the form of huts for holidaymakers and divers.

In the dry season (April to September), diving from Perhentian can be excellent, and the waters on the South China Sea side of the island are quite clear. The reefs are generally fairly shallow, although they extend deeper on the northern sides of the islands. There are some hard corals though not that many, plenty of beautiful soft corals and some impressive gorgonians on the outer reefs.

On a good dive you can expect to come across schools of trevallies, jacks, glasseyes and rainbow runners. There are some blacktip sharks in the area. Visibility here averages 12 meters, though it can fall. Among the pelagics often encountered around the Susu Dara group of isles just northwest of Perhentian—probably the best dive location— are whale sharks, but mantas, sailfish, barracudas and large groupers are also common.

Lang Tengah

Some 8–9 nautical miles (15 km) south of Perhentian lies the 120-ha island, Pulau Lang Tengah, another good spot for diving. A new resort has been built here with an emphasis on diving and snorkeling, and more and more good dive sites are being identified around the island.

Because of the surrounding

Opposite:
Nemanthus anna-mensis, the gorgonian wrapper or whip coral anemone, on a gorgonian. *Photo by Jones/Shimlock.*

By bumboat from coastal towns and from island resorts

Fair, 8–20 m

Usually negligible to light

Good condition, fine variety in most places

Usually coral gardens

Schools, reef fish, pelagics

Whale sharks, manta rays; wall at Tenggol

deep waters and its isolation, Lang Tengah has good corals, both hard and soft, hosting a proliferation of marine life. Six good dive sites have been identified in the vicinity including one with a large area of *Dendronephthya* and another of table corals. On a regular 15-meter dive, you should find yourself amidst schools of jacks and trevallies, yellowtails and rainbow runners. Late afternoon is a particularly good time for diving. A resident blacktip shark is often sighted near the resort while two large groupers have established a home practically at the resort door. Occasionally, bumphead parrotfish come into the reef in front of the resort. For the macro-photographer there are some great nudibranchs. The best time to dive here is in the dry season, from April to October.

Redang

The premier dive spot on the East Coast, Redang comprises nine islands. It is accessible from all the coastal towns mentioned earlier, or on the fast boat from Tanjong Marang, operated by the new resort itself. Once home to a few fishing families, it is now one of the country's newest tourist destinations. Its powdery white, sandy beaches and excellent coral reefs are a powerful magnet, and divers who want to explore the nearby reefs and islands further afield should book for at least 5 days to do the area justice.

The reefs around Rendang have suffered the minimum of damage over the years because of their relative distance from the mainland.

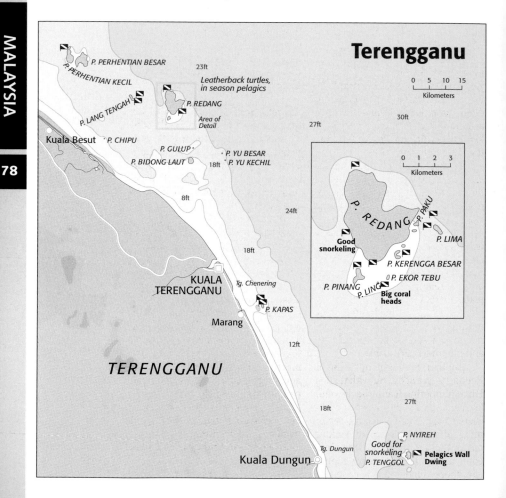

Consequently the reefs offer a fine variety of both hard and soft corals, which host a wealth of marine life.

Around the southeastern end of the main island there are some small offshore isles, Kerengga Kechil and Kerengga Besar, Pulau Ekor Tebu, and the large rock known as Ling. The reefs here are shallow in depth and you'll encounter a veritable forest of mushroom corals on the southwestern tip of Kerengga Besar. A huge area of *Porites,* rising over 5 meters from the seabed, is a favorite dive site around Ling, while staghorn corals are also predominant. The main island has some good shallow patches of coral— ideal for snorkeling or a repeat dive—which drop to deeper levels on the east coast.

The instructors and divemasters operating from Redang Island Resort have identified some eight good sites for diving, amongst which the reefs off the northeastern part of the main island and around Pulau Paku Besar and Pulau Paku Kecil come up a repeat favorite. A bit further eastwards, Pulau Lima has deep coral reefs, while the reefs around Pulau Pinang are very shallow and suffer from the run-off from the river Rendang.

So what are the highlights? In season (April to November, before the monsoons arrive) you can expect to see plenty of schools of fish: jacks, golden trevallies, groupers, coral trouts, snappers and barracudas. The macro-photographers should keep their eyes open for Spanish dancers—pink, purple and orange delights. The seabed is the place to find stingrays (there are plenty), while pelagic highlights inevitably include whale sharks, manta rays and the occasional tiger and hammerhead sharks.

Another highlight of diving in Redang is an encounter with turtles. Huge lumbering leatherbacks often lay their eggs in the beaches of the islands, and can be spotted swimming offshore. It's worth looking out for them at night, too, when they come ashore to nest. As mentioned elsewhere, turtles are a protected species in Asia and any encounter is a truly fascinating experience.

Although the diving is good throughout the summer months, it can be very good early November and again sometimes in late April. Visibility averages 10–15 meters and it can occasionally clear to 18 meters.

Kapas

Accessible from Kuala Dungun, the beautiful island of Kapas is known for its white, sandy beaches rather more than for its diving. However, it does have pretty corals in the shallows and this appeals particularly to snorkelers. The reef shelves gradually from 3 to 12 meters but it is symptomatic of the reef's condition that you'll find plenty of sea urchins! Look out for clownfish and their host anemones, small nudibranchs, damsels and sergeant-majors.

Tenggol

The island of Tenggol is situated further south from Redang and some 12 nautical miles offshore. It comprises one main island with a beautiful sandy beach of fine white sand and two small isles. On the western side of the island lies a sheltered bay.

However, the big attraction at Tenggol is wall diving, for the island has steep rocky cliffs on the eastern, South China Sea side of the island, which drop dramatically to the seabed. In addition, there are some pristine coral formations and a number of submerged rocks with excellent coral growth on them. Diving at Tenggol goes down to 48 meters, to the seabed, and divers who are more interested in fish than in corals and tunicates will find bumphead parrotfish, lizardfish, large schools of jacks, some whitetip sharks, and an occasional whale shark and manta ray. The rarely seen ghost pipefish is also known to make its home here.

—*Fiona Nichols*

Tioman & Aur

Playground for Divers and Holidaymakers

From the very first glimpse of its white sandy beaches, azure waters and often mist shrouded mountains, the island of Tioman exerts an almost mystical pull. Nearly 40 years ago it delighted film-goers, and it continues to delight romantics today. Tioman has become renowned as a great place to holiday. Indeed, during the late April to September season, visitors arrive

Above: A coral grouper, *Cephalopholis miniata*. This fish, a common inhabitant of caves and ledges, preys on small fishes and crustaceans. The younger specimens are more brightly colored. *Photo by Jones/Shimlock.*

from Kuala Lumpur, Johor and Singapore—so book in advance.

But Tioman is not a divers' paradise, but a paradise in which divers can dabble in their favorite sport. The once pristine corals have suffered through illicit dynamite fishing, run-offs from the rivers and the effects of being a popular resort.

In 1985, however, the waters around Tioman were designated part of a large marine park where sustainable fishing is permitted but dynamiting, cyanide poisoning and spear fishing are outlawed. Similarly, the islands off the coast of Johor—Rawa, Tinggi, Besar and

Sibu—were put under protection.

Although the visibility is usually in the region of 8 or 9 meters, it can very occasionally reach 12 meters. On an average dive, you'll meet schools of jacks, trevallies, coral trout, pufferfishes, a few stingrays and a number of moray eels. The crown-of-thorns starfish, which has done much damage to the reef, seems to be less prolific nowadays. We've heard stories about meeting a dozen hammerheads on one dive, but such sightings are uncommon. There are sharks—blacktip, nurse and even a whale shark from time to time. We have seen mantas on many trips and even the occasional sailfish.

There are some five or six favorite dive spots around Tioman, most of which can be accessed in less than an hour by the regular, converted fishing boats.

Some 15 minutes from the main resort, Magician Rock is the place for whale sharks and mantas when they pass. Schooling fish hang out here. There are plenty of fans for the photographers. Off the east coast, Juara is a good spot to see barracudas, snappers, stingrays, and to enjoy the hard corals. There is a submerged pinnacle here that attracts plenty of fish. Off the northeast, Sri Buat is renowned for its beautiful hard corals and some exceptionally tall soft corals.

Adjacent islands with good coral include Labas and Tulai. Check out the Napoleon wrasses at Tulai (it has a beautiful beach, too), and look out for the schools of trevally and barracuda. There are angelfishes and coral trouts for the

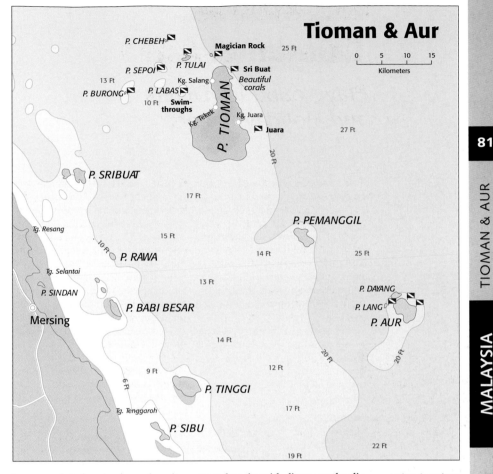

Tioman & Aur

P. CHEBEH

Magician Rock   25 Ft

0   5   10   15
Kilometers

P. SEPOI   P. TULAI

13 Ft   Kg. Salang   Sri Buat

P. BURONG   P. LABAS   Beautiful corals

10 Ft   Swim-throughs

P. TIOMAN

Kg. Tekek   Kg. Juara

Juara   27 Ft

20 Ft

P. SRIBUAT

17 Ft

P. PEMANGGIL

Tg. Resang

15 Ft

P. RAWA   14 Ft   25 Ft

10 Ft

Tg. Selantai

13 Ft

P. SINDAN   P. DAYANG

P. BABI BESAR   P. LANG

Mersing   P. AUR

14 Ft

20 Ft   20 Ft

9 Ft   12 Ft

6 Ft

P. TINGGI

Tg. Tenggaroh   17 Ft

P. SIBU

22 Ft

19 Ft

keen eyed. Labas is also a favorite for its rock formations and swim-throughs.

Tiger Reef has two huge pinnacles where there are schools of yellowtails, angelfishes and snappers. Nurse sharks are often sighted here. There are also some impressive sea fans and lovely soft corals. Diving is also excellent on the Jubilee Shoals, some 80 minutes by speedboat—it's pioneer diving on a virgin shoal—but only for those with GPS facilities.

Pulau Aur

This small island, 65 km from the Malaysian coast, is home to an active fishing community. Together with the neighboring islands of Dayang and Lang, Pulau Aur is a great favorite with divers, as the distance from the mainland has ensured its corals remain in good condition while its relative remoteness contributes to a better-than-average visibility for this part of the coast. Because of its distance, live-aboard diving is the norm (either from Mersing or Singapore) although some bungalows on Pulau Dayang offer accommodation.

Expect to find trevallies, sweetlips, coral trout, wrasses, plenty of parrotfishes, anemones and a wide variety of nudibranchs. Night diving in the main bay is also fun. Further from the shelter of the island, currents can be strong, especially on the surface, but as a compensation there are more large fish, and sighting a whale shark or even a hammerhead is possible.
—*Fiona Nichols*

By bumboat from Tioman or live-aboard dive trips from Mersing and Singapore

Fair, average of 9 m; Aur averaging 12 m

Variable

Fair in Tioman; good in Aur

Coral gardens

Good numbers, fair variety

Whale sharks, mantas; beautiful beaches

Langkawi

Diving the Marine Reserve at Pulau Payar

Below: The anemonefish *Amphiprion perideraion* in the magnificent anemone, *Heteractis magnifica.* The larger fish of an anemonefish pair is the female. *Photo by R.C. Anderson.*

This marine park encompasses four islands, Pulau Payar, Pulau Kaca, Pulau Lembu and Pulau Segantang, and is located 19 nautical miles south of the island of Langkawi, and 40 nautical miles north of Penang. The park's pride lies in its wide variety of habitats and the largest number of coral species in the country, including the most colorful soft corals.

The Marine Park was conceived to protect the natural marine wealth, while specific zones have been marked for research and educational activities as well as for recreation.

Coral Garden At the southwestern tip of Pulau Payar, this site offers a scenic dive with multi-colored soft corals, mainly *Dendronephthya.* The panorama is one with steep gullies and crevices which hide plenty of jacks, titan triggers, moray eels, blue-ringed angelfishes, lionfishes, porcupinefishes and many barrel sponges. Don't expect gin-clear visibility—it's around 10 meters usually, but can extend up to 16–20 meters.

Grouper Farm Named for the large groups of groupers which dwell here, this nearby site also pro-

Boat from Kuah to marine platform, 50 min

Fair, 2–10 m

Negligible

Best variety in Malaysia

Coral gardens, artificial reef

Fair variety

Ease of access; great for snorkelers

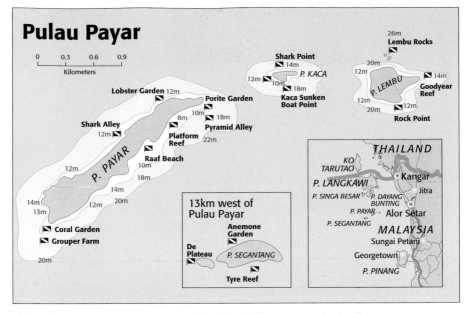

Pulau Payar

Map labels:

26m — Lembu Rocks
Shark Point — 14m
12m — P. KACA — 10m — 18m
Lobster Garden — 12m
Porite Garden — Kaca Sunken Boat Point
20m — 12m — 14m — Goodyear Reef — P. LEMBU — 12m — 20m — 12m — Rock Point
8m — 10m — 18m
Shark Alley — 12m
Pyramid Alley
Platform Reef — 22m
P. PAYAR
Raaf Beach — 10m
12m — 18m
14m — 20m
14m — 13m — 12m
Coral Garden
Grouper Farm
20m

THAILAND
KO TARUTAO — Kangar
P. LANGKAWI — Jitra
P. SINGA BESAR — P. DAYANG BUNTING
P. PAYAR — Alor Setar
P. SEGANTANG — MALAYSIA
Sungai Petani
Georgetown
P. PINANG

13km west of Pulau Payar
Anemone Garden
De Plateau — P. SEGANTANG
Tyre Reef

0   0.3   0.6   0.9
Kilometers

---

vides a home to mangrove snappers (*Lutjanus argentinaculatus*) and barracudas. Visibility, unfortunately, is usually very poor and only reaches 10 meters on a good day. However, the groupers are worth coming to see.

Sriwana Beach At the southeastern side of Pulau Payar, in front of the newly installed reef platform, a coral reef at a depth of between 6 and 8 meters is a great place for a snorkeler or diver to explore coral. Look out for the staghorns (*Acropora nobilis, formosa, and florida*), brain and *Montipora* corals. There are also sponges, anemones with their associated anemonefishes, jacks, black-tipped fusiliers, groupers and Moorish idols. Keep an eye open too for young blacktip sharks; the fish life here is prolific.

Kaca Sunken Boats Point An artificial reef has been created off the southern tip of Pulau Kaca by the sinking of confiscated fishing boats. These have proved a haven for fish life. Japanese jacks, lionfishes, mangrove snappers (*Lutjanus argentimaculatus*) and giant groupers are all frequently encountered, while you'll also come across ramose *Murex* shells.

Tyre Reef The steep vertical walls at Tyre Reef extend down to 20 meters before sloping down gently to a sandy bottom depth of 26 meters. Fish life is plentiful with large shoals of barracudas, sergeant-majors, red snappers, mangrove snappers, jacks and Javan rabbitfish. Sea fans, black corals, wire and whip corals are common in the deeper waters.

Anemone Garden Sea anemones cover the surface of most of the rocks and boulders on the northern side of the island. Large *Murex* shells, helmet shells, spiny lobsters and moray eels are all common.

Langkawi Coral Langkawi Coral operates a 25-meter, high-speed catamaran designed to carry 162 passengers to Pulau Payar on a daily basis. The cruise takes 50 minutes. On arrival, the catamaran moors at a large reef platform. The platform's underwater observatory, glass-bottom boats and snorkeling equipment allow visitors of all ages, even non-swimmers, a close-up look at the marine life.

All dives are led by qualified BSAC instructors. Resort dives for beginners are also available.
— *Danny Lim*

Diving in the Philippines

Hundreds of Sites and a Well-developed Dive Industry

As a diving destination, the Philippines is hard to beat. Walls, drop-offs, coral reefs, wrecks, submerged islands and lagoons abound. Divers can choose from a staggering array of locations, both easily accessible and hard to reach. Choices range from off-the-beach resort diving to dive safaris and exploration dives from boats. Among these options are a variety of live-aboard boats and other vessels which visit not only the popular and well-known sites, such as the Sulu Sea and the Visayas, but also the untouched, remote locations.

Whether you're a humble scuba enthusiast with a limited budget or a wealthy aquanaut with a taste for the luxurious, the Philippines can accommodate your every whim at a price to suit your pocket.

Scuba Potential

Since the early 1960s, when scuba diving first started to gain popularity, entrepreneurs were quick to realize the potential of a country with 7,107 islands (counted at high tide), each with its own unique coral and reef formations.

Anilao in Batangas Province, to the south of Manila, became the very first dive center in the country, and probably one of the first in Asia. Since those distant days, diving has caught on in a big way. Resorts all over the country have invested in diving equipment, and there are scuba diving instructors and divemasters everywhere.

In fact, the Philippines is an outstanding place to learn diving or to upgrade your certification level. A typical Open Water Course costs between US$200 and $300 in most places, and can be taught in languages as varied as English, French, German, Italian, Hebrew, Swedish, Japanese, or various Chinese dialects, by multi-lingual instructors of many nationalities who have made the Philippines their home. You'll find international certification agencies such as PADI, NAUI, SSI, ADSI and CMAS are well established here, and there are three resident PADI course directors running PADI Instructor Development Courses frequently throughout the year. These are usually in La Union, Anilao, Puerto Galera, Boracay and the Visayas.

Diving is most commonly done from native *banca* boats, motorized outrigger canoes which can vary in size from 6 to over 25 meters. As a general rule, the smaller the boat, the less stable it is likely to be. Care should be taken when stowing gear and selecting a place to sit, as the balance can be critical, especially in smaller *bancas*. The driest part of such a *banca* is usually right in the front, beneath the plywood covering the bow. Stow items you want to keep dry there. Let the *bancero*, or boatman, take charge of this and try not to make any sudden movements. Inform the boatman when you are about to enter the water or get back on board after a dive, as he may have to provide counterweight to avoid capsizing. Another useful tip is to arrange the price for your trip before leaving and pay when you get back. There are, sadly, uncommon but verifiable stories

Overleaf: A rhizostome jellyfish, maybe family Thystanostoma. The fish visible above the jellyfish's bell is a juvenile jack, which uses the jelly's stinging tentacles for protection. *Photo by Lynn Funkhouser.*

Opposite: A videographer explores a soft coral covered "bommie." *Photo by Mark Strickland.*

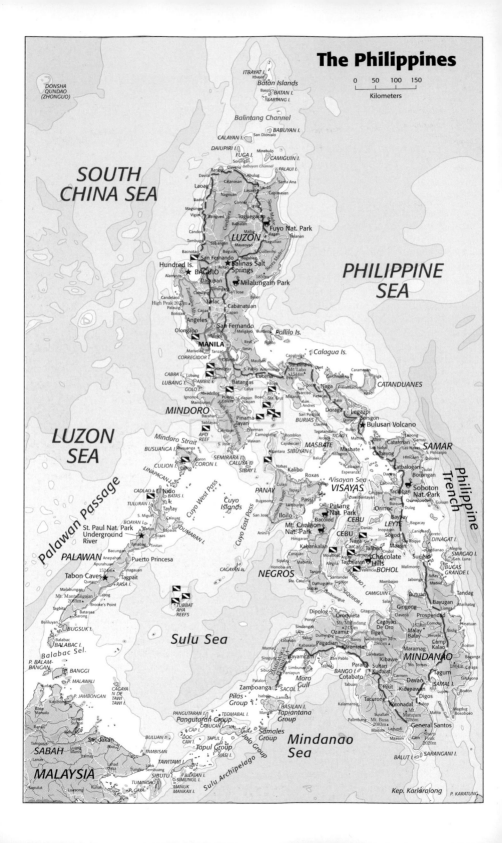

The Philippines

0 50 100 150
Kilometers

DONSHA
QUNDAO
(ZHONGUO)

SOUTH CHINA SEA

PHILIPPINE SEA

ITBAYAT I.
Itbayat
Batan Islands
Basco
BATAN I.
SABTANG I.

Balintang Channel

BABUYAN I.
CALAYAN I.
San Dionisio
DAIUPIRI I.
FUGA I.
Minabulo
Sorongan
CAMIGUIN I.
Babuyan Channel
PALAUI I.
Abulug
Bangui
Davila
Santa Ana
Calanasan
Laoag
Lal-lo
Capisayan
Nagnuan
Lasam
Conner
Iguig
Badoc
Tuguegarao
Magsingal
Babalan
Vigan
Bangued
Malig
Ilagan
Balanan
Candon
Sablangan
Mayaoyao
Negulian
Tamburac
Baguio
S.Guillermo
Bacnotan
Arlao
San Fernando
Bagabag
Hundred Is.
BAGUIO
Salinas Salt Springs
Alaminos
Dagupan
Milalungain Park
Candelaid
Umingan
San Jose
1800m
High Peak 2037m
Camiling
Baler
Palayag
Tarlac
Cabanatuan
Botolan
Gapan
Capas
Angeles
San Fernando
Olongapo
Malyog'n
Burdeos
Pollilo Is.
Real
Pollilo
MANILA
Tanay
Mariveles
Tanza
CORREGIDOR I.
Calamba
Mauban
Capalonga
Calagua Is.
Nasugbu
Lipa
S. Pablo
Antimonan
Mt. Labo
CABRA I.
Lubang
AMBIL I.
Lucena
1544m
CATANDUANES
LUBANG I.
Abra
Pitogo
Naga
Presentation
GOLO I.
Batangas
Calapan
Boac
Sta. Cruz
San Andres
Mamburao
Puerto Galera
Naujan
Mabini
Doraga
Legazpi
San Pablo
Pasacao
Sorsogon
MINDORO
Barahan
Pinamalayan
Clavera
BURIAS I.
Bulusan Volcano
Sablayan
Camogtong
Masbate
Tagatanduan
TICAO I.
Matnog
Mindoro Strait
Calintaan
Romblon
APO REEF
S. Jose
Wawan
Cajibocan
MASBATE
San Isidro
SIBUYAN I.
Balud
Catarman
S. Policarpo
BUSUANGA I.
Buruanga
SEMIRARA I.
Cawayan
SAMAR
Esperanza
Hinicaan
CULION I.
CALUYA I.
Nabas
Kalibo
Dolores
CORON I.
SIBAY I.
Catbalogan
CADLAO I.
BATAS I.
Roxas
Culasi
Visayan Sea
Daram
Borongan
LINAPACAN I.
Bugasong
Tapas
Cabra
El Nido
Passi
VISAYAS
Soboton Nat. Park
TULURAN I.
Cuyo Islands
San Jose
Ilolio
Patang Nat. Park
Tacloban
Taytay
Bacolod
Ormoc
Baybay
BOAYAN I.
Anini-y
CEBU
Danao
Calauag
S. Miguel
Mt. Canlaon Nat. Park
LEYTE
St. Paul Nat. Park
Barton
Hingaran
Naga
Carcar
Maasin
SIARGAO I.
Underground River
Tinitian
Kabankalan
Talibon
Chocolate Hills
Sungad
Gen. Luna
PALAWAN
Bacungan
Tagbilatan
BOHOL
BUGAS GRANDE I.
Puerto Princesa
Canayan
Valencia
Malimono
Apurahuan
Sta. Catalin
Santander
Tandag
Tabon Caves
1524m
RASA I.
Damaguete
Siguijor
Mambajao
Butuan
Bayugan
Quezon
Inagauan
CAGAYAN Is.
NEGROS
SIQUIJOR I.
Salay
Gingoog
Prosperidad
Malinao
Labog
CAMIGUIN I.
Gitagum
Clavera
Brooke's Point
Batarasa
Sipalay
Zamboanga
Dipolog
Oroquieta
Cagayan De Oro
Malay Balay
BUGSUK I.
Ponot
Mt. Malindog
2435m
Camp Kalao
BALABAC I.
Sindangan
Ozamiz
Iligan
Maramag
Balabac Sel.
Siraguan
Siaguan
Kalatungan Mts.
P. BALAM-BANGAN
Salug
Pagadian
Boroy
2866m
Sto. Tomas
MINDANAO
P. BANGGI
Mamao
Lambatan
Baganga
P. MALAWALI
Siraguan
San Pablo
Kibawe
Kapalong
CAGAYAN N DE TAWI TAWI
Limbuan
BANGO I.
Sultan Kudarat
Tagum
P. JAMBONGAN
Patalon
Paniapon
Cotabato
SAMAL I.
Kudat
Tumindao
Isabela
Tabuan
Davao
Tamparong
SABAH
Sandakan
PANGUTARAN I.
TEOMABAL I.
BASILAN I.
Rikit
Kidapawan
Digos
P. TAMBISAN
Pilas Group
Pangutaran Group
Tapiantana Group
Kalamansig
Kotonadal
Sulop
MALAYSIA
CAP I.
CABUCAN I.
Surallah
Mt. Busa
Magdug
BULUAN Is.
DOC CAN I.
TAPUL I.
Samales Group
Palimbang
2083m
General Santos
Lahad Datu
TAPUL I.
SIASI I.
Maitum
Lagundi
Tapul Group
Jolo Group
Mindanao Sea
Sharp Peak
2020m
SIBUTU I.
BILATAN I.
SIMUNUL I.
Sulu Archipelago
BALUT I.
SARANGANI I.
TAWITAWI I.
TUMINDAO I.
MANUK MANKAS I.
Kep. Karleralong
P. KARATUNG

LUZON

LUZON SEA

Palawan Passage

Cuyo West Pass
Cuyo East Pass

Sulu Sea

Moro Gulf

Mindanao Sea

Philippine Trench

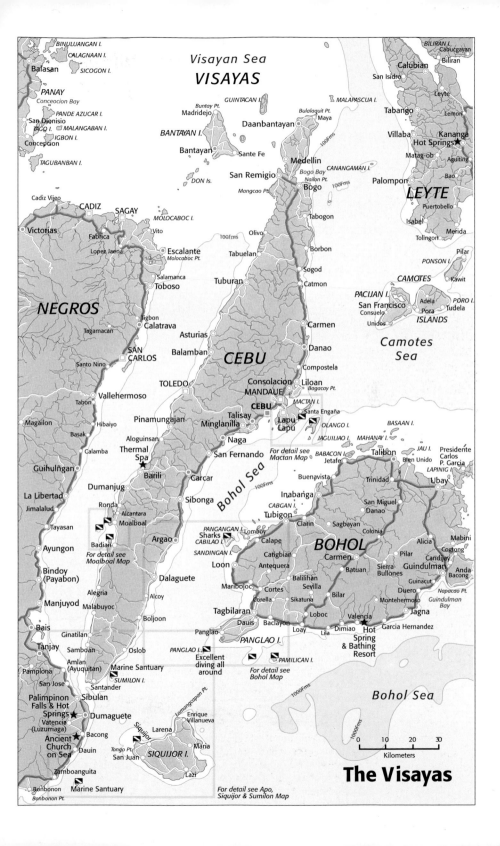

The Visayas

of divers who have paid up front and then been left to fend for themselves once they are in the water.

If the *banca* has no steps to get back on board, another useful tip is to take a length of rope, tie one end to the outrigger close to where it joins with the hull and tie a stirrup, or loop, at the other end at about water level. Then, by placing a foot in the stirrup and standing up, you can avoid the embarrassment of struggling to get back in the boat, otherwise accomplished by pulling oneself up by the arms.

Protecting the Seas

Spear fishing and the collection of corals and shells is illegal in the Philippines, but that doesn't seem to worry the many fishermen and gatherers who make their living from the sea. Dynamite fishing is still widely practiced and the damage is horrendous in some places. Sodium cyanide and other poisons are sometimes used to stun fish for collection for the aquarium and live food fish trade, a practice that burns dead patches into the coral and invertebrate cover. Then there is *Muro Ami* fishing, where teams of swimmers bounce rocks, tied to string with streamers attached, across entire reefs to drive the fish into a net at one end. This practice strips a reef of its fish and destroys the coral at the same time—yet another major factor in the continuing degradation of the Philippines' estimated 27,022 sq km of coral reef at the 10-fathom level.

While various attempts have been made to cope with the problem, local politicians and influential supporters in many areas have effectively negated any serious effort to stop the devastation. The coast guard suffers from a lack of vessels and other resources: this means that policing of marine sanctuaries and other likely targets of the *dynamiteros* is a haphazard and arbitrary affair. In a country in which millions rely on the fishing industry for their livelihood, it is ironic that the fishermen themselves, through the harmful techniques they employ, are the main culprits behind the continually declining fish stocks which they so vocally complain about.

The scuba diving industry in the Philippines has always been at the forefront of the struggle to protect the magnificent resources nature has bestowed on the Filipinos. In Anilao, for example, there is a long history of co-operation with the coast guard, and an ongoing, aggressive, pro-environment sentiment among the large scuba diving community there. In Puerto Galera, the industry has developed in harmony with the local population who can see the benefits that tourism has brought to their little corner of paradise. As with Anilao, there are some superb sites around the area because of this concern.

In the Visayas, the story is the same. On Mactan Island, there can be no doubt that the presence of so many scuba diving operations over the years has considerably slowed down the ravages of illegal fishing. Sites that are frequently visited by divers—and there are a lot of divers in the water every day around the island—are perceived as too risky by most illegal fishermen. While there are areas bombed out beyond hope, there are also some incredible spots just waiting to be discovered, and no shortage of knowledgeable guides to take them there.

Around Bohol, especially at Panglao and Balicasag islands, the locals seem to have held their marine resources in higher regard than some others, because they are precious jewels in the crown of Visayan diving. Apo Island, to the south of Cebu and east of Negros, is another outstanding, pristine site not to be missed.

Obviously, the remoteness of a location can be its salvation, though some *Muro Ami* vessels are quite seaworthy and can stay at sea for long periods, over 6 months if necessary. The Sibuyan Sea, to the northeast of Boracay and southeast of Marinduque Island, is largely unexplored by divers. Banton Island, at the western extremity of the Sibuyan Sea, is now accessible from Marinduque, and returning divers sing its praises with gushing superlatives. Other, remoter sites which have been visited by "frontier divers," often on live-aboard vessels on transition runs, are reported as either fantastic or devastated, with few assessments of anything in between.

Professionalism in the Industry

The Philippine Commission on Sports Scuba Diving (PCSSD) was formed in 1987 to promote the development of the sport, oversee the conservation of the country's marine resources and to register and license dive establishments and professionals in the industry. This regulatory body has done a lot to improve and develop scuba diving in the country.

At the start of 1994, over 72 dive establishments and 57 diving professionals were registered with the PCSSD. Air from registered dive centers is tested twice annually, and licensees are required to conform to an ethical and environmental code. It is always a good idea to check that a dive center is registered with the PCSSD as it may say a lot about the integrity of the operation. The PCSSD works closely with the industry to promote the country as a diving destination, and visitors are always welcome at their office in the Department of Tourism Building in Manila. The PCSSD also maintains a recompression chamber in Cebu, at which over 80 people of various nationalities have been treated since it started operations in 1989.

In the private sector, the Diving Industry Association of the Philippines (DIAP), a registered Non-Governmental Organization (NGO), also works to preserve the reefs and maintain the integrity of the industry. The Haribon Foundation is another effective environmental group working with divers, as is Mario Elumba's *Scubasurero* project at Anilao. *Scubasurero* is a play on the Tagalog word for a garbage collector, a *Basurero*, and that's what participating divers do: pick up plastic bags and other garbage strewn over affected reefs.

Prices for all Pockets

But don't be put off by tales of dynamite and plastic bags. A visiting scuba diver is not short of superb destinations from which to choose. For most, deciding which area to choose will be based on financial considerations and the amenities on offer. From a US$500 a night resort to a US$6 hut on the beach, the choice is yours. In the US$20–$40 range, the possibilities are almost

Below: Specimens of an unidentified species of porcelain crab. The pattern is similar to *Neopetrolisthes maculatus*. *Photo by Gerald Allen.*

endless. These days, most dive centers have good equipment, many offering niceties such as rental of dive computers and underwater videos, and are run by professional, competent businessmen.

Various consultants and specialized tour operators, such as Whitetip Divers and Dive Buddies, both located in Manila, can give valuable tips on most areas as well as up-to-the-minute information on weather and dive conditions around the islands, advice on travel, accommodation, amenities, night life, dining and other points of interest.
—*Heneage Mitchell*

La Union
Calm Waters and Pleasant Beaches

Opposite: Blotched hawkfish *(Cirrhitichthys aprinus)*. Photo by *Mike Severns.*

Only a 5-hour bus ride from Manila, La Union was one of the first beach resorts to be developed in the Philippines. The US Air Force had around 150 men stationed at Wallace Air Station until 1992, many of whom learned scuba diving in the warm, clear waters of La Union's Lingayen Gulf.

Unfortunately, indiscriminate dynamiting and other illegal fishing techniques have wreaked havoc over the years on the once prolific inner reefs. Nonetheless, there are enough interesting sites in the usually calm and gentle waters of the gulf to justify several days of lingering around to enjoy both the diving and the beaches of Bauang, Paringao and San Fernando.

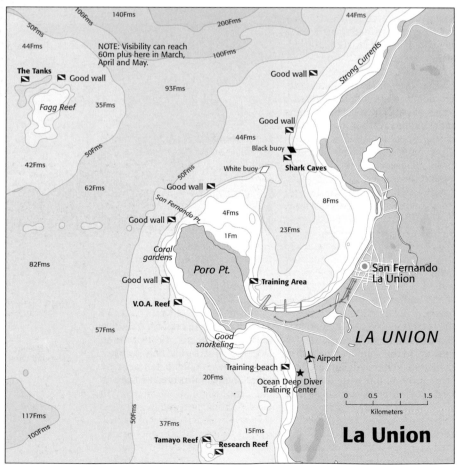

140Fms
50Fms
100Fms
200Fms
44Fms
44Fms

The Tanks

Good wall

NOTE: Visibility can reach 60m plus here in March, April and May.

100Fms

Good wall

Strong Currents

Fagg Reef   35Fms

93Fms

Good wall

44Fms

Black buoy

42Fms

50Fms

White buoy

Shark Caves

62Fms

50Fms

Good wall

San Fernando Pt.

8Fms

Good wall

4Fms

23Fms

1Fm

Coral gardens

82Fms

Poro Pt.

Good wall

Training Area

San Fernando
La Union

V.O.A. Reef

57Fms

LA UNION

Good snorkeling

Airport

Training beach

20Fms

Ocean Deep Diver Training Center

0   0.5   1   1.5
Kilometers

117Fms

100Fms

50Fms

37Fms

15Fms

La Union

Tamayo Reef   **Research Reef**

The Tanks

This is the most famous dive in the gulf. Resting 39 meters down on a ledge protruding from the almost vertical western wall of Fagg Reef, a mile or more off Poro Point, these three World War II-vintage M10 tanks are now home to a variety of marine life, including a 65-kg moray eel. It's best to check if he is at home before sticking your head into the turret of the middle tank.

Currents can be tricky this far out, but it is usually possible to come up from this deep dive and drift across the top of the reef while decompressing and still see plenty of interesting stuff. I have come across pelagic whitetip and whale sharks on the wall at Fagg, as well as wrasses, dorados, the occasional Spanish mackerel, king barracuda and leopard rays. There used to be plenty of hawksbill turtles, but sadly they are rare now.

The caves on Research Reef are another popular dive, with an average depth of around 15 meters. A series of easily penetrable tunnels and canyons rather than actual caves, expect to see lobsters (usually young), parrotfishes and lionfishes, as well as almost any kind of other tropical reef fishes, though usually small and timid, at this site. It's an excellent site for a night dive.

Voice of America Reef

In the next cove to the north, you'll find VOA Reef, so named because of the half-million watt Voice of America transmitting station which still occupies a large section of Poro Point. From the white, coral sand at 6 meters to the bottom of the wall at 22 meters, VOA is a delightful, easy dive. In common with the other local sites, there is a profusion of table, basket, staghorn, brain, star, flower and finger corals, together with a wide variety of soft corals and anemones. La Union makes up in shell life for what it lacks in fish,

and following trails in the sand will usually lead to something interesting. There are eggshell, map and tiger cowries all over the place, as well as green turbans, a variety of augers, cones (be careful!) and murex. There is generally more fish life—groupers, parrotfishes, squirrelfishes, snappers and lionfishes—at the southern, deeper end of the wall, but visibility lessens here too.

Visibility in the Lingayen Gulf is unusually good year round. In peak season (March to June), it can get to over 60 meters. In the middle of the rainy season (from June to December) it rarely falls below 7 meters, and is often better at many sites. The Gulf is protected from all but the worst weather by the Cordillera Mountain range to the east, and is well north of the usual typhoon tracks, and so enjoys mild weather year round.

— *Heneage Mitchell*

Banca boats, 20–90 min

Good, 20–50 m in season

Usually negligible

Damaged but pretty in certain places

Rocky: crevices, caves and corals

Skittish, fair variety, small numbers

M10-1A World War II tanks; caves

Subic Bay

A Choice of Wrecks in a Perfect Natural Harbor

Just a few hours northwest of Manila are the newly discovered corals and wreck sites of duty-free Subic Bay. During the years the US Navy held sway over the perfect natural harbor in the bay, diving and fishing were off-limits in many areas. Now that they are gone, new sites are being discovered almost weekly. Visibility can reach over 40 meters in the bay, though it is usually between 5 and 15 meters. There is virtually no current and the water is almost always calm enough to dive.

Probably the most accessible wreck, and the most interesting one

Below: Close-up of the hull of the *El Capitan* wreck, Subic Bay.
Photo by Jack Jackson.

to dive on, is the battleship USS *New York*. Built in 1891, she saw service in the Philippine American War, the Chinese Revolution and World War I. Decommissioned in 1931, she rode at anchor in Subic Bay for the next 10 years until she was scuttled by retreating US forces to prevent her massive 17-inch cannons from falling into Japanese hands. She lies on her port side in 27 meters of water between the Alava Pier and the runway at Cubi Point, and is home to a variety of marine life, including barracuda, lionfishes, spotted sweetlips, groupers, lobsters and spotted rays. The cannons are still intact and the photo opportunities are outstanding.

A Sunken Freighter

Not to be missed is the *El Capitan*. Lying on its port side, the stern is in only 5 meters of water while the bow rests at 20 meters. A small freighter, the *El Capitan* is safely penetrable. The accommodation area is now taken up by a wide variety of tropical fishes; look out for glasseyes, wrasses, tangs, gobies, spotted sweetlips, lobsters, crabs and clownfishes. Visibility is usually between 5 and 20 meters, depending on the tide.

There are several other wrecks visited regularly by local dive centers, including the *Oryoku Maru*, an outbound passenger ship carrying over 1,600 prisoners of war when it was attacked and sunk 400 meters off Alava Pier. Despite having been flattened by US Navy demolition

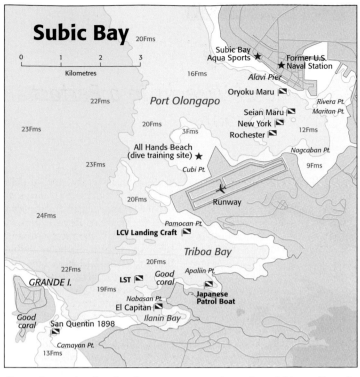

divers for navigational safety reasons, this is still a good dive with plenty to see, including a resident shoal of barracuda patrolling the site overhead.

Good Coral and a Spanish Galleon

Coral reef fanatics are also well served in Subic. Apart from the ever popular sites at nearby Grande Island, a former R&R centre for US servicemen, several new sites in pristine condition have recently been discovered. These include sites such as the coral gardens off Nabasan Point in Triboa Bay. Their healthy condition is due to the fact that they have been protected from fishing and divers for many years. Expect to find outstanding examples of brain, table and star corals, as well as a profusion of crinoids, sponges and crustaceans.

Brian Homan, who has been discovering wrecks around the Philippines for over 15 years now, conducts regular explorations and excursions aboard his replica of a Spanish Galleon, *La Gallega*. Plunging into the waters of Subic Bay from this outstanding and unusual vessel is an experience in itself. As there is probably no-one around with better local knowledge than Brian, divers are strongly recommended to check out his operation.

Subic is now a duty-free port and is a good place to buy diving equipment: remember to take your passport. You should also try to visit the recompression chamber on the former base, still maintained and operated by a team of well-trained and dedicated professionals. This chamber is one of three available to careless sport divers and ignorant, hose-diving fishermen who resort to recompression all too often to save their lives after diving accidents. Complete diver training is offered at several centers from Olongapo to Barrio Barretto, a popular, laid-back beach resort area a few miles to the north of the city of Olongapo.

— *Heneage Mitchell*

Banca boats,
5–60 min

Usually fair,
10–25 m

Usually none

Fair variety in places

Sand, mud bottom,
some corals

Good variety,
prolific in places

Excellent wreck
diving

Nasugbu

Easily Accessible from the Capital

A few hours' drive by bus to the south of Manila, in the province of Batangas, is the sleepy little coastal town of Nasugbu. Facing the South China Sea, the region has long, volcanic sand beaches and no shortage of good diving.

Fortune Island

Perhaps the most famous dive sites around here are at Fortune Island, a small, privately owned resort island a few miles out to sea west of the town itself. Except for the Bat Cave, visibility here is usually excel-

lent, reaching 50 meters and even more.

On one particular site, the Blue Holes, there are large groupers, sweetlips and parrotfishes everywhere, as well as angelfishes, puffers, wrasses, gobies, butterflyfishes and damselfishes—to name but a few. Squid and cuttlefish are also common. The corals and other reef organisms are prolific and diverse—you'll find gorgonians and barrel sponges, vast slabs of star coral with plume worms all over them, and anemones galore. There are three sink holes which converge into an open cavern, and a

By boat,
10–60 min

Depending on site,
5–50 m

Can be strong in
places

Good variety,
prolific in places

Walls, drop-offs

Good variety

Fortune Island,
walls and caves

coral overhang at 28 meters. Hawksbill turtles and shoals of leatherjackets frequent the area, and several species of pelagics often swim by.

Also at Fortune Island are the remains of an old freighter lying in 20 meters or so of water. Not much is left now except box sections, but the wreck is very penetrable and excellent for photography. Beware: there are large scorpionfishes and lionfishes all over the place.

The Bat Cave is also a popular site, another 20-meter dive which leads to a semi-submerged cave with bats hanging around inside. Cuttlefish breed here, and there are abundant soft corals around.

Sumo Bank

Several miles further out, this is another excellent local dive. Among other features is an abundance of cauliflower-

shaped corals which cover the sandy bottom. Whitetips and other sharks roam these waters, and a wide variety of tropical reef fish make their homes here. The corals, soft and hard, are prolific, and the area is well suited for the more experienced diver.

Closer inshore are Twin Islands, really two large rocks jutting up out of the sea. There are several good dives here, the Pink Wall being our favorite. An almost sheer drop-off starting at 8 meters, the wall is covered by thousands of soft, pink corals. There are lots of small tropical fish here all the time and a few turtles sometimes.

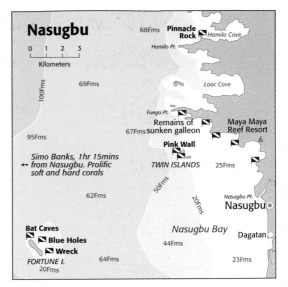

Nasugbu

68Fms Pinnacle Rock — Hamilo Cove

0 1 2 3
Kilometers

Hamilo Pt.

100Fms

69Fms

Looc Cove

Fuego Pt.
Remains of sunken galleon
67Fms

95Fms

Maya Maya Reef Resort

Pink Wall

Simo Banks, 1hr 15mins ← from Nasugbu. Prolific soft and hard corals

TWIN ISLANDS 25Fms

50Fms

62Fms

20Fms

Nasugbu Pt.
Nasugbu

Bat Caves
Blue Holes
Wreck
FORTUNE I.
20Fms

64Fms

Nasugbu Bay
44Fms

Dagatan

23Fms

Visibility doesn't usually exceed 20 meters, but the diving is always memorable.

Sunken Booty

At Fuego Point, almost directly north of Twin Islands, a boulder-strewn bottom hides artefacts from a long ago sunken galleon. The remains of the anchor, rope and chain can still be seen. The fish life is perhaps not so impressive, but there are lots of small tropicals swimming around. Visibility is not normally much above 15 meters but the drop-off, which goes past 30 meters, usually enjoys a little better visibility—between 12 and 25 meters—and is draped with colorful gorgonians, and other hard and soft corals. Tuna and other pelagics cruise the waters, and there are plenty of small tropical reef fish to keep the average diver happy.

The dive sites around Nasugbu are not visited as frequently as one might expect, given its proximity to Manila. However, the PADI dive center at popular Maya Maya Reef Resort is an excellent place to go to discover what many local divers have been missing for all these years.

— *Heneage Mitchell*

Opposite: The green sea turtle *(Chelonia mydas)* is the most commonly encountered turtle in the Southeast Asian region, where it can weigh up to 200 kg. *Photo by Mark Strickland.*

Above left: *Photo by Mark Strickland.*

Anilao

Birthplace of Philippine Scuba

A two-and-a-half-hour drive through the lush Southern Luzon countryside from Manila, Anilao can justifiably claim to be the birthplace of scuba diving in the Philippines.

In the mid 1960s, Dr. Tim Sevilla transplanted an entire coral reef onto a large rock formation a short distance off shore from his Dive 7000 resort. At the time, the conventional thinking about coral reef growth regarded transplanting a coral reef to be futile, but Dr. Sevilla proved them wrong. And to this day, Cathedral Rock is a much visited site, a vibrant, colorful dive with a profusion of small reef fish, soft and hard corals and even a small underwater shrine.

The shrine is in the form of a cross, and was blessed by the Pope and placed at about 40 ft (13 meters) between two coral carpeted pinnacles in 1982 by Lt. General Fidel V. Ramos, who would later become the President of the Philippines.

Anilao has remained at the forefront of the scuba industry since then, and is still an excellent place for snorkelers, novices and experienced aquanauts alike.

However, don't expect to find much beachfront along the rugged Balayaan Bay coastline—you don't come to Anilao to laze around on beaches—trips here are definitely focused on water sports, and scuba diving in particular.

Photographers inevitably have a field day here, and professionals come in time and time again from around the world to shoot the area's diverse sites. The macro-photographer will enjoy the legendary photo opportunities this dive destination affords while wide-angle enthusiasts won't be disappointed either.

Unfortunately, the pressures of an ever increasing population has put a lot of stress on the local ecosystem, typical of many premier dive destinations elsewhere. Being "just round the corner" from a major port, Batangas City located at the mouth of Batangas Bay, Balayan Bay has not escaped the negative effects of shipping and constant water movement.

The many thousands of Filipino divers who trained and still dive regularly in Anilao have long been on the cutting edge of the social,

Below: This cross at Cathedral Rock was laid by President Fidel Ramos and blessed by Pope John Paul II. *Photo by Jack Jackson.*

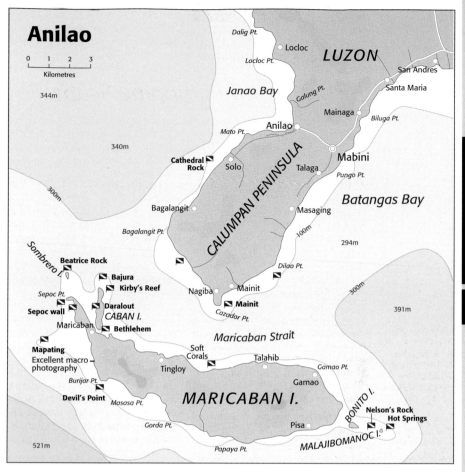

Anilao

0 1 2 3
Kilometres

344m

340m

300m

Dalig Pt.

Locloc

Locloc Pt.

LUZON

San Andres

Santa Maria

Janao Bay

Galung Pt.

Mainaga

Biluga Pt.

Mato Pt.

Anilao

Mabini

Cathedral Rock

Solo

Talaga

Pungo Pt.

CALUMPAN PENINSULA

Bagalangit

Masaging

Batangas Bay

Bagalangit Pt.

100m

294m

Sombrero I.

Beatrice Rock

Dilao Pt.

300m

391m

Bajura

Kirby's Reef

Nagiba

Mainit

Sepoc Pt.

Sepoc wall

Daralout

CABAN I.

Mainit

Cazador Pt.

Maricaban

Bethlehem

Maricaban Strait

Mapating
Excellent macro
photography

Soft
Corals

Tingloy

Talahib

Gamao Pt.

Gamao

Burijar Pt.

Devil's Point

Masasa Pt.

MARICABAN I.

BONITO I.

Nelson's Rock
Hot Springs

Gorda Pt.

Pisa

MALAJIBOMANOC I.

521m

Papaya Pt.

environmental and political issues affecting all marine areas of the Philippines from Mactan to Marinduque. Dynamite and other illegal fishing techniques, collection of corals and shells, overfishing and pollution: these are just some of the harmful influences that have put immense pressure on the environment. Action is being taken against such practices at many levels and by a increasing number of people throughout the islands.

Anilao has led the way in programs such as the *Scubasurero* (a play on the Tagalog word for a garbage collector) clean-up operation and has attracted wide interest from such prestigious organizations as the Haribon Foundation and the PADI AWARE Program. This is not to say that diving around Anilao is any way deficient: far from it. But it is important to recognize Anilao's importance to the development and to the future of scuba diving in the Philippines. The fact that the local diving continues to attract many thousands is testament to the continuing struggle between the ecologically aware locals and the diving community on one hand, and the forces of industrialization and the unending demands for resources, on the other.

Anilao is still, and plans on continuing to be, an extremely popular year-round destination, and there is certainly no shortage of excellent diving available here. Most of the better sites are not actually in Balayan Bay but around the islands of Sombrero and Maricaban, each located a short *banca* boat ride to the south of Anilao.

Banca boats,
10–60 min

Usually fair,
10–40 m

Can be stiff in
places

Prolific and varied

Walls, drop-offs

Prolific in places

Outstanding macro-
photography

Sombrero Island

Uninhabited, this island has a delightful beach which is often used as a picnic spot between dives. The diving is good all the way round the island but perhaps the best site is Beatrice Rock, just off the northern point. From depths of 6 meters down to 25 meters, there are plenty of good hard corals. Currents are often strong, which encourages pelagics to visit the site. Several species of ray can be found here, including the occasional eagle ray, as well as rainbow runners and yellowtails. Look out for another small statue placed here at a depth of around 13 meters.

At nearby Bajura, east of Sombrero and north of Caban Island, the reef is over 1 km long and descends from 12 meters to around 37 meters. There are lots of caves and overhangs, often providing a temporary home to sleeping sharks. The drop-offs and walls here are covered in a profusion of table, staghorn, mushroom and other hard corals, as well as a wide variety of crinoids and gorgonians. The prolific fish life is impressively diverse, with plenty of parrotfishes, butterflyfishes, triggerfishes, wrasses, lionfishes, scorpionfishes, plenty of moray eels, aggregations of sweetlips, the occasional octopus, some angelfishes, a few batfishes, schools of surgeons and snappers, and from time to time, eagle rays and whitetip sharks. However, you should take care here as the currents are unpredictable and can be strong, but as this is an excellent dive you shouldn't be dissuaded by this possibility.

At Mapating, off the northwest shore of Maricaban, the reef has excellent soft corals and small fish in depths of only 3–12 meters. As with most sites around Anilao, the macro-photography here is outstanding: the wide variety of nudibranchs are an ever-popular subject. Then there is a big, long wall starting at 18 meters which drops off to over 60 meters. Another shelf at 20 meters has some good hard corals and provides temporary shelter to the occasional nurse and cat sharks. Schools of snappers and surgeons often swim by when the current is running, as do some very large southern rays and whitetip sharks. For those who are qualified

Below: Juvenile striped eel catfish, *Plotosus lineatus*. As juveniles, these fish gather into large schools, actually more like wriggling *balls*. Their dorsal and pectoral spines are venemous, a fact perhaps advertised by their contrasty coloration and busy movements. *Photo by Jones/Shimlock*.

to make a really deep dive, there is a huge cave between 37 and 43 meters.

Pinnacles and Points

To the southeast at Devil's Point there is a large, submerged rock between 6 and 12 meters with pleasant corals and lots of small fish. The rock formations are picturesque but, again, watch out for the current.

At Mainit, which means "hot" in Tagalog, there is a rocky, ridged slope with a good selection of hard and soft corals on it. At 18 meters you'll find a submerged pinnacle while there's also a shark cave at 6 meters. Generally the site hosts an abundance of small reef fish. Currents can be awkwardly strong, but they also produce a few pelagics when they are running so it's usually worth the effort. Afterwards, check out the hot springs on the beach.

Just off Layaglang Point on the northeastern tip of Caban Island is Kirby's, a pinnacle which goes down to 28 meters. There's a small wall with morays, lionfishes

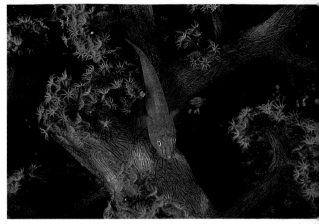

as well as lots of colorful crinoids.

Between Culebra and Malajibomanoc (which means "chicken feather" in Tagalog) islands is Nelson's Rock, which tops out at 16 meters and drops down to a depth of over 30 meters. The pinnacle is carpeted, most of the time, by a profusion of blooming coral polyps, and large gorgonians, while the water is usually a haze with lots of damsel fishes. You'll also see caves that often host sharks, some stingrays, and a few pelagics when the current is running.

A little to the east are the Hot Springs—a very unusual dive site. At 21 meters, hot volcanic gas bubbles out of holes in the seabed, and you can place an egg to cook on one of the holes while you swim off into a fairytale landscape of multi-hued pastels, bright greens and vivid yellows. Because the water is warm, the visibility here is always good. Walking fishes (the frogfish or anglerfish) are common in one spot, and shark and rays frequent the site. When you are ready to ascend, don't forget to collect your egg—it should be hard boiled by the end of your dive.

It is hard to include all the favorite dive sites in and around Anilao—this choice is inevitably very subjective. Suffice to say that Anilao has plenty to offer divers of all levels.

—Heneage Mitchell

Above: Soft coral goby *Pleurosicya* (maybe *boldinghi*) on *Dendronephthya* soft coral. *Photo by Gary Bell.*

Verde Island
A Fabulous Wall and Good Corals

Below: At Verde Island Wall, sea fans and anemones billow in the constantly moving water. Depicted here is a crinoid on a sea fan. *Photo by Jones/Shimlock.*

This is a favorite dive spot for regulars in the Puerto Galera and Anilao area. Situated in the aptly named Verde Island Passage between southern Batangas on the mainland of Luzon, and the northeastern tip of Mindoro, Verde has one of the best wall dives north of Palawan. There are several beaches which divers use to picnic on between dives: please make sure you clean up afterwards!

Currents can be a problem here, but they do create some interesting drift dives. The island's west coast has gentle drop-offs starting from the shore and sloping down to abyssal depths. There used to be the remains of the keel of a Spanish galleon sitting in a few meters just off the beach. History relates that the galleon had just left Manila bound for Spain with a cargo of silks and spices from China when it ran aground. No-one was killed, but the incensed crew and passengers immediately constructed a gallows and hanged the unfortunate navigator. The keel has now been raised and preserved in the National Museum. However, the ardent treasure hunter can still sift the sand where the galleon sank and come across a few ballast stones or, even better, fragments of pottery or an ancient musket ball.

Jumping into the sea anywhere off this west coast will put a diver onto the gentle slopes of the fringing reef, which is criss-crossed with gullies and ravines. The current usually provides a free ride, but care should still be taken. There are lots of soft and hard corals, but not so many reef fish around because most of these lurk in the gullies out of the current. It is worth investigating the various patches of sand with coral heads blooming out of them, as they are home to anemones and clownfishes, spotted rays, as well as a variety of crustaceans.

The Verde Island Wall

But it is the Verde Island Wall which attracts most divers to the

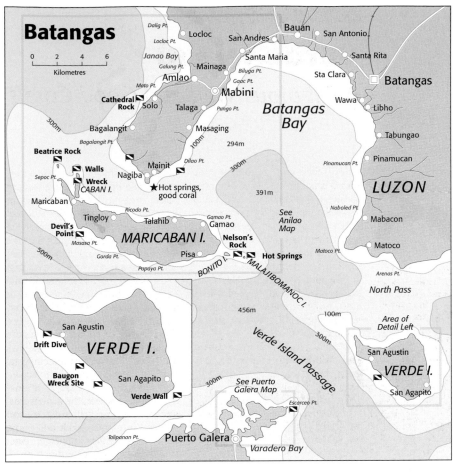

Batangas

0 2 4 6
Kilometres

Dalig Pt.
Locloc Pt.
Locloc
San Andres
Bauan
San Antonio
Santa Rita

Janao Bay
Galung Pt.
Mainaga
Santa Maria
Biluga Pt.
Gaac Pt.
Sta Clara
Batangas

Mato Pt.
Amlao
Mabini
Wawa
Libho

Cathedral Rock
Solo
Talaga
Pungo Pt.
Batangas Bay
Tabungao

Bagalangit
Masaging
294m
Pinamucan

Bagalangit Pt.
100m
Pinamucan Pt.

Beatrice Rock
Dilao Pt.
300m

Walls
Mainit
391m
LUZON

Sepoc Pt.
Wreck
Nagiba
Naboled Pt.
Mabacon

CABAN I.
Hot springs, good coral

Maricaban
Ricodo Pt.
See Anilao Map
Matoco

Tingloy
Talahib
Gamao Pt.
Gamao
Matoco Pt.

Devil's Point
Nelson's Rock

Masasa Pt.
MARICABAN I.
Pisa
Hot Springs
Arenas Pt.

Gorda Pt.
North Pass

Papaya Pt.
BONITO I.
MALAJIBOMANOC I.

456m
100m
Area of Detail Left

San Agustin
Verde Island Passage
300m

Drift Dive
VERDE I.
San Agustin

Baugon Wreck Site
San Agapito
300m
See Puerto Galera Map
VERDE I.

Verde Wall
Escarceo Pt.
San Agapito

Talipanan Pt.
Puerto Galera
Varadero Bay

island. Easily identifiable by the rocks sticking out of the water off the southeastern tip of the island, the wall descends from the surface almost straight down to seemingly unfathomed depths. Around the corner from the drop-in point, the wall curves in a bit, which allows divers to collect themselves in calm waters before starting to explore the surroundings.

There are vast slabs of star corals draped all along the wall, as well as giant gorgonians and large, cascading soft corals. Sea fans and anemones billow in the constantly moving water, and you can't help but be amazed by the impossibly diverse colors that meet the eye everywhere.

The first time I visited Verde, I encountered two large Napoleon wrasses who casually swam up and inspected our party. On other dives, we have seen mantas, eagle rays, whitetip and blacktip sharks. Schools of jacks and tuna are not uncommon, and there are plenty of sweetlips, batfishes, wrasses, emperors, surgeons, soldiers and tangs everywhere.

You must take care to control buoyancy and watch the depths on this particular dive. As the reef starts at the surface, safety stops can be made while still on the wall. Watch for schools of curious unicornfishes coming in close to check out decompressing divers. Serious photographers should bring two cameras: one for the larger animals and one with a macro lens to capture the nudibranchs which are generally plentiful around here.

— *Heneage Mitchell*

By boat, 30–180 min

Usually good, 15–40 m

Very strong in places

Prolific, colorful and good variety

Walls, drop-offs

Often prolific and good variety

Pristine wall, excellent corals and fish

THE PHILIPPINES

Puerto Galera

Diving from a Popular Holiday Resort

The discovery of an ancient inter-island trading vessel laden with Chinese Dragon Jars and other ceramic goodies in the picturesque Batangas Channel of Puerto Galera was the precursor to the incredible growth of the scuba diving industry that thrives there today.

Local dive operators lay claim to 25 excellent dive sites within an hour of whichever of the many coves or beaches you may be staying at locally. Usually, there is fine snorkelling just offshore. At press time, there were 16 dive centres doing business in the area, with more on the way.

A place of outstanding natural beauty, Puerto Galera's underwater delights are some of the most popular diving sites in the country.

Probably the most famous dive hereabouts is the Shark Caves off Escarceo Point. Prone to treacherous currents (one local veteran has been swept away into the Verde Passage twice now, fortunately surviving to tell the tale), this is not a dive for the timid or the inexperienced. The divemaster assesses the current and the divers descending to 18 metres. This is often a drift dive. You swim over a ledge to a patch of sand, and there, under the ledge, you can usually spot a few whitetip sharks resting, often with large grouper and other big fish. A little deeper and there is another, narrower cave which also accommodates sleeping shark. This cave is popular with photographers as one can get really close to the sharks, but it is quite deep (28 meters), so bottom time is limited.

Ascending from here to around 12 metres you'll find the Pink Wall,

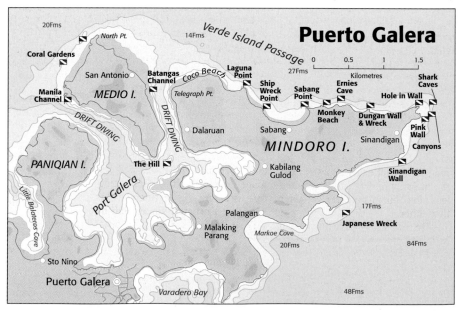

so named for the profusion of soft Cauliflower corals that have created an impressive overhang. A great spot for photography, and a popular night dive.

The Canyons

The Canyons is probably the most visited dive site in Puerto Galera, especially popular with Technical divers. Usually starting at the Hole in the Wall, a natural hole that's large enough to pass through one at a time, divers swim along a wall and then into a series of canyons. These are encrusted with all sorts of soft and hard corals, sponges, sea fans and feather stars. The sea is alive with morays, lionfish, sweetlips, jacks, tuna and frequently whitetip sharks. If you're lucky, you may even catch a glimpse of Barnacle Bill, a hawksbill turtle who often hangs around here. The dive ends at an old anchor covered with soft corals and small sea fans, home to two large lionfish.

Sabang Point is another site worth visiting. A booming coral reef starting at seven meters and descending to 18–20 meters, the reef is covered with feather stars, pot sponges, sea whips and sea pens. At one point there is a beautiful wall covered with different corals and home to morays, multicolored nudibranchs and fluorescent blue triggerfish.

Eight kilometers to the west of the town of Puerto Galera proper, past the secluded White Beach and out from Talipanan Beach is another reef for the serious diver, with strong currents, pelagic fish and stunning corals of all kinds. This reef, being a little further away from the majority of dive sites, is visited less often, but is none the worse for that either.

Dorado and spanish mackerel have been spotted there, as well as tuna and other pelagics. Expect to find humphead wrasse, parrotfish, sweetlips, angelfish, lionfish and the peculiar crocodile fish, which, although difficult to spot, is quite

common around Puerto.

Visibility in the area can reach 35 meters, but is typically 20 meters or less, depending on the site and the season. As mentioned earlier, currents can be very tricky, even on some seemingly innocuous shallower dives, so always plan to go with a professional dive guide or you could end up in trouble.Puerto is increasingly being visited by passing live-aboard boats, and is also a jump off point for regular live-aboard trips to Apo Reef, Coron Bay and the Suibuyan Sea. Trips are usually arranged at short notice.

Local dive operators own an interesting variety of vessels between them, from *MV Tabibuga,* a very seaworthy 70 ft (18 meter) steel boat sleeping up to 14 divers to large *bancas,* custom dive boats, yachts, catamarans, v-hulls and converted local wooden fishing boats. Ocean kayaks are available for rent, popular with snorkellers.

An active dive store owner's association works hard to ensure visiting divers have healthy reefs to dive on. They provide mooring buoys at popular dive sites and promote environmental and infrastructure projects. Six artificial reefs have been created since 1996 by sinking derelict vessels in the area. This professional attitude to safety and service that has developed over the years explains why so many divers just keep coming back to Puerto Galera.

—*Heneage Mitchell*

Above: The nudibranch *Chromodoris magnifica* and the yellow sea cucumbers *Cholochirus robustus* in front of soft corals and a red sponge.
Photo by Jack Jackson.

Banca and custom dive boats, 10–30 m

Usually fair, 10–30 m

Very strong in places

Prolific, colorful and good variety

Walls and coral gardens

Often prolific, good variety

Shark caves, coral gardens

Marinduque

Outstanding Sights in the Tablas Straits

A short flight or a five-hour bus and ferry ride south of Manila finds you in Marinduque. Famous for its Moriones festival, Marinduque and environs are far more rewarding to the diver for the profusion of outstanding underwater sites.

Wreck divers, wall divers, reef divers, cavern divers and photographers are well catered for, and many experienced divers who have visited some of the outlying islands in the Tablas Straits reckon them to be superior to anything they have seen anywhere, including the Red Sea, the Great Barrier Reef and the Sulu Sea too. High praise indeed.

To get to the choicest spots, it is necessary to plan full day trips and dive safaris of several days. Trips usually originate from Puerto Galera or Boracay. There are 11 main diving areas adjacent to Marinduque, from Natanco in the north west to the Maestre de Campo Islands to the south west and Banton Island to the south east. Each has something special about it, and has more than one dive site to recommend it.

Natanco and Balanan

Natanco is noted for its walls and drift diving. On one section we found an unbelievable coral structure, white, like a huge avalanche of snow stretching for several meters, at another wall we stumbled onto a huge shoal of tuna at 20 meters. We also found some great gorgonians and some big groupers.

At Balanan, the Japanese torpedo boat. is not a dive for amateurs.

This small (35 metre long) casualty of World War II is sitting upright with a badly smashed bow in 36 to 40 meters of water. The visibility can be a problem sometimes, and averages around 10 meters. The prop is missing, but there's still a multi-barrelled gun on the deck and, to our horror, several depth charges still in their racks.

Elephante Island

Elephante Island, an private resort, is home to the other dive shop servicing Marinduque. Catering mostly to Japanese package tourists, there are a couple of good dives here. To the north, there is a wall off the beach with a fairly stiff current, (3 knots or more at times). The bottom of the wall is deep, we reached 40 meters at one point and it still kept going. Large gorgonians adorn the face. A little further south, there's an area with more of that incredible white coral, this time flatter and resembling a snow covered field. There are a lot of color-fulfish here, and photo opportunities abound. Unfortunately, sometimes the resort guests think it's fun to buzz slow moving boats following divers on jet skis.

Balthazar

At Balthazar, to the west, there is a cave you can enter at 20 meters and exit at 28 meters. There are lots of Stonefish everywhere, so be careful. The gorgonians are particularly beautiful here, too. A little to the

Opposite: Diver exploring table corals *Acropora elathrata*. *Photo by Mark Strickland.*

Live-aboard boats, 1–5-day trips

Good, 10–50 m in season

Can be strong in places

Outstanding variety and prolific

Walls and drop-offs

Many species, great numbers and all sizes

Pristine diving, superb corals and fish, wrecks

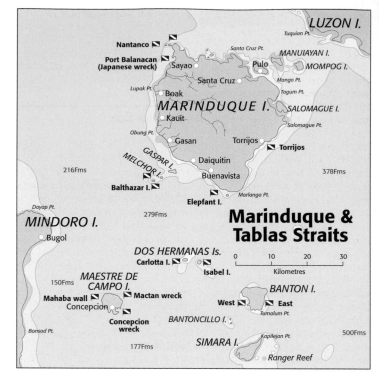

Marinduque & Tablas Straits

south is a great night dive with prolific corals and plentiful fish life and an army of Spiny Lobsters.

Further south and west again, at Maestre de Campo, there are several excellent dives, including the *M.V. Mactan,* a ferry boat which went down 20 years or so ago. In good condition, she lies north to south on a sandy slope from 25 to 55 meters. The bow is to the south. sweetlips, grouper, barracuda and a lot of lionfish and clouds of small tropicals have made this wreck their home.

At Port Concepcion, there are two Japanese wrecks in the harbour. A little scratching around in the muddy bottom usually rewards the searcher with bottles and other relics. The visibility is not so good, careful finning is the order of the day on these sites.

There are also the remains of World War II planes dotted around the place, and there is good coral diving on the west side of the island.

At Isabella in Dos Hermanos to the east, there is a maze of crevices

and lots of corals and reef fish. The area is often visited by local hookah fishermen, however, and the fish are skittish. A little to the west there is an excellent night dive area.

At Torrijos, on the east side of Marinduque, there's a shallow (15 meters) dive with cracks, fissures and canyons everywhere full of interesting things to explore, and a wall with large Gorgonians, colourful sponges and lots of big fish. Expect to see tuna, barracuda, grouper, sweetlips, shoals of tropical reef fish of all shapes and sizes and *Tridacna* clams. The current is not usually too bad here.

Banton

Further south and east again finds the island of Banton. The inhabitants of Banton process copra, and many of the younger Islanders have found work abroad, apparently remitting sufficient funds to maintain their families comfortably. Perhaps that's the reason the locals don't fish the surrounding reefs, and that's the reason the reef fish are so abundant and frisky around the island. The west side has areas of stunning coral encrustation, hard and soft corals of all kinds everywhere, with pennant butterflies, huge grouper, snapper and sweetlips darting in and out of the holes and cracks in the reef. Several species of shark and ray are sometimes seen, as are dolphins, which are very common all around the surrounding Sibuyan Sea.

The North-West wall, easily found by the graffiti 'Class of '93' scrawled above it, is simply awesome, one of the best wall dives you will find anywhere.

The weather can kick up on this exposed westerly side, making it a site you should plan to visit during the relatively benign months of March, April and May.

On the west coast of Banton, the story is pretty much the same, pretty, white sand coves, some with fantastic, unspoiled diving in coral gardens which reach 20 meters.

The Slab, a block of rock in a few meters of water about a third of the way south along the west shoreline, has an interesting cave that stretches into the darkness and is penetrable for several meters.

Visibility often exceeds 35 meters here during season, (December to June), and the profusion of pelagic and reef fish of all sizes is staggering.

Sibuyan Sea

The Sibuyan Sea, which stretches south and east of here, is almost completely unexplored by divers. Due to its remoteness and inaccessibility, it is only now that a few intrepid operators are beginning to open up this frontier. Some areas which have been visited over the last few years are reported to be heavily devastated by illegal fishing techniques. Others are spoken of in awe by the few divers lucky enough to have reached them. These days, several dive operators such as La Laguna Beach Club of Puerto Galera arranging custom trips for small groups who want to dive this virgin territory, and some of them are surprisingly reasonably priced.

One last point to make about Marinduque is that, up to now, scuba instruction is not easily available.
—*Heneage Mitchell*

Below: Generally docile and harmless unless bothered, the nocturnal leopard shark spends much of its day resting on the bottom. *Photo by Mark Strickland.*

Boracay

Stunning Beaches with First-class Dive Sites Nearby

The fabulous, powdery white sand beaches of Boracay have been famous for quite a few years as some of the world's best. Yet despite the island's popularity, scuba diving was slow to catch on. Today there are at least 12 dive centers doing good business around this small island, making it an excellent place to learn scuba. Courses range from Discover Diving to PADI Master Instructor.

Several dive outfits operate safaris to hard-to-reach locations such as the Sibuyan Sea, Tablas, Romblon and to Semirara Island, as well as to the west coast of Panay and the outlying reefs and islands.

Closer to Boracay, there are some first-class dive sites catering to divers of all levels, and some good, easily accessible snorkeling.

Friday's Rock, close to the west shore and at a depth of between 10 and 18 meters, is a favorite dive site. Here you will find a variety of soft and hard corals, butterflyfishes, wrasses, tangs, damselfishes, snappers and stingrays, and big scorpionfishes and lionfishes. Most divemasters can take you to a fish feeding station where the fish swarm around divers.

A little to the northwest of Friday's Rock there are two dive sites

By boat,
10–90 min

Usually good,
7–25 m

Strong in some areas

Good variety and quite prolific

Walls and coral gardens

Prolific in places, good variety

Easy access, awesome walls

named Punta Bonga 1 and 2. One is shallower, a drop-off to 24 meters, and the other starts at 30 meters and goes down to 50 meters. On the shallower dive, the top of the reef is covered with soft corals. Triggerfishes, groupers and angelfishes are commonly seen. Diving on the deeper wall, you'll find large gorgonians of all colors and big stingrays. There are plenty of sizeable sweetlips and tuna about, and occasional barracuda and shark.

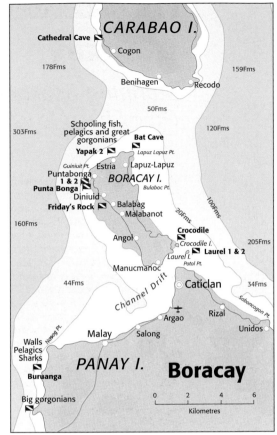

Crocodile Island

Southeast of Boracay, Crocodile Island (named for its shape, not any resident reptile) is another popular site, but one with current as it is right in the channel between Boracay and Panay. The bottom of the wall is around 24 meters at its deepest, the top of the reef is about 10 meters. You'll find just about everything here: sweetlips, triggerfishes, wrasses, butterflyfishes and snappers. There are a few banded sea snakes too—we've seen some over 2 meters long—but no-one has been bitten by one. Look out too for the pretty blue gorgonians.

Another excellent dive close by is Laurel Island. Currents can get very strong here, but it is these currents which encourage the corals to open up their fantastic yellow and orange polyps to feed on microscopic elements, festooning the walls of an 8-meter-long tunnel at the tip of the island. There are also big sponges and large gorgonians.

At the northern end of Boracay is Yapak, a deep wall starting around 30 meters and descending beyond 60 meters depth. Currents are often tricky here and the water is usually rough, but for experienced divers and lovers of big animals, this is the best Boracay has to offer. Covered with a profusion of soft corals, there are also some outstanding gorgonian fans hanging off the wall. Snappers, sweetlips, surgeons, pennants and rainbow runners are all plentiful as are barracudas, whitetip and grey reef

sharks. Occasionally a hammerhead will fin by. Manta rays have also been spotted from time to time. This is not a dive for beginners.

To the north, nearby Carabao Island has some fairly good spots. Cathedral Cave, a wide-mouthed cave at around 28 meters, is our particular favorite for its plentiful groupers and colorful soldierfishes.

Neighboring Panay

To the southwest of Boracay, the west coast of Panay has some excellent sites. At Buruanga, off Nasog Point, Black Rock and Dog Drift, the walls and drop-offs start at around 10 meters and go down to 40 meters. A variety of hard and soft corals are home to snappers, sweetlips and big triggerfishes. Keep an eye open for large pelagics.
— *Heneage Mitchell*

Left: Beaked butterflyfish *(Chelmon rostratus)*. Butterflyfishes are a favorite of underwater photographers, displaying a remarkable array of color patterns.
Photo by Mike Severns.

Mactan

A Popular Resort with Fair Diving

Looking a little unprepossessing from the air, the island of Mactan, 45 minutes from the heart of Cebu, comes alive underwater. Visited by thousands of divers every year, Mactan's east coast has several good dive sites along its walls. The Hilutangan Channel, which separates Mactan from adjacent Olango Island, is extremely deep and, as a consequence, one can hope to see several species of large animals on a lucky diving day. Although visibility can exceed 30 meters it usually averages around 18 meters, and divers should note that currents are a factor to be reckoned with.

Dive off the Resorts

The Tambuli Fish Feeding Station, just off the 5-star resort of the same name, is an excellent opportunity to get to know many smaller species of fish which abound in the warm and generally clear waters off Mactan Island. Photographers will appreciate this dive, as literally hundreds of fish swarm all around proffered bread or other snacks which dive guides bring along.

The soft corals off Mar y Cielo Resort are another interesting dive, a gentle slope covered with ele-

Local boats, 10–100 min, also live-aboards

Often excellent, 10–50 m

Can be stiff in places

Good variety, pristine in places

Walls and drop-offs

Good variety, good shells

Fans, gorgonians and pelagics

phant ear coral and barrel sponges.

Although a little deep with an entrance at 26 meters, the Marigondon cave is another popular dive well worth making the effort to visit. The cave stretches inward for about 45 meters and comes to end at a depth of 25 meters where there is a small grotto, home to dozens of flashlight fish. These fish have adapted to life in the dark by developing a neat patch of bio-luminescence under each eye. Divers poke their heads into the narrow opening and turn off their torches to be rewarded with a weird and wonderful light show as the fish dart around and hundreds of eyes appear to be winking back out of the dark recesses. A very unusual sight, indeed!

Good Walls

Just to the south of the cave on Marigondon Reef, there is a wall starting at 12 meters and descending to around 45 meters. Its attraction is that the face is covered in a wide variety of colorful sponges, soft corals, brain corals and gorgonians, a feature that characterizes most dives off Mactan. Not to be missed here is a sizeable colony of garden eels. There is usually a fair current—most dives are drift dives. A little to the north is Pang Pang, another wall dive very popular for night dives. Occasionally, lucky divers see whale sharks here, and sometimes manta rays, too.

The wall just off Kon Tiki Resort is another fine site. A short swim from the resort finds one on a gently sloping coral covered rocky seabed at 5 meters. This soon gives way to an impressive drop off, festooned with fan corals, sea stars, feather stars and myriad crinoids. Barracuda and solitary whale sharks can also been seen.

Olango Island

Across the Channel at Olango Island, there are a couple of sites of

interest, including Santa Rosa. A white sand bottom with a profusion of soft corals leads to a steep drop off at 15 meters. It bottoms out around 50 meters where big grouper can be seen in the small caves which are dotted about.

Also at Olango is Baring, just off the northwestern tip of the island. A sloping, sandy bottom starting at around 15 meters with several small caves, this area is

Below: Mactan's east coast has several good dive sites along its walls. *Photo by Ashley Boyd.*

home to large fish. Sharks can be seen here as well.

Mactan is a major jump-off point for divers wanting to visit outstanding, remoter dive sites around the Visayas, such as Cabilao, Panglao and Apo Island. Most dive centers on the island organize dive safaris, lasting from a couple of days up to a week or more aboard a variety of boats.

— *Heneage Mitchell*

Above: The broad-armed cuttlefish, *Sepia latimanus,* is the largest cuttlefish found in Southeast Asian waters. It can reach a half-meter in length. *Photo by Ashley Boyd.*

North Cebu

A Less Crowded Alternative to the Southern Resorts

Below: *Goniopora djiboutiensis* looks superficially like a soft coral, but the stalked tentacles of the colony are attached to a typical hard coral skeleton. *Goniopora* is most common in turbid waters of coastal reefs and lagoons. *Photo by Mike Severns.*

Due to the somewhat sparse diving infrastructure in this area, most of the coastal dive sites visited regularly by divers in the north of Cebu tend to be close to the town of Sogod, on the east coast, which has two resorts offering scuba rentals and guides.

However, all is not lost for visitors staying elsewhere on the island of Cebu. Some of the Mactan-based dive operators, in the central part of the island of Cebu, head north regularly, usually to visit Capitancillo, Gato and Calangaman islands.

Capitancillo Island

Capitancillo Island has a mushroom-shaped wall on its south side with outstanding coral formations and impressive gorgonian fans. Large manta rays are occasionally seen roaming around the teeming waters of the reef, and you can also hope to see shoals of yellowfin tuna and large groupers. The bottom is deep here—you still can't see it when you are down at 45 meters—so care should be taken at all time to monitor depths.

Local boats, 10–100 min, also live-aboards

Often excellent, 10–50 m

Can be stiff in places

Good variety, pristine in places

Walls and drop-offs

Good variety, good shells

Fans, gorgonians and pelagics

As a diversion after diving, you'll find an old lighthouse on top of this small rocky island. It is worth the climb, for the view from the top is impressive.

North of Capitancillo lies Calangaman, another dive site visited by the adventurous few who enjoy diving on so-called "virgin" dive sites. Both of these sites are within relatively easy striking distance and visited often by divers from Club Pacific, a Sogod-based resort.

Quatro Island is another location frequented by northern Cebu divers, who rave about its caves and reef formations. The hard and soft corals are outstanding here, and snorkelers favor the place as there is plenty to see—even in only 1 or 2 meters of water. There are actually four different reefs at this site, with walls descending to 150 meters, but don't even consider trying to get anywhere near the bottom of the wall. It is as well to remember that although there is a recompression chamber in Cebu City, it is far away.

At Kimod Reef, another one of those sunken islands, you are quite likely to run into a wide variety of pelagic life, including several different species of shark, as well as eagle and manta rays.

Gato Island

Another popular spot. Between November and May it's a good area for whitetips and other reef sharks. Here you'll find plenty of soft corals, gorgonians of all colors, sponges and hard corals. Gato Cave, actually a tunnel underneath the island, is also frequented by sharks and banded sea snakes. It is not for the faint hearted, but definitely a must for the thrill-seeker. Currents are usually a bit stronger here than at the previous locations mentioned, so drift diving is sometimes the order of the day.

Malapascua Reef is an excellent site for a night dive as it is at a depth of only 8–12 meters. Apart

from a profusion of corals, there are several interesting species of nudibranch, some of which grow up to 35 cm in length. The shell life is also plentiful, and you will find quite a number of moray eels here as well.

Closer to Sogod, there are a number of inshore sites worth a look. Dive boats typically anchor in 3–12 meters. There is a series of lagoons with sheer drop-offs going

Below: Due to its great size and graceful swimming action, the manta ray is a favorite with divers. They are often easier to approach on snorkel. *Photo by Jones/Shimlock.*

down to a maximum of 40 meters then it slopes gently to several hundred meters. All kinds of soft corals, sponges, nudibranchs and other invertebrates flourish in these waters. Chances are you will encounter dolphins and hawksbill turtles, and discover many different species of shells. The relatively rare golden cowrie has even been found around here.

—*Heneage Mitchell*

Above: Nudibranch *(Flabellina sp.)* feeding on the hydroids coating a sponge. *Photo by Mike Severns.*

Moalboal & Pescador

A Small but Superb Site Away from the Crowds

A few hours' drive southwest of Cebu City, across the dusty mountain roads of the interior to the west coast, is Moalboal.

One of the original dive centers of the Philippines, Moalboal owes its popularity almost entirely to scuba diving. A few steps off the beach from the main resort area of Pangasama lies a reef which is home to a wide variety of marine life. The ubiquitous fan corals and gorgonians are, of course, very much in evidence, as are sponges and crinoids, nudibranchs and several different species of shells. There are sweetlips, tangs, gobies and lionfishes all

over the the dive site. A little careful exploring will usually reveal some interesting shell life too.

Tongo Point, at the south end of the beach, is covered with little cracks and caves, home to soft corals and many tropical reef fish. Anemones and clownfishes, nudibranchs and a host of other invertebrates make this a popular photographer's dive. Visibility can be changeable, depending on the weather. A great dive for novices and a popular second dive.

An underwater "island," Lambug, lies about a 45-minute *banca* boat ride away. Really an underwa-

From the beach or by boat, 10–60 min

Often excellent, 10–50 m

Can be strong in places

Outstanding—great variety and prolific

Walls and drop-offs

Good variety, prolific in places, big pelagics

Pescador, Sunken Islands

ter mountain, Lambug is reached after descending through blue water for 27 meters before reaching the peak. There is often a strong current here too, so this really is not a dive for amateurs but for those who are up to it. Lambug is an outstanding experience. Large pelagics cruise by all the time; we saw several king barracudas, a lone tuna, two manta rays and a whitetip shark as well as groupers, snappers and a huge shoal of Talakitok, or jackfish, on one 25-minute dive last year.

Pescador Island

But the jewel in the crown of Moalboal's diving is tiny Pescador Island. About 2 km offshore, Pescador has been described as "a different dive every five meters." It is quite possible to circle the island on a shallower dive. Utterly superb drop-offs, buttresses and impressive overhangs are the main features of this site, with a shallow reef running around the island. Between 22 and 25 meters is a large, funnel-shaped structure of about 15 meters, called the Cathedral. When the sunlight hits it in just the right position, the corals and sponges are dappled with beams of light, making it a beautiful sight.

Lionfishes, snappers, groupers, scorpionfishes and sweetlips are found at every depth, and on deeper dives whitetip sharks and hammerhead sharks are not uncommon, especially between the months of November and April. Less frequently, tiger and thresher sharks put in an appearance. The

Photo by Jones/Shimlock

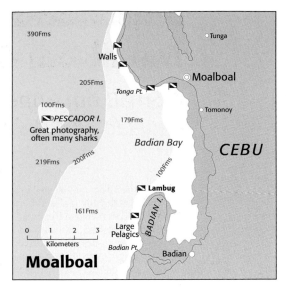

gorgonians are perhaps less profuse than one might imagine, but there is a lot of black coral around, as well as sea fans, sponges of all types and nudibranchs. Divers often see Spanish dancers wriggling their way sensually around the reef.

Pescador takes on a totally different perspective after dark, and it is a favorite local night dive.

Nearby, Badian Island is another spot worth visiting, though the marine life is neither as prolific or as exciting as Pescador and Lambug. However, whitetip sharks are quite common, and you may well see a banded sea snake or two, together with the inevitable anemones and sponges.

Several Moalboal dive centers arrange excursions further afield, to Bohol, Cabilao, Apo Island and other, remoter dive sites on an ad hoc basis. The communication revolution hasn't quite reached this sleepy little hamlet yet, so it's best to arrive and plan when you get there. Whatever you may end up doing, rest assured that Moalboal is sure to satisfy even the most jaded diver, and has the advantage of excellent off-the-beach diving of a quality which few other dive areas in the Philippines can match.

—*Heneage Mitchell*

Opposite: The common lionfish *(Pterois volitans)*. This animal sometimes travels in packs, lurking around vertical formations such as coral outcrops or shipwrecks. *Photo by Fiona Nichols.*

Bohol

Great Diving off Cabilao, Panglao and Balicasag

Bohol, in the Western Visayas, has long been regarded as home to some of the best diving in the Philippines. Panglao Island, connected to the mainland by a bridge, is the easiest dive area to reach and has a number of excellent sites for both divers and snorkelers.

At Arco Point, near Bohol Beach Club, there is a colony of sea snakes and a tunnel starting with an entrance at 8 meters, exiting at around 18 meters. Covered with a garden of soft corals, the interior has clouds of small tropical fish, including wrasses, butterflyfishes, tangs and copper sweepers.

The northwest tip of the island has a gentle drop-off leading to a bottom which becomes deeper the further south you swim. Currents can be quite strong here, so you should go with a guide. The gorgonians are particularly impressive although there is a good mix of hard and soft corals, as well as sponges.

There are several other spots well worth diving around the island, including the wall at Tangnan. Starting at around 6 meters, the wall falls away steeply to over 35 meters. Here, you'll find a series of small caves that are fun to explore.

Bancas,
10-300 min,
live-aboards

10–35 m

Can be stiff in
places

Good variety,
pristine in places

Walls, drop-offs and
coral gardens

Good variety,
good shells

Fans, gorgonians
and pelagics

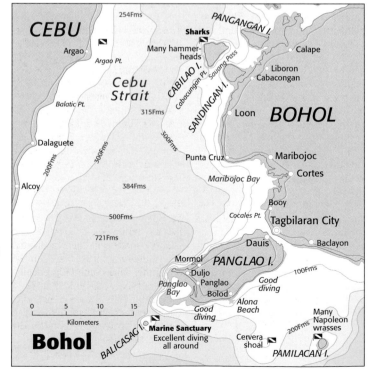

Big groupers dart in and out of the holes in the corals and rocks, but look out as well for wrasses, soldierfishes, surgeons and the occasional barracuda, jacks and whitetip sharks.

Marine Sanctuary

Diving aficionados should make sure that they take the time to venture a little further afield to Balicasag Island, to the southwest of Panglao, which contains a superb marine sanctuary and has what most visitors regard as the best diving in the Visayas. Drop-offs and bottomless walls, overhangs, plentiful fans, huge table and star corals, large clumps of black coral and big fish are the main features of Balicasag. But that is not all that the sanctuary has to offer.

Shallower spots with a variety of hard and soft corals, sea whips, feather stars, crinoids, tunicates, anemones and sponges are a photographer's delight. On a good day you'll encounter schools of barracuda and jacks, batfishes, big parrotfishes and groupers. There are plenty of lionfishes about, and veritable clouds of small reef fishes.

To the east of Balicasag and southeast of Panglao lies Pamilacan Island. Pamilacan means "resting place of mantas" in the local dialect, and you may be lucky enough to swim with one of these impressive creatures. A marine sanctuary has been set up on the northwestern side of the island, and it is here that you'll find superb gorgonians and hard corals along the walls, as well as an assortment of soft corals, anemones, tunicates, sponges and sea fans.

Between Pamilacan and Balicasag is the Cervera Shoal. An under- water

island just beneath the surface, dropping off to 20 meters, is home to a large colony of banded sea snakes. The corals are not particularly impressive, but it is the pelagics which are the attraction here. You can expect to see several species and occasional whitetip sharks, as well as butterflyfishes, scorpionfishes, damsels and surgeons.

Cabilao

This island is located further north, off the west coast of Bohol. Cabilao is a two-and-a-half-hour boat ride from Mactan, and it is from this island that most divers start their trip. Off the lighthouse on the northwestern tip of the island there are a series of overhangs, cracks and coral gardens. Gorgonians, crinoids, sponges and soft corals adorn the walls and drop-offs, making this a very pretty dive.

But it is the hammerhead sharks for which the island is most famous. Schools of these awesome beasts congregate around the island, usually quite deep at around 40–45 meters, between December and June. Also commonly encountered in this excellent spot are barracudas, jacks, mackerel, tuna, triggerfishes, butterflyfishes and humphead wrasses feeding in the strong currents.

— *Heneage Mitchell*

Above: Alona Beach, Bohol. *Photo by Mike Severns.*

Below: The butterflyfish *Chaetodon lunula. Photo by Gerald Allen.*

Apo Reef

A Speck in the Midst of the South China Sea

Apo Reef, in the South China Sea off the west coast of Mindoro, is actually an underwater lagoon. Between March and June, the peak season, water visibility is usually excellent, extending to 30 meters and more at most sites. But from July to January, the sea can be turbulent, making access uncomfortable to downright unpleasant. Trips to Apo are arranged through Pandan Island Resort on the west coast of Mindoro and from Puerto Galera, 125 km away. Most live-aboards feature Apo Reef on their itineraries too.

Wall diving is spectacular along many parts of the perimeter, and you don't need to go too deep to discover plenty of neat marine life.

A favorite spot on the reef itself is the wreck of a small fishing boat with a bridge which divers and snorkelers love to have their photographs taken in. Lying in shallow water, the hulk used to attract snappers and groupers, as well as hard and soft corals, sponges and a variety of other tropical marine life. The bottom has patches of table corals but visiting fishermen continue to wage war with nature very effectively, despite Apo's status as a marine sanctuary.

Dramatic Drop-offs

The northern edge of the lagoon has spectacular walls, dropping off radically from generally 5 to 10 meter depths. The walls are covered with gorgonians and fans due to the currents which can get quite stiff, attracting lots of pelagics as well as

Below: Friendly batfish *(Platax teira)* often escort divers during safety stops. *Photo by Mark Strickland.*

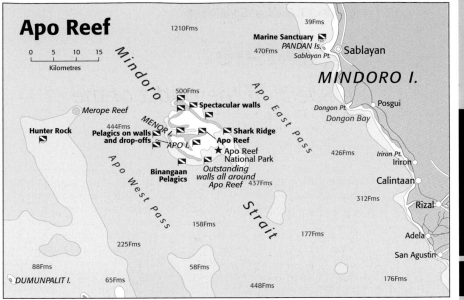

Apo Reef

0 5 10 15
Kilometres

1210Fms

39Fms

500Fms

Mindoro

MENOR I.

444Fms

Merope Reef

Hunter Rock

Pelagics on walls
and drop-offs

APO I.

Spectacular walls

Shark Ridge
Apo Reef

Apo Reef
National Park

Binangaan
Pelagics

Outstanding
walls all around
Apo Reef

437Fms

Apo West Pass

Apo East Pass

Marine Sanctuary
PANDAN Is.
Sablayan Pt.
Sablayan
470Fms

MINDORO I.

Dongon Pt.
Dongon Bay

Posgui

426Fms

Iriron Pt.
Iriron

Calintaan

312Fms

Rizal

Strait

158Fms

177Fms

Adela

225Fms

San Agustin

88Fms

58Fms

DUMUNPALIT I.

65Fms

448Fms

176Fms

encouraging more impressive coral formations. Watch out for the tuna, jacks, humphead wrasses, and from time to time, mantas and hammerheads. The remains of an old steamer in shallow water on the north of the reef are also quite interesting.

To the east, Shark Ridge is renowned for, of course, sharks—whitetips and blacktips most commonly—as well as mantas. The coral is not so impressive on this sloping bottom which gives way to sand and detritus at about 25 meters, but the animals are big and the diving can get wild!

To the southwest is another excellent wall, the Binangaan drop-off. Impressive gorgonians and hard and soft coral formations and schools of humphead parrotfish are seen here, as well as tuna and groupers, snappers, lots of interesting shells and some large pelagics.

Around Apo Island, to the west of the reef, there are also a number of superb sites to dive, mostly walls and drop-offs. Once again, mantas are not uncommon visitors all around the island, and the gorgonians are outstanding. Schools of tuna and other pelagics, turtles and groupers, snappers and wrasses, triggerfishes and parrotfishes seem to be everywhere. Lobsters and

other crustaceans scuttle about under rocks, in crevices and fissures, while along the perimeter, blacktip, whitetip and hammerhead sharks, remoras and barracudas fin silently past. Currents are often strong, but snorkeling can be good.

Snakes Galore

Some 21 km west of Apo Reef, Hunter Rock is an underwater island and not easy to find unless you're with a good guide. Our guide, Frank Doyle of Lalaguna Beach Club, had no trouble at all, dropping us onto the shallowest point of the reef at a depth of 9 meters or so.

"Follow a sea snake down," he said, and he wasn't joking. There are hundreds of them on Hunter Rock, in crevices, under coral heads and swimming about the reef. During mating season (June through July), literally thousands of snakes appear, and the sea is sometimes unnervingly carpeted with them. The reef itself is a profusion of corals and sponges, alive with schools of tropicals—butterflyfishes, snappers, sweetlips—and larger, predatory reef fish.

— Heneage Mitchell

Boat from Pandan Island, 1 hour; live-aboards, 1–5 days

Usually good, 15–50 m

Can be stiff in places

Prolific and varied

Walls and coral gardens

Prolific in places

Outstanding macro-photography

Sumilon

A Species-rich Marine Sanctuary

At the southeastern tip of Cebu lies Sumilon Island. While there are other sites around South Cebu visited by divers from Cebu and Bohol dive centers, Sumilon is a favorite, being the very first marine sanctuary created in the Philippines, though it has suffered considerable damage despite this status. Today, Sumilon enjoys better protection than before, and visiting divers are asked to contribute a small sum to help preserve it once again.

The waters are outstandingly clear around the island, especially between December and May, and there are stunning drop-offs and walls to be enjoyed with breathtaking fans and plentiful gorgonians, especially at deeper depths.

All kinds of pelagics swim around Sumilon, including leopard and manta rays, yellowfin tuna and jacks. Several shark species have been noted, not only the ubiquitous whitetips but also hammerheads and the occasional whale shark.

Dive safaris from
Cebu and Bohol

Usually outstanding,
15–50 m

Can be strong

Outstanding, prolific
and abundant

Walls, drop-offs

Many species,
prolific and large

Fans, gorgonians
and pelagics

fishes, surgeons, squirrelfishes, butterflyfishes, glasseye snappers, drums and several species of parrotfishes are all there in quantity.

Pelagics are plentiful, and there is every chance of an encounter with blacktip and whitetip sharks, as well as barracuda, tuna, and game fish such as dorado and Spanish mackerel.

Apo is conical in shape, and the

Apo Island

To the south of Sumilon is Apo Island (not to be confused with Apo Reef in the South China Sea, off the southwest coast of Mindoro). Apo is widely regarded as one of the best sites in the Visayas. In fact, many dive enthusiasts claim that it is THE best site. The marine sanctuary on the southeast side of the island is a fairytale land of hard and soft corals, with thousands of tropical reef fish blotting out the light in all directions. Gobies, tangs, wrasses, chromis or pullers, damsel-

untouched coral reef fringes the island at about 15–20 meters. All over the reef, there are veritable hills of star and brain corals, magnificent barrel sponges, a variety of stinging crinoids, pillar and staghorn corals. On the walls, you'll find magnificent gorgonians and fan corals. An outstanding dive site!

There are no dive centers on either Apo or Sumilon Island, and trips to both are arranged regularly by dive operations from Mactan, Moalboal, Bohol and several of the smaller resorts in southern Cebu. The best time to visit Apo Island is between December and May.

Siquijor Island

Between Apo and Sumilon, and a little to the east, is Siquijor Island. The inhabitants of this island are renowned (and feared) throughout the Philippines as mystics and spiritualists. Unfortunately, this has not prevented serious damage being inflicted on the reefs and shoals, and many of the great dive sites of yesteryear are history, reduced to algae-covered skeletons of coral.

There are still one or two sites worth visiting, however, including Tonga Point on the northwest coast. Here, a wall drops off quite rapidly from the relatively shallow fringing reef. Soft corals are plentiful here, and you'll find some reasonable gorgonians as you drift along the wall. Don't expect an abundance of fish life around this area, except at Apo Island, as the local fishermen are adept at harvesting everything that moves. Divers are urged to avoid dive outfits which encourage spear fishing.

— *Heneage Mitchell*

Below: Blue and gold fusilier *(Caesio teres)* form big, colorful schools, sometimes composed of several species, and frequently swarm around divers. *Photo by Takamasa Tonozuka.*

Coron Bay

Exploring a World of Wrecks off Busuanga Island

On September 24, 1944, Admiral "Bull" Halsey, seeking a safe passage through the uncharted Calamian Islands, sent out several waves of photo reconnaissance planes, When analysts compared the pictures taken, they noticed several "islands" had changed position relative to the surrounding land. Realising that they had discovered a camouflaged Japanese fleet, Halsey immediately ordered an air strike. Upon their return, US Navy pilots claimed 24 vessels sunk.

Fifty years on, 12 of these wrecks have been discovered in the protected waters of Coron Bay, lying in depths between 15 and 40 meters.

Due to their former inaccessibility and lack of diving infrastructure, its only recently that divers have started visiting the wrecks and outstanding coral reefs of the area. Most agree that the diving is superb, easily as good as Truk Lagoon in Micronesia but much shallower.

Irako and Kogyo Maru

The southernmost wreck visited frequently by local divers is the *Irako*. The *Irako* was a refrigeration ship, about 200 meters long displacing 9,570 tons. Now it is home to big groupers and shoals of yellowfin tuna. Lying in over 40 meters of water, the deck of this relatively intact wreck is at 28 to 33 meters.

To the north is the 140 meter

Below: Exploring a wreck in shallow water near the entrance to Barracuda Lake, Coron Island. *Photo by Jack Jackson.*

Coron Bay

Concepcion

TANTANGON I.

DICOYAN I.   Tae Maru
              (Concepcion wreck)

15Fms
CALUMBUYAN I.

0   2   4   6
Kilometres

Bintuan

BUSUANGA I.

Cayangcanan

17Fms   Akitsushima
LAJO I.   (Flying boat tender)

MANGLET I.

Olympic Maru

16Fms

LUSONG I.

APO I.

14Fms

LAMUD I.   Gunboat

TANGAT I.   Gunboat

Kogyu Maru
(Tangat wreck)

MARILY I.

25Fms

Mamiya Maru   Irako   BATUNAN I.

NAGLAYAN I.   29Fms

14Fms

BAKBAK I.

LAPUT 1.

CHINDONAN I.

29Fms

Siuk

PACHIRI I.   Tabulsit

BUGUR I.   INLULUCUT I.

Balanga

Coron Bay

CULION I.   Palumpung

Baldat   Culion   25Fms

long freighter *Kogyo Maru*. Also
known as the Tangat Wreck, she is
lying upright in about 30 meters of
water. Divers come onto the deck
at between 18 to 24 meters. The cargo holds are easily penetrable, and
there are shoals of fish all over it.
Look for giant pufferfish, especially
around the masts, bow and stern.
Soft corals and sponges, as well as
some small hard corals, have
attached themselves to the remains,
and this is a good first wreck dive
for beginners.

Mamiya Maru

West of the *Kogyo Maru* is the
Mamiya Maru, another freighter
about 160 meters in length. Lying
on its starboard side in 34 meters
of water, the wreck is easily penetrable in some places. The cargo
holds are still full of construction
materials, and anti-aircraft weapons
remain on the deck. Lots of grouper
have made their home on the
Mamiya Maru, and the port side
has many hard and soft corals and a

variety of fish life, including snappers, wrasse and lionfish.

To the north east is a small
gunboat about 35 meters long on
the other side of Tangat Island.
Lying in only 18 meters of water,
this wreck is a good snorkelling
site, as the bow is in only three
meters.

Olympic Maru

North west of the gunboat is the
Olympic Maru, 120 meters long and
lying on its starboard side in 25
meters of water. Once again, there
are plenty of grouper on this wreck,
and the port side, which is only 14
to 18 meters underwater is covered
in hard corals. Easy penetration of
the cargo holds and engine room
make this an interesting dive, but
watch out for scorpionfish which
are all over this area!

Tae Maru

Further away, to the north west, is

Banca boat,
30–120 min,
live-aboards

10–35 m

Moderate

Good variety,
prolific in places

Walls, coral gardens
and wrecks

Wide variety,
prolific

Wrecks galore!

the *Tae Maru,* or Concepcion wreck, a Tanker about 200 meters long lying upright in 26 meters of water. You come onto the deck at between 10 and 16 meters. The bow is completely smashed, allowing for easy penetration, and the wreck is covered in hard and soft corals and sponges. Sweetlips, grouper, lionfish, surgeons, wrasse, tang and soldierfish have made this wreck their home, and barracuda occasionally swim by overhead. The currents can be treacherous sometimes, and can take an unwary diver by surprise, especially when rounding the stern or bow.

The Akitisushima

Due south is the *Akitisushima,* my personal favorite, a 200-meter-long flying boat tender lying on its starboard side. The flying boat is long gone, but the huge crane used to put it into the water and retrieve it is still in one piece, twisting away from the wreck into the sandy bottom at 38 meters. More or less intact, the gaping hole in the side which caused it to sink immediately is quite apparent.

A good boatman will put a diver onto the highest point of the wreck at about 20 meters, and the average depth of a dive is usually around 28 meters. Shoals of barracuda, tuna and yellowfin circle the wreck, and grouper, batfish, snapper and many other species of tropical reef fish have made their home here. Apart from the wrecks, Coron also has some outstanding coral dives, and these should definitely not be missed.

Coral Diving

Off the northwest coast of Busuanga lies the island of Dimaky. Adjacent to this island are a number of excellent coral dives. On the west side of the island, a gorgeous coral garden with tame reef fish is a popular dive. A slope dropping to 17 meters is home to tunicates and

Opposite: Coron offers some outstanding coral dives. Photo by Ashley Boyd.

sponges as well as groupers and several species of parrotfish. At the far end of the wall, there's a large swathe of staghorn coral, with an abundance of barracuda, rainbow runners and goatfish. Manta rays and turtles are occasionally seen here and more frequently at the northern end of the island.

At Dibuyan Island, the reef starts around 13 meters, sloping gently to 28 meters. Whitetip, blacktip and grey reef sharks are commonly seen here, as well as surgeonfishes and batfishes. Mantas, too, are occasionally seen. In the shallows, a profusion of small tropical reef fish can be found.

Busuanga is at the frontier of the struggle to preserve the natural resources of the Philippines. Among the creatures whose fates are inextricably linked with man's actions over the next few years is the harmless *Dugong dugon,* a relative of the manatee, or sea cow. They are only occasionally seen by divers, but their tender flesh is a favored delicacy among native fishermen, which may doom them to extinction in local waters despite the best efforts and intentions of several conservation groups operating in the area.

Barracuda Lake

Coron also has one of the most unusual divesites in the Philippines, Barracuda Lake. To get to the lake, you have to climb up a limestone mountain for 15 or 20 minutes.

The water temperature in the lake varies from between 30 to 38 degrees Celsius: you can actually see the thermoclines. After simmering and boiling for a while your host, a resident 1.5 meter king barracuda, usually appears to guide you around until its time to leave, providing an great opportunity for photographers to get excellent close ups!

—Heneage Mitchell

El Nido

Fabulous Seascapes and Year-round Diving

A stunning collection of islands with high limestone cliffs predominates the idyllic seascapes of El Nido in northwestern Palawan. As one might expect, there is no shortage of fine diving to be enjoyed here. Lots of pelagics, some rare and unique species, and excellent wall and drift diving; the marine life is diverse and in places very prolific.

Diving Dilumacad

Below: High limestone cliffs and stunning islands dominate the idyllic seascapes of El Nido, Palawan. *Photo by Photo Bank.*

A popular site west of El Nido town itself, situated in the southern bowl of Bacuit Bay, is on the north side of Dilumacad Island. A year-round dive site, except when a strong north wind is blowing, this location features a tunnel with a cavern in the center of it, at about 15–20

meters, and an entrance wide enough for two divers to swim abreast. Not far in, the tunnel widens out into the cavern with a bottom of sand, and there are clouds of small fish as well as crabs roaming the floor. The 10-meter-long way out is narrower, so only one diver can pass at a time. It exits at about 22 meters nearby lots of large rocks which frequently have big fish hanging around. Recently, while searching for the rubber cover of his depth gauge which had fallen into a crack, my buddy collided rather suddenly with a very large Spanish mackerel. Hard to tell who of the two was more surprised!

Further west around Miniloc Island, where the luxurious resort at El Nido is located, there are several worthwhile sites.

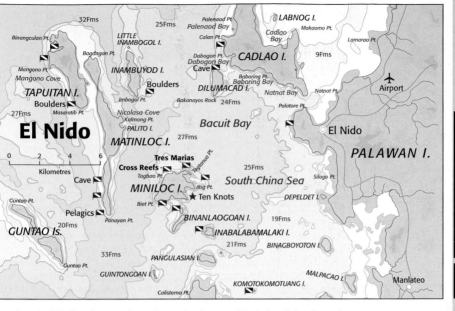

South Miniloc has a dive site between 13 and 21 meters with abundant lettuce corals, sponges and a colony of blue ribbon eels. Visited by jacks and barracuda, squids, cuttlefish and angelfishes also make their homes here. A sheltered spot, this is one of several year-round dive sites worth a visit.

To the north is Twin Rocks, another year-round site. It is characterized by a sandy bottom at depths varying between 13 and 21 meters, and is dotted with table corals, sea whips, corals and sponges, amongst which there are small stingrays and angelfishes.

Boulders and Big Fish

Off the northwest point of Miniloc Island lies tiny Tagbao Island. The local boatman probably knows it as Tres Marias, in reference to the three coral reefs wrinkled between the two land masses. To the southwest is a series of vast boulders, some as large as two-story houses. Because of the relatively shallow depths, the potential for snorkeling is good here, and you'll find plentiful reef fishes and colorful corals, as well as painted crayfish.

South Tip or Banayan Point on the larger Matinloc Island to the west is for lovers of pelagics. Most divers don't notice the richly coral-encrusted rocks as they are too busy avoiding mackerel, tuna and jacks finning by in the, often stiff, currents. It's best to head for the western side of the island, especially between March and June, as the east coast is generally a lot less attractive, though accessible all year round. Bakanayos Rock, known locally as Picanayas, has yet more boulders on the southwest side with a crew of whitetip sharks poking in and out of the holes.

To the southwest of adjacent Inbogal Point (Inambuyod) there are some impressive gorgonians and green corals on a steep wall that drops down to 35 meters. Jacks, tuna and mackerel pass by, and this site is home to a unique species of angelfish, *Pomacanthus annularis*, distinguished by its additional stripe. It is only known here and at Tres Marias.

Of the many local dives in the area, Black Coral Forest off the west of Entalula Island deserves a mention. On a steep drop from 35 to 40 meters, there are lots of acropora and clumps of black coral sprouting out in several places.

—*Heneage Mitchell*

Banca boat, 10–120 min live-aboards

10–45 m

Usually negligible, strong in places

Outstanding in places; soft coral covering past dynamite damage

Walls, drop-offs and coral gardens

Varied, prolific; some unique species here

Walls and pelagics

The Sulu Sea

Diving the Reefs of Tubbataha, Jessie Beazley and Basterra

The Sulu Sea is bounded on the west side by the long, thin island of Palawan, and on the east by the islands of Panay, Negros and Mindanao. Some of the best diving in the Philippines, and perhaps the world, is to be found at several remote locations within the Sulu Sea, most famous of which is Tubbataha Reefs.

Despite its inaccessibility and its relatively short season—mid-March to mid-June—berths on any of the several live-aboard boats visiting Sulu Sea are much sought after. It's best to book as early as possible to avoid disappointment.

Tubbataha Reefs

Tubbataha Reefs National Marine Park consists of two atolls, North and South Tubbataha, separated by 4 nautical miles of water with depths reaching an incredible 650 fathoms. Most live-aboards, and the one or two large pump boats which make the trip regularly in season, start out from Puerto Princesa, capital of Palawan, and take 10 hours or so to motor to the Reefs. Puerto Princesa is actually located 98 nautical miles to the northwest of the Reefs.

The first stop is most likely to be the southern reef, sometimes called Lighthouse, as it encloses a small islet with a solar-powered lighthouse which identifies the area. It is worth climbing up the lighthouse, for the view of the reef and the large lagoon inside it is truly spectacular from this vantage point.

Underwater, the east side of the reef is like gently rolling hills of hard and soft corals and sponges. A wide variety of squirrelfishes, angelfishes, groupers, parrotfishes and butterflyfishes hover and swim about in an underwater fiesta of colorful abandon. You may even see a crocodilefish on the bottom between coral heads.

The reef slopes down to 18–24 meters in a few spots before reaching the edge of the wall stretching north for about 12 km.

What remains of the *Delsan* wreck lies partly submerged near the edge of the drop-off. The vertical walls are covered with a wide variety of soft corals, tube sponges and sea fans. Moorish idols, triggerfishes, surgeons and other schooling tropicals are quite common near the drop-off, while whitetip and blacktip sharks cruise deeper along the wall. Occasionally a barracuda, either solitary or in a pair, will cruise by, and if you are really lucky, manta rays may pass by close enough for a good photograph.

The west wall starts more abruptly. Winding slowly towards the northwest for almost 11 km, the drop-off has large pink, purple and burgundy colored soft corals. Red and violet sea fans reach outward, and occasionally small schools of crevale jacks swim by. When the current is running, mackerel, tuna and shark cruise close to the wall.

The north side of the reef, known for its turtles, has the same gently sloping incline leading to the actual wall, but the drop-off is not so steep in places. Hawksbill and

Live-aboard boats from Puerto Princesa

Mostly excellent, 20–50 m

Variable

Outstanding variety, pristine and prolific

Walls and coral gardens, sand banks

Awesome variety, prolific in all sizes

Probably some of the best diving anywhere

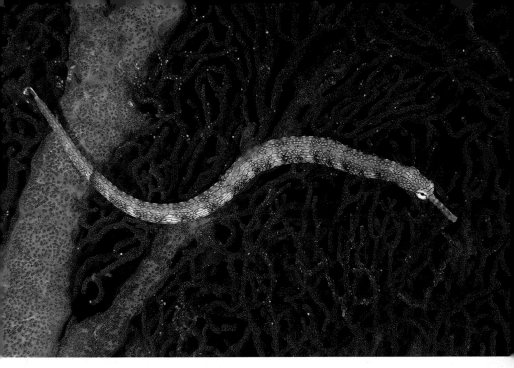

green turtles are usually to be seen, either resting or gliding leisurely near the edge of the reef. Around the area called Black Rock there are likely to be currents. Unpredictable and often swift, these can catch an unwary diver and cause problems.

Amos' Rock on North Tubbataha is in the south among the sandy cays. Here you will find a gently sloping bottom covered mostly with branching hard corals interspersed with soft corals, sponges and sea squirts. Sandy patches at around 6–10 meters are home to sea pens and Cerianthid anemone. This area is ideal for night dives, when a good variety of cones, cowries and olive shells are found by sifting through the white sand. With a bit of patience and close observation, we invariably spotted a fine assortment of species including several Triton shells.

On the west side of the islet, the reef winds from the southwest to the northeast. The walls are not so vertical but numerous varieties of sea whips, sea fans and soft corals abound among the hard corals. Coral fishes hover about, facing

mild currents, and further off the wall are schools of surgeonfishes and jacks. The wreck of a small-sized tugboat, now inhabited by plenty of small fish and an increasing number of coral colonies, sits near the wall's edge, offering good snorkeling or a shallow second dive.

The north wall, near Bird Island, starts in 5–8 meters. Numerous fissures lead into the near vertical wall and open up into the shallows. Crevices and horizontal ledges cut into the drop-off where nurse sharks and, less commonly, leopard sharks may sometimes be caught resting or sleeping.

As you swim along further to the northeast, the edge drops gradually deeper. Black coral adorns the wall as well as plentiful lush soft corals and tube sponges. The sandy bottom that slowly rises to the shallows, is dotted with coral heads and wide table corals. It is not unusual to find lobsters underneath these corals. Look underneath, also, for sheltering blue-spotted stingrays and small sharks.

Keen-eyed divers have often found guitarfish (also called the

Above: Banded pipefish *(Corythoichthys intestinalis)*. Photo by *Mike Severns.*

shovel-nosed shark) motionless on the sandy bottom, while we have often had good sightings of manta rays in the slightly deeper waters.

The north islet is known also as Bird Island for the thousands of terns and boobies that inhabit this pocket handkerchief of land. It is an excellent spot for bird watching and photography, but take care as the boobies lay their eggs in the sand.

Jessie Beazley Reef

This reef lies about 18 km northwest of North Tubbataha. It is a small, circular reef that rises up almost to the surface of the sea. The surrounding blue water plunges to depths of over 500 fathoms. Marked by the shifting sand cay and the contrasting greens of the shallows, Jessie Beazley has similar features as Tubbataha Reefs, except that it is only half a kilometer in diameter. During calm, sunny days, water visibility averages an impressive 27–37 meters though currents can be quite strong in places.

The reef typically slopes to 7–12 meters before the edge of the wall itself, which drops off to over 50 meters. The shallows are predominantly covered with Porites and Acropora corals. Near the edge, at depths of 16–19 meters, are cave-like crevices with a colony of lobsters (*Panulis versicolor*). Turtles are occasionally seen perched among coral heads. Hanging off one side of the reef is an old anchor, encrusted with a variety of colorful corals.

Anthogorgia sea fans, den-

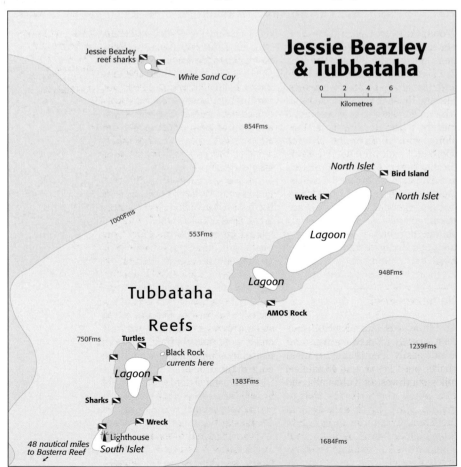

Jessie Beazley reef sharks

White Sand Cay

Jessie Beazley & Tubbataha

| 0 | 2 | 4 | 6 |

Kilometres

854Fms

North Islet

Bird Island

Wreck

North Islet

1000Fms

553Fms

Lagoon

948Fms

Tubbataha

Lagoon

AMOS Rock

Reefs

750Fms

Turtles

1239Fms

Black Rock
currents here

Lagoon

1383Fms

Sharks

Wreck

48 nautical miles to Basterra Reef

Lighthouse

South Islet

1684Fms

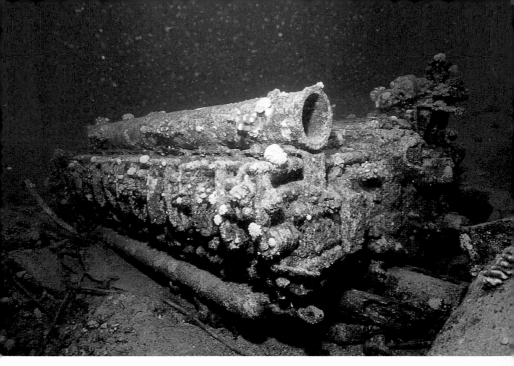

Above: The engine of the wreck of a Tristar B at Basterra Reef. *Photo by Jack Jackson.*

dronephthyrya and antipatharian black corals lace the wall as you descend the steep face. The wall itself is etched with small undercuts and ledges at 21–35 meters. Massive basket sponges, some of which measure as much as 3 meters, cling to the rock face along with a diversity of tube sponges. Small whitetip and black-tip sharks are commonly seen, and sometimes a nurse shark can be found resting on the sandy ledge. On the larger end of the scale, hammerhead, mako and thresher sharks have been spotted cruising the clear, blue waters of the reef from time to time.

Basterra Reef

Also known as Meander Reef, this reef is rarely marked on maps and is not easily identifiable on most charts, but it lies around 48 nautical miles southwest of Tubbataha and 110 miles southeast of Puerto Princesa. It is much smaller than the Tubbataha reefs and slightly bigger than Jessie Beazley, but what it lacks in size it makes up for in real fish action.

Surrounded by waters plunging to 1,000 fathoms, Basterra Reef pushes up to the surface, a massive pinnacle capped by a sand bar, and a wreck, the *Oceanic II,* lies to the north. The majestic walls and corals of Basterra are bursting with myriad forms of marine life. In fact, the almost-round reef is considered by many to be the best diving spot in the entire Sulu Sea.

At Barracuda Slope you'll find a gentle slope of white sand, with porites and acropora corals almost breaking the surface, shelves to the edge of the wall at about 16 meters. Multitudes of small, colorful fish such as anthias, swarm like confetti around large coral heads and the table corals. These become more and more dense as you approach the edge of the wall. Perciform fish swim around in the light current and a large school of red snappers is usually seen cruising around the edge of the drop-off.

Then, at a distance, you should be able to pick up what appears to be a silvery-grey cloud in the water. At first sighting it seems stationary, suspended in mid-water, but as you move closer you realize that the cloud is a thick school of almost motionless barracuda which regularly inhabit this area and after whom this site has been named.

The white, sandy slope is also an excellent place for night diving. A wide variety of shells, including terebras and murex, make their home here, as does a colony of garden eels, which can be spotted peering from their holes during the day. Deeper down the wall, the common blacktip and whitetip sharks are almost always present.

From the southwest to the west side of the reef, a thick growth of massive brown corals, piled almost on top of one another, borders the impressive vertical wall which drops off from 5 to 10 meters to unfathomable depths. Squirrelfishes, bigeye jacks, assorted snappers and butterflyfishes join schools of Moorish idols and bannerfishes. Check out the crevices, too, for lobster are found here. Coral encrusted fishing lines stretch out almost horizontally from the wall, which is covered with a profusion of soft corals, sponges, black corals and gorgonians.

As one swims along, you'll see another silvery cloud cascading from the shallow reef to the depths in the distance. Closer inspection reveals it to be thousands of jacks, mingling with a large school of sweetlips and surgeonfishes.

Moving northward along the wall, in the shallower parts of the reef, there are a series of depressions that are etched into the wall. The most prominent one resembles a crater and is home to multitudes of small tropical fish, including the uncommon leaf fish. Deeper, you'll come across boulder-like formations of massive corals at 12–15 meters, and this is where the current may start to move in the opposite direction, attracting plenty of fish. Look out for the surgeonfishes amidst jacks and tuna. From here, the action really begins.

Named Expressway for the current's speed at this dive site, the reef hosts an abundance of fish life which includes large manta rays, grey reef sharks and even whitetip

sharks. Not as creviced as other areas around Basterra, the edge of the wall starts at around 3–4 meters before plunging radically to unrecorded depths, forming an awesome cliff which angles inward to create a truly impressive overhang. This is one dive which cannot fail to excite any diver, however comprehensive his diving experience! If you can tear your gaze away, common black corals and dendrophillias are scattered sparsely along the wall.

A Wreck, Too

The scattered wreck of a large twin-hulled boat, complete with well-established coral growth, provides shelter to a variety of snappers, groupers and spade fishes, as well as smaller fishes like wrasses, chromis and thousands of sergeant-majors. What used to be one of the engines lies in 13 meters of water close to the nesting site of some triggerfish.

Near the *Oceanic II* wreck, to the north, the reef is characterized by a thick growth of a variety of hard corals. Here you may see manta rays, mating pairs of hawksbill turtles and a few solitary barracuda. Patches of coral rubble near the edge of the wall at 18–24 meters are favorite hangouts of sharks. Barracudas, dogtooth tuna and mackerel are common off the wall that gradually curves away to the east.

Further south, the slope steepens then drops vertically from depths of 18–22 meters on the east side of the reef. Every so often, divers should watch the blue water to the east for sightings of grey reef sharks, mantas, tuna, jacks and turtles. Unicornfishes and other varieties of surgeonfish are quite common in this part of Basterra. The beautiful and colorful clown triggerfish may be seen in the shallower areas, where brightly hued clams also thrive. Check out the crevices, too, for blue triggerfish and tangs.

— Louie and Chen Mencias

Opposite: Divers' accommodations in Bonito.
Photo by Mike Severns.

Diving in Thailand

A Kingdom Straddling Two Seas

Thailand's great diving has been kept somewhat of a secret from the world. Residents of Southeast Asia and those more adventurous divers from Europe and North America, however, discovered long ago the wondrous attractions that dwell in our undersea kingdom.

Thailand is blessed with two bountiful seas, the Gulf of Thailand in the east and the Andaman Sea—part of the eastern Indian Ocean—in the west. The riches that these oceans contain are a delight to those of us that have had the pleasure of diving here. Furthermore, the Thai Kingdom is blessed with a remarkable history and culture, friendly natives who offer friendly service, beautiful national parks, a wide range of accommodation possibilities at every price level and some of the most delicious and extraordinary food—including tropical fruits—in the world.

Often referred to as the "Land of a Thousand Smiles," Thailand is a joyous country to travel in. One of the first Thai phrases travelers learn is *mai pen rai,* which literally translates to "it is nothing." It also is used in the same ways that "never mind" or "that's OK" are used in English. However, *mai pen rai* is more than that—it is almost a philosophy that teaches one to hide problems and keep one's "public face" smiling and happy. For the visitor this attitude creates a feeling of burdens lifted. It makes you feel satisfied, content and cheerful. While exploring the country you'll feel carefree, lighthearted and safe—you'll feel *mai pen rai.* Is it any wonder so many of us expatriates have

decided to stay, or does it surprise that people visit Thailand time and time again?

Thailand's territory stretches from the eastern border with Cambodia to the western border with Myanmar (formerly Burma), and then south to Malaysia. Because of its varied topography and delightful people, Thailand offers the visiting diver diverse undersea experiences along with an unbelievable amount of top-side recreation. It's the perfect place for a diving holiday. World-class diving, heavenly tropical islands and immaculate white sand beaches await the explorer. With water visibility often exceeding 30 meters, an average ocean temperature of around 25°C, and uncommonly calm sea conditions, Thailand has some of the most comfortable and safe diving environments to be found anywhere in the world.

Development of the Diving Industry

Every year more and more is published on the diverse marine life that prowl the depths of Thailand's oceans, and every year more and more divers visit the country. There are three reasons for this. First, new destinations, such as the Burma Banks and the Andaman Islands in the Andaman Sea, Ko Tao in the Gulf and Ko Chang near the Cambodian border, have opened up and been made more accessible to a wider variety of visitors. Second, Thailand's infrastructure has vastly improved, making it easier to com-

Overleaf: The whale shark, *Rhincodon typus,* is the largest fish known. This is a small specimen, and it has been known to reach 15 meters. *Photo by Ashley Boyd.*

Opposite: Peering through a natural porthole at a clown triggerfish *Balistoides conspicillum.* These are rather bold and territorial fishes. *Photo by Mark Strickland.*

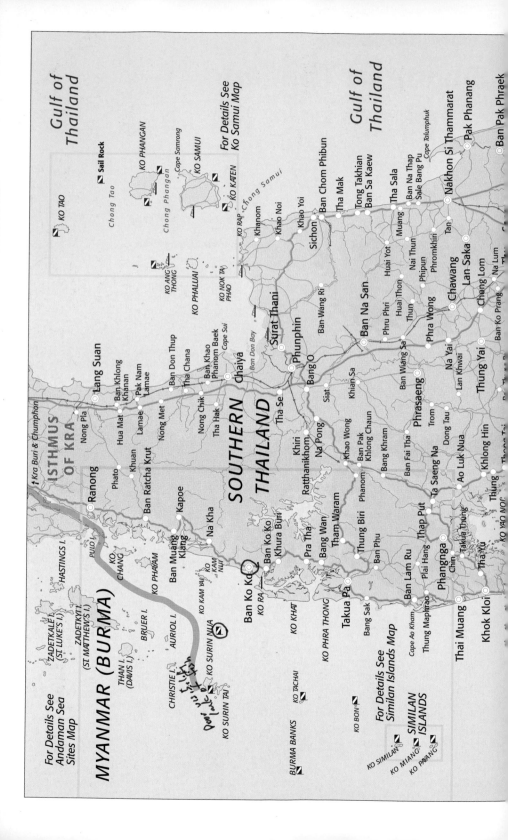

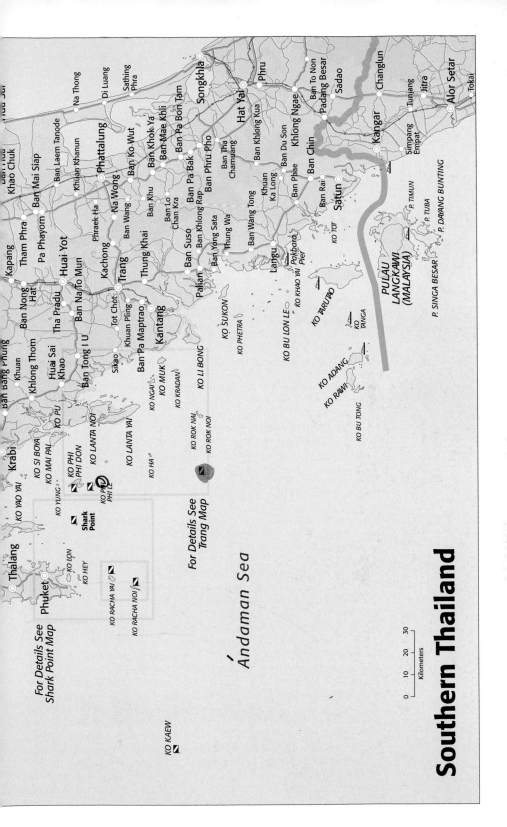

Southern Thailand

Andaman Sea

*For Details See
Shark Point Map*

*For Details See
Trang Map*

Thalang
Phuket
KO YAO YAI
KO SI BOYA
KO MAI PAI
KO YUNG
KO PHI PHI DON
KO PHI PHI LE
Shark Point
KO LON
KO HEY
KO RACHA YAI
KO RACHA NOI
KO KAEW

Krabi
Ban Bang Phung
Khuan
Khlong Thom
Huai Sai
Khao
Ban Tong I U
KO LANTA NOI
KO LANTA YAI
KO HA
KO NGAI
KO MUK
KO KRADAN
KO ROK NAI
KO ROK NOI

Kapang
Ban Nong Hat
Tham Phra
Pa Phayom
Tha Pradu
Ban Na To Mun
Huai Yot
Sikao
Khuan Pling
Ban Pa Maptrao
Kantang
KO LI BONG

Khao Chuk
Ban Mai Siap
Ban Laem Tanode
Na Thong
Di Luang
Sathing Phra

Na Wong
Phraek Ha
Kachong
Trang
Tot Chot
Palian
Ban Suso
KO SUKON
KO PHETRA

Phattalung
Ban Khu
Ban Wang
Thung Khai
Ban Lo Chan Kra
Ban Khlong Rap
Ban Yong Sata
Thung Wa
Langu
Pakbara
Pier
KO BU LON LE
KO KHAO YAI
KO TARUTAO
KO ADANG
KO RAWI
KO BU TONG
KO TANGA

Khuan Khanun
Ban Ko Wut
Ban Khok Ya
Ban Mae Khli
Ban Pa Bon Tam
Songkhla
Ban Pa Bak
Ban Phru Pho
Ban Tha Chamuang
Ban Wang Tong
Khuan Ka Long
Ban Du Son
KO TOT

Phru
Ban To Non Padang Besar
Sadao
Changlun
Hat Yai
Khlong Ngae
Ban Chin
Ban Rai
Satun
Ban Phae
Kangar
Sumpang Empat
Tunjang
Jitra
Alor Setar
Tokai

PULAU
LANGKAWI
(MALAYSIA)
P. TIMUN
P. TUBA
P. SINGA BESAR
P. DAYANG BUNTING

0   10   20   30
Kilometers

municate with the people who offer the diving—the dive centers. Third, the diving boats, diving resorts, diving operations and diving staff have improved their services and amenities so considerably that they now cater to the most discerning diver.

Professional level diving services are the norm in Thailand. The diving industry has exploded over the past 7 years or so, and the standard of service and professionalism in Thailand is unequalled in Southeast Asia. Most dive centers are affiliated with PADI, but SSI and NAUI instruction is available in many places. Prices vary depending on what you are doing, where you are going, and how comfortable you want to. It is always best to contact diving centers before arriving to arrange your holiday, since at certain times of the year—especially in Phuket where the diving is considered to be the best—dive boats are frequently full. If you are planning a live-aboard to the Burma Banks or to Similan, pre-booking is essential.

Most diving activities are supervised by a diving guide, either Thai or *falang* (western foreigner). If you are a beginner, it is generally suggested that you find out as much about the dive site and the guide as possible before booking. Not all dive sites in Thailand are suitable for beginners, and like anywhere, not all guides are as competent as others.

Most dive centers offer beginning dive courses, as well as advanced and professional-level courses. Very high-quality underwater photography courses are available, especially on Phuket's better live-aboard dive boats. All courses are generally of the highest quality, and prices are reasonable. One advantage of learning in Thailand is that the normal class size is small, averaging between four and six students, often less.

Diving takes place in three general areas: Pattaya, near the capital of Thailand, Bangkok; around the southern islands of the Gulf of Thailand; and in the two triangles of diving in the Andaman Sea on the west coast of Thailand's isthmus. The pages that follow will describe these areas in detail and will give you an idea of what to expect.

The Andaman Sea To the northwest of the island of Phuket lie the most popular, famous and best-loved dive sites in Thailand, the Similan Islands, visited by many live-aboards. Approximately 180 km to the northwest of these islands lie the relatively unexplored Burma Banks, a group of underwater mountains rising from depths of over 350 meters to just below the surface. These banks are only accessible by professionally equipped live-aboard boats. About 350 km further to the northwest are the newly opened Andaman Islands. Then there is Richelieu, known for its whale sharks.

South of Phuket lie a number of islands, most of which can be enjoyed in a day's diving excursion. Look out for trips to Ko Racha Yai and Noi, Shark Point and the delightful Phi Phi Islands. Further to the south lies the largely unexplored area of Trang, which can offer diving quality on par with the Similans. Live-aboard operators from Phuket are now diving here.

Gulf of Thailand The friendly laid-back islands of Ko Samui and Ko Tao are located a relatively short distance from Thailand's east coast city of Surat Thani. Originally coconut plantations, these islands have developed into a paradise for people searching for a completely relaxed life-style. Exotic dive site names such as Ko Wao, Hin Bai and Chumpon Pinnacle all lie within easy reach of Ko Tao and Ko Samui, and some of the diving here can be spectacular. These sites present the casual diver with a pleasant diversion from such sybaritic activities as relaxing on the beach, drinking from cool coconuts fresh off the tree, or dancing to the sounds of reggae music at one of the local night clubs. Interesting diving combined with a very pleasant stay on the islands ensure an all-around great time.

East Coast Frequently referred to as "Southeast Asia's Fun Resort," Pattaya is located just a short 2-hour drive from Bangkok. A weekend escape for those living a life in the chaotic capital, Pattaya's dive sites stretch from Pattaya Bay to the newly explored areas near the border of Cambodia. Although mainly a popular place in Thailand for diving instruction, the waters around Pattaya can offer the experienced diver the opportunity to dive on ship wrecks and at the same time stay in Thailand's most comprehensive tourist resort.

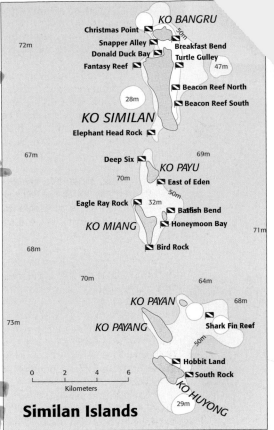

Similan Islands

Environmental Protection

Protecting the environment is a fairly new concept in Thailand and Southeast Asia, but fortunately more and more people are developing an awareness for it.

Divers have long been aware of damage to coral reefs through dynamite fishing and anchoring, but only recently have dive centers started to recognize the damage done by the divers themselves. For this reason, most centers have developed a hands-off policy. This has resulted in Thailand having some of the most environmentally progressive dive shops in the world, which has helped to keep our reefs healthy and beautiful. Divers are asked to respect the wishes of the diving community by not gathering or collecting any corals or shells, even from the beaches (removing dead shells also deprives a creature, such as a hermit crab, of a potential home). Marine items from shell shops should also be avoided.

Environmentally, Thailand's diving fraternity has been a leader in coral reef protection in Southeast Asia. Many of Thailand's best dive sites have become protected under law. Over the past 7 years, I have personally seen major improvements in the quality of diving in almost all regions around the coun-

try. While other areas in Southeast Asia and the rest of the world have suffered major degradation of their reefs, Thailand's government and its dive centers have instigated sound policies in controlling damage to the coral and fish populations. These policies have included educating people regarding the destruction of reefs by dynamite, mooring projects in the Similans, Ko Racha, Ko Phi Phi, Ko Samui and Ko Tao, and a strict hands-off policy for divers enjoying our undersea treasures.

As long as this positive trend continues, diving in Thailand's seas will bring pleasure, enjoyment and thrills to many people—and hopefully to their children and grandchildren as well. You'll find Thailand's waters, islands and culture full of life, full of wonder—and full of surprises.

— John Williams

Similan Islands

Nine Gems Offering Some of Asia's Best Diving

Overnight by live-aboard boat

Great,
18–30 m plus

Variable,
sometimes strong

Excellent condition,
unbelievable variety

Boulders,
coral walls

Small sizes
but fantastic

Unusual formations,
dramatic scenery,
swim-throughs,
large fans, and
beautiful beaches

Ko Similan is by far the most beautiful group of dive sites in Thailand and one of the best areas for diving in the entire world. Many divers find that the most unusual aspect about the Similans is that there are two radically different types of environments neatly packaged together into one destination.

The Similans, located about 100 km northwest of Phuket, are composed of nine granite islands covered in tropical jungle, washed by a clear, blue tropical ocean and blessed with some of the world's finest beaches. The word Similan is a corruption of the Malay *sembilan*, which means "nine," and history has it that it was a Malay fisherman who named the group "The Nine Islands." Today, the islands are identified by a Thai name and a corresponding number: for example, Ko Huyong (Island #1), located at the southern end of the chain.

In the last decade, the islands have achieved national park status, and thus are fully protected under Thai law. The National Park Authority maintains their presence on two of the islands: Ko Similan (Island #8) the largest, and Ko Miang (Island #4). Recently, the islands have come to the special attention of the Thai Royal Family, which, we hope, protects them even further from any possible abuse.

By drawing an imaginary line from north to south, the area divides into the two separate types of environments. The east coast with its powdery beaches features hard coral gardens which slope dramatically from the surface down to approximately 30–40 meters, where sand takes over as the water depth increases. On this side, the most popular activity is drift diving among healthy coral gardens and their reef inhabitants. In several sites, large coral heads or bommies rise from the bottom and are covered with soft corals, sea fans and an enormous amount of critters and unusual fish. Here the diving is easy and navigation simple, allowing each buddy pair to explore at his or her own pace.

The west coast, just a short boat ride away, can offer faster-paced, more exhilarating diving, as currents swirl around the huge granite boulders—some larger than the largest of houses. These smooth, rounded boulders create dramatic underwater formations, holes and overhangs or "swim-throughs" where divers can enjoy swimming with the current through the openings. The drama of just looking up through the clear water at these huge rocks is satisfaction enough for some divers, as there are very few places like this on earth. Growing on these boulders are some of the most colorful soft corals imaginable, in many places so thick that the rock is no longer visible. In the larger passages between the boulders the fans grow to a size sometimes 3 meters across, and are often so tightly bunched together that it makes it impossible to swim through the channels. Most of the dive sites on the west coast are best seen with a guide, since navigation can be tricky. By diving with an experienced guide you'll no doubt increase your enjoyment of the area.

If you enjoy watching and photographing small fish, the Similans are hard to beat for the sheer numbers and varieties of tropicals. Large fish, however, are a different story, and the Similans are not well known for consistent big fish action. For this kind of diving, you must travel further to the Burma Banks. However, luck brings an occasional whale shark, while large cow tail rays are fairly common. And, of course, the leopard shark makes his appearance on a regular basis. Whitetip and blacktip sharks are also sighted once in a while, and a few times over the years we've seen pods of false killer whales.

Like diving in all areas of Southeast Asia, you should enjoy the Similans for what they are justly famous for: wild, unspoiled beaches, magnificent coral growth, prolific fish life, crystalline waters and sensational underwater rock formations. Because of the distance from the mainland, the best way to visit the Similans is on a live-aboard boat.

Boats in Thailand vary widely in style and comfort. For those less worried about comfort, sleeping in one big cabin or even on deck might be a cheap option. At the other end of the scale, several boats are available with large, private air-conditioned cabins, professional photography services, modern communications and other little extras such as gourmet meals, video and sound systems. These boats also have the stability, the range and the navigational equipment to explore areas north and west of the Similan Islands, such as the Burma Banks and Richelieu Rock.

Trip lengths vary from 3 to 5 days; they are often longer if the boat is including the Similans as another stop on the itinerary. One-day trips are sometimes possible, but in general are not to be recommended.

The high season in the Similans is from October until May, but diving is possible all year round. The water tends to be clearest in the summer and in the fall, but then again, the visibility is usually fairly good in the Similans, averaging approximately 18–25 meters and at times exceeding 40 meters! There are well over 20 charted dive sites in the Similan chain, and the following short descriptions of a few of the favorites should give you an

Below: A snorkeler explores the sunlit shallows of Ko Similan. *Photo by Mark Strickland.*

idea of what kind of diving to expect.

Christmas Point, Island #9, Ko Bangru One of the most dramatic dives in the Similans, this dive begins with a series of large arches at a depth of about 24 meters. The soft coral growth and sea fans are as large as they are anywhere, and the fish action is fast here. We often encounter small schools of blue-fin trevally feeding on schools of small fry. End your dive near the island for the best swim-throughs in the Similans, and keep your eyes open for surprisingly large jacks that hide in these passageways.

Breakfast Bend, Island #9, Ko Bangru A typical east coast dive, this is a favorite way to begin a trip. The light is beautiful early in the morning—hence its name—and the coral is in great shape. Down deeper in the sand there has been a large increase of garden eels over the past few years. In the shallows, leopard sharks are often seen resting in the sand. Recently we've spotted a Napoleon wrasse—a rare fish in the Similans.

Fantasy Reef, Island #8, Ko Similan One of the most popular dive spots in the Similans, these underwater rock formations cover a huge area. The friendliest fish in the Similans hang-out here, including a few approachable clown triggerfishes—normally a fish difficult to get close to. Depths range from 15 meters down to past 40 meters, and this is one of the best dives for enjoying the spectacular, huge boulders.

Beacon Reef (south), Island #8, Ko Similan One of my favorite dives, probably because this is where I saw my first whale shark, this reef features a steep drop-off with striking diversity of hard corals from a depth of 35 meters almost all the way to the surface. This dive could easily have the largest variety of healthy hard corals in the Similans, probably

exceeding 300 species. There are plenty of nudibranchs around the coral heads, as well as rare, nervous firefishes (*Nemateleotris magnifica*), one of the most beautiful fish in the tropical sea. One of the ugliest residents of this reef are the bigeyes (*Priacanthus hamrur*) that slowly cruise the reef flats. These fishes have an amazing ability to change from a deep red color to a contrasting vivid silver. It almost appears as if they are changing their color to fit their mood.

Elephant Head, Island #8, Ko Similan Probably the most famous dive in the group, the site is named after an unusually shaped rock that juts out of the water just south of Ko Similan. The three rocks that form Elephant Head also create a natural amphitheater that feels like diving in a huge aquarium. Yellow goatfishes and snappers always hang around at the deepest level of the bowl, as well as several species of lionfishes, coral trout, and the occasional hawksbill or Ridley's turtle. The swim-throughs at deeper depths are dazzling and worth the dive experience alone.

East of Eden, Island #7, Ko Payu A typical east coast dive, this particular site has one of the most incredible underwater bommies in the Similans. Beginning at a depth of about 21 meters and rising to 12 meters, the concentration of marine life is unequalled in the Similans. During a recent summer, we had the opportunity to photograph, repeatedly, a cute pink frog fish as he stayed, regally poised, in the same spot for over 2 months.

One last but important comment about the Similan Islands—they are unique for another reason as well. Mooring projects and other environmentally protective measures have been introduced over the past few years, and, happily, the diving has actually improved. One thing is for sure, the Similan Islands will give all that you ask for—and more.

—*John Williams*

Opposite: Diving at Fantasy Reef, one of the most popular dive spots in the Similans. *Photo by Ashley Boyd.*

The Burma Banks

Pioneer Diving in Pristine Conditions

In the early 1990s, several dive operators out of Phuket, looking for new diving frontiers in the Andaman Sea, began exploring an area 90 nautical miles northwest of the Similan Islands that came to be known as the Burma Banks. In a very short time, the banks became recognized as the place for serious divers to observe sharks up close and personal, and experience sadly lacking in Thailand's waters.

Though the banks lie in international waters, by the middle of the decade the Myanmar (Burmese) authorities became concerned about the diving activity off of their coastline, and asked the operators to get official permission from the government before diving there. After three years of negotiations, the Myanmar authorities in 1997 consented to allow diving in not only the now famous Burma Banks, but also off the islands of Myanmar's inshore waters. As we approach the millennium, divers have been given the opportunity to explore one of the last pristine environments on earth—the Mergui Archipelago.

Lush, Unexplored Area

Historically, the archipelago had been an important area for trade between the east and the west. But after World War II, with the major political changes that took place in Burma and rest of Southeast Asia, the archipelago fell into obscurity. With more than 800 islands, some of the them the size of Singapore and most of them completely uninhabited, the area has unlimited potential as a playground for divers, yachties, naturalists, and other pleasure seekers. Steps have already been taken to preserve the islands, and the government seems to be very interested in developing the area in a positive way.

Inshore, the islands are lush with vegetation and primary jungle, and contain some of the last jungle cats and other large mammals to be found in Southeast Asia. Here the water is not very clear, thus of little interest to divers. Offshore, the islands are smaller—and drier—and lie in deep enough water to afford good visibility. Here the corals, sea fans, and fish life are similar to that found in Thailand, but with one major difference; there are an abundance of sharks. This makes the diving more exciting than in the waters further south, and is attracting people looking to dive with these awesome creatures.

The Burma Banks, located in

Below: *Acropora elathrata* tables grow to immense proportions at Rainbow Reef, Burma Banks. *Photo by Mark Strickland.*

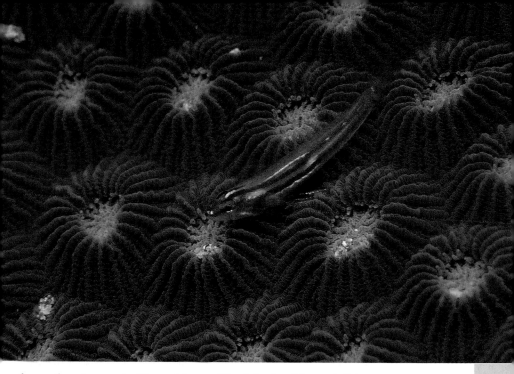

the southwestern part of the archipelago, are a series of sea mounts which rise up from over 300 meters to just below the surface. Completely underwater, depths average 15–22 meters on the flat areas on top, dropping off slowly on the edges. The currents are often strong and unpredictable, and diving here requires careful planning. Guided drift dives are the norm, usually starting on the edge of the banks in 35 meters of water, where divers stare out in the blue looking for large silver-tip sharks.

Face to Face with Sharks

Silver-tips are full-bodied, two-meter-long animals easily identified by the white trailing edges on their pectoral fins and caudal, or tail fins. Curious, but not aggressive, they approach divers close enough to make for incredible photo opportunities. Seven species of sharks have been reported on a single dive in Burma, including bull sharks, nurse sharks, mako sharks, and one of the most beautiful sharks I've ever seen, the open water black-tip shark (*Carcharinus limbatus*).

The islands with good diving are of two types. Some of them—like North and South Twin—look like the Similan Islands, both above and below the surface. Lush soft corals, large sea fans, huge bolders, and very clear water make the diving interesting for experienced as well as intermediate divers. The best diving is at the tips of the islands, and on offshore, underwater pinnacles.

Others—such as Western Rocky and Black Rock—rise straight out of the sea and plunge almost straight down. Vegetation is sparse and beaches are rare or nonexistent. These sites feature caves going through the islands, vertical walls, very interesting rocky outcroppings and deep canyons. Some of the caves are full of lobsters.

The Mergui Archipelago is only just being explored, and many new dive sites will undoubtedly be discovered over the next few years. It's an exciting time and the possibilities are virtually unlimited. Although perhaps not for everybody, those looking for shark encounters and the thrill of diving in strong currents will be in heaven.

—*John Williams*

Above: Tiny creatures like this goby escape the attention of many divers. *Photo by Mark Strickland.*

Several days by live-aboard boats

Variable, 6–50 m

Strong in many areas

Varies from excellent to poor

Sloping mountains, coral and sand

Fantastic, large schools, many sharks

Big sharks and rays, beautiful islands, Pristine diving

Ko Tachai & Richelieu Rock

Plus the Sites at Ko Bon and Ko Surin

North of the Similans lie Ko Bon, Ko Tachai, the Surin Islands and Richelieu Rock. All of these areas, with the exception of Surin, offer world-class diving that differs from the Similan Islands. You should endeavor to make this part of your itinerary when you visit the south of Thailand.

Ko Bon This island is located about 20 km north of Similan Island #9, and features one of the few vertical walls in Thailand. The dive site is on the southwestern point and consists of a 33-meter wall facing a small cove, and a step-down ridge that carries on to depths of over 45 meters. Leopard sharks are common on the ridge and on the sandy flats below the wall. Although the soft corals are not as high-profile as they are in the Similans, the colors of the corals are radically different and include shades of turquoise, yellow and blue, besides the more common pinks and purples. Ko Bon is one of the better places to see

manta rays, especially towards the end of the season (April and May) when there is more plankton in the water.

Ko Tachai Twenty-five kilometers north of Ko Bon, this isle has an offshore underwater ridge that runs perpendicular to the island. This is considered to be one of the finest dives in the Kingdom, and is famous as a place to see not only the more common species of corals, fans and schooling tropical fish, but larger animals such as rays, leopard sharks, nurse sharks and hawksbill turtles. Whale sharks make an appearance on a regular basis. Tachai also boasts a breathtakingly beautiful sandy beach on its northeastern shore.

Surin Island Although visited by several dive operators from Phuket, these islands are more appropriately famous for their beautiful coves, bays and dense jungle than they are for their diving. Spending a few idyllic days on a sail boat or other yacht here is the stuff dreams of paradise are made of, yet the serious diver will be bored easily after a few dives because of the generally poor visibility and lack of fish. This area is also accessible directly from Ban Ko Ko, on the mainland, and takes around 4 hours.

Richelieu Rock Surin's ace, however, is a small submerged rock about 18 km east of Surin. Richelieu Rock—just exposed at the lowest of tides and thus a navigational hazard for those boats not equipped with a GPS navigation system—rates as

Below: The unmistakable silhouette of a whale shark at Richelieu Rock. *Photo by Mark Strickland.*

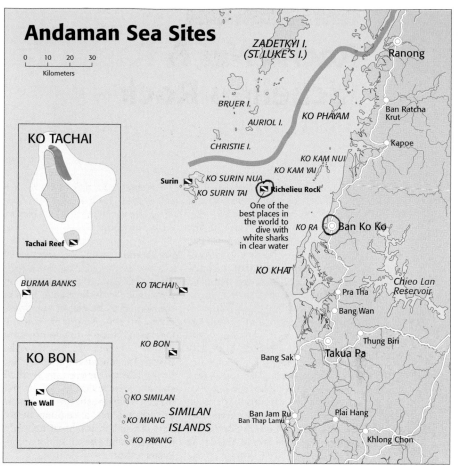

Andaman Sea Sites

0 10 20 30
Kilometers

ZADETKYI I.
(ST. LUKE'S I.)

Ranong

BRUER I.

AURIOL I.

KO PHAYAM

Ban Ratcha Krut

Kapoe

CHRISTIE I.

KO KAM NUI
KO KAM YAI

Surin

KO SURIN NUA

KO SURIN TAI

Richelieu Rock

One of the best places in the world to dive with white sharks in clear water

KO RA

Ban Ko Ko

KO TACHAI

Tachai Reef

KO KHAT

Chieo Lan Reservoir

Pra Tha

Bang Wan

BURMA BANKS

KO TACHAI

KO BON

Thung Biri

Bang Sak

Takua Pa

KO BON

The Wall

KO SIMILAN

KO MIANG

SIMILAN ISLANDS

KO PAYANG

Ban Jam Ru
Ban Thap Lamu

Plai Hang

Khlong Chon

one of the best places in the world for swimming with our gentle giant, the whale shark. Encounters with these animals—the largest of all—are rare, almost any place in the world. But for some reason, Richelieu attracts more than its fair share. Swimming with such a large animal, known to grow to lengths of 20 meters or more, has to be a high point for any diver. Sightings occur 50–70 percent of the time spent diving there, depending on the time of year. Generally, February, March and April are the best times for a visit.

Besides the appearance of the whale shark, Richelieu Rock offers lush soft corals, large schools of pelagic fishes, as well as countless small organisms clinging to the rock. Octopuses are abundant. Recently we had a chance to observe cuttlefish in their courtship behavior on almost every dive. The ritual can be likened to a dance as their tentacles wave wildly in all directions, and go through rapid color changes which almost appear to be like a quick change of costume between dance acts. Richelieu is good, too, for shell spotters. Murex, cowries and cones are there in abundance. Lastly, at Richelieu the guitar shark (family Rhinobatidae), one of the ugliest creatures alive and growing to over 2 meters in length, can be seen lying quietly on the bottom.

All of these sites are visited by the Burma Banks operators on their regular, extended charters. Most depart directly from Phuket by boat, while others take to the road and then set sail from ports like Bon Ko Ko, further north.

— *John Williams*

Live-aboard boat

Good, 15–30 m

Variable, sometimes strong

Excellent

Walls, ridges, pinnacles, boulders

Fantastic

Whale sharks, guitar sharks, soft corals in a rainbow of colors, schooling pelagics

THAILAND

Racha Noi & Racha Yai

Fun Diving in Phuket and the Isles Nearby

Though most serious divers will immediately book a longer live-aboard boat to the Similans and beyond when contemplating a Thai diving holiday, Phuket does offer some fine day trips and shorter overnight cruises to its west coast and off-shore islands. One- and two-tank, half-day and full-day diving excursions are available through most of the dive centers in both Patong and Kata, as well as from some of the new hotels in the Bang Tao area near the airport.

Phuket's west coast offers casual diving, usually from a local longtail boat. Although not the easiest of boats to dive from, they do have the advantage of being able to pull right up to the beach and, are relatively inexpensive to hire.

Some of the dive areas off the west coast include Patong Bay, Freedom Beach, Paradise Beach, Bang Tao, Kata Beach and Ko Pu. All of these spots are popular training areas and actually do offer some pleasant, easy diving, although Phuket's off-shore areas are much better. One of the best areas is right off the beach in Kata, where the coral reef parallels the bay's northern rocky point. Averaging a depth of only 5–6 meters, the amount of marine life surprises the most seasoned diver. I've seen all sorts of unusual fish here including a ghost pipe fish, dragon wrasses, a crocodilefish and sea robins. I've also had a lionfish swim up to a diving class and peer into each student's individual mask as if looking for an explanation. Expect the unexpected on Phuket's west coast.

To the south of Phuket lie the twin islands of Ko Racha Yai (Big Racha) and Ko Racha Noi (Small Racha), which offer significantly better diving than do Phuket's western beaches. Almost all diving operators offer 1-day trips to both of the islands (although not on the same day), and some offer a 2-day live-aboard trip every week.

Ko Racha Yai

Racha Yai's best diving is off its east coast which makes it especially attractive during Phuket's off-season in the summer. Although visibility varies, it can be as good as 25 meters or more. A typical dive is a gentle drift along a sloping rocky face that is sprinkled with hard

Below: Yellow-tail damselfish *Poma-centrus* sp. *Photo by Mark Strickland.*

coral forests of many, many varieties. Especially prominent are staghorn corals of blue and tan. Many times there are large schools of false barracudas hovering over the reef, while on the reef itself you'll see octopuses and cuttlefishes in addition to the more common tropical species. Divers of all levels of experience and snorkelers can visit Racha Yai without concern over dive hazards as the diving is easy and gentle. Water depths range from 3 to 30 meters.

Ko Racha Noi

This spot is popular for the more experienced diver, as depths are generally greater and the currents frequently stronger than at its sister island to the north. The northern tip features a large pinnacle where spotting larger marine life is possible, while the southern point is a nice drift dive with the added bonus of having a beautiful little beach to visit during your surface interval. There is also a wooden shipwreck at about 27 meters on the southwest coast of the island, an enjoyable deep dive. Not

much grows on the wreck yet, but it attracts large amounts of reef fish. The diving here is definitely more challenging than at Racha Yai, but the rewards can also be much greater.

Accommodation is available on Racha Yai in both of the pristine little bays on the northern side of the island. Muslim farmers and a few fisherman have lived on Racha Yai for years now, harvesting coconuts, marijuana (now prohibited!) and fishing the waters surrounding the islands.

— *John Williams*

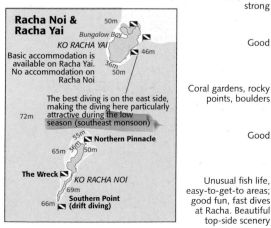

Racha Noi &
Racha Yai
Bungalow Bay
50m
KO RACHA YAI
Basic accommodation is
available on Racha Yai.
No accommodation on
Racha Noi
46m
36m
50m

The best diving is on the east side,
making the diving here particularly
attractive during the low
season (southeast monsoon)
72m

55m
Northern Pinnacle
65m 36m 50m

The Wreck
KO RACHA NOI
69m
Southern Point
66m (drift diving)

Above: This octopus, bleached with exhaustion, has been driven to the surface by clumsy, pestering divers. Please don't do this.
Photo by Fiona Nichols.

Half-day and full-day trips arranged by dive centers

Average to poor, west coast. At Racha, 10–30 m

Variable, can be strong

Good

Coral gardens, rocky points, boulders

Good

Unusual fish life, easy-to-get-to areas; good fun, fast dives at Racha. Beautiful top-side scenery

Shark Point

Shark Point and Anemone Reef: Surprisingly Excellent Diving

By far the best and most popular dive sites by day-trip from Phuket or Phi Phi, these two pinnacles are located approximately 25 km east of Chalong Bay in Phuket. Given official marine sanctuary status in 1992, these two dive sites are the only day-trips in Thailand that offer truly world-class quality diving, and except for the limited visibility, these are two of the better dives in the world. The rock pinnacles explode with life; the sheer density of marine life makes diving here a wonderful, sensual experience.

Shark Point, or Hin Musang (Shark Rock, as it translates), rises out of the water from surrounding depths of only about 18–20 meters. Considering the small extent of the rock above the water, the actual size of the reef underwater is a big surprise to most divers. Beginning from the relatively steep main rock

Below: Two local divers at Shark Point. *Photo by Mark Strickland.*

pinnacle, the reef flattens out to the south until it rises towards the surface again about a half-kilometer away. This second rock does not break the surface, and, depending on the current, is an excellent place to begin the dive.

Like many places in Thailand, Shark Point's most colorful feature is the profusion of purple and pink soft corals that cling to the rocks. The strong currents sweeping over the pinnacle provide food a-plenty for hundreds of different species of hard corals and Indo-Pacific tropical fishes.

The name of the site comes from the common leopard (zebra) shark *(Stegastoma varium)*, a docile creature that hangs out in the sand surrounding the pinnacle. These completely approachable, trusting sharks grow to lengths of a little over 2 meters, and most divers

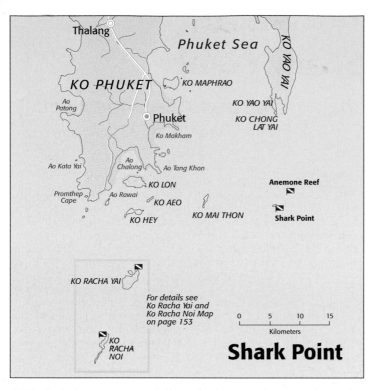

Thalang

Phuket Sea

KO PHUKET

KO MAPHRAO

Ao Patong

KO YAO YAI

KO YAO YAI

Phuket

KO CHONG LAT YAI

Ko Makham

Ao Kata Yai

Ao Chalong

Ao Tang Khon

KO LON

Anemone Reef

Promthep Cape

Ao Rawai

KO AEO

KO HEY

KO MAI THON

Shark Point

KO RACHA YAI

For details see Ko Racha Yai and Ko Racha Noi Map on page 153

0   5   10   15
Kilometers

KO RACHA NOI

Shark Point

think that they are one of the "cutest" sharks in the ocean. Divers who are not accustomed to seeing sharks are genuinely surprised at how big and approachable they are. Unfortunately, many times these sharks are taken advantage of and handled unnecessarily. Handling by divers can injure the animal and expose it to infection. Touching an animal in no way benefits it and—more often than not—seriously harms it.

Anemone Reef

Hin Jom (Submerged Rock or Anemone Reef) lies just under water, about 600 meters to the north of Hin Musang. As the Thai name makes clear, no part of the pinnacle is exposed, and under water the rock drops off more dramatically to a depth of between 20 and 27 meters until reaching a bottom of sand and oyster shells. Although not as colorful as Shark Point, the fish life here is excellent as well and our friends, the leopard

sharks, are often seen free-swimming at the top of the rock in 6 meters of water. A couple of years ago, my dive buddy and I counted 92 lionfishes in less than 20 minutes at this dive site! Although this is not an everyday occurrence, I know people who have spent years diving without seeing this many in total—much less on one dive. This gives you the idea of just how dense the marine life is in these areas.

Located just south of Ao Phang-nga and all of its fresh water rivers, visibility averages around 10 meters, often less. Although conditions such as this are not what divers dream of when they think of the "perfect dive," the amount of marine life more than makes up for the often limited visibility. On days when the water becomes gin-clear, diving here feels like taking a breath of fresh air. Conditions are virtually impossible to predict. The only down-sides of these sites are the visibility and the occasional strong currents, making both locations unsuitable for beginners.

—*John Williams*

Full-day trips through dive centers

Variable, 2–25 m

Variable, often strong

Unequalled

Coral gardens, rock

Quantities and varieties excellent

Leopard sharks, large moray eels, unbelievable amounts of marine life, great soft corals and fans

Phi Phi Islands

*Beaches, Bommies
and Birds' Nests*

Over the past several years, Ko Phi Phi (pronounced "pee pee") has grown from a peaceful little Muslim fishing village to one of the busiest international tourist destinations in the country. It now boasts at least 10 diving centers, several expensive international hotels and a variety of cheaper bungalows and guest houses. Literally thousands of people visit Ko Phi Phi daily, but after the last boat leaves, around mid-afternoon, the island regains much of its peaceful allure.

Located about 45 km east of Phuket, the Phi Phi Island group—actually part of Krabi province—is composed of the islands Ko Phi Phi Don, Ko Phi Phi Lae (translating as "Phi Phi of the Sea"), Ko Yung (Mosquito Island), and Ko Mai Pai (Bamboo Island).

Although the scuba diving is generally not considered to be at the world-class level—depending on your definition—Ko Phi Phi offers the keen diver a wide range of diving possiblities and occasionally some absolutely fantastic diving. It is a delightful place to spend a few days relaxing on its exquisite beaches, exploring its numerous coves and bays, climbing its steep vertical peaks, investigating the huge caves that hide the edible nests of swifts and—last but not least— enjoying some colorful and enticing scuba diving.

Dramatic Scenery

What sets Ko Phi Phi apart from other dive destinations in Thailand are two features: the first is the amazing limestone cliffs that rise dramatically out of the sea and plunge equally spectacularly straight down underwater; the second is the remarkable variety of dive sites that are concentrated in such a small area.

Nature has created the limestone rock formations and islands which form Ko Phi Phi and which have become known the world over

Opposite: At Ko Phi Phi, amazing limestone cliffs rise dramatically out of the sea.
Photo by Ingo Jezierski.

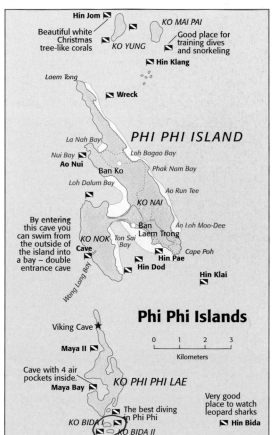

Hin Jom

Beautiful white Christmas tree-like corals

KO MAI PAI

Good place for training dives and snorkeling

KO YUNG

Hin Klang

Laem Tong

Wreck

PHI PHI ISLAND

La Nah Bay

Nui Bay

Ao Nui

Loh Bagao Bay

Ban Ko

Phak Nam Bay

Loh Dalum Bay

Ao Run Tee

KO NAI

By entering this cave you can swim from the outside of the island into a bay – double entrance cave

KO NOK

Ton Sai Bay

Cave

Ban Laem Trong

Ao Loh Moo-Dee

Cape Poh

Hin Pae

Hin Dod

Hin Klai

Wang Long Bay

Phi Phi Islands

0   1   2   3

Kilometers

Viking Cave

Maya II

Cave with 4 air pockets inside.

Maya Bay

KO PHI PHI LAE

The best diving in Phi Phi

KO BIDA I

KO BIDA II

Very good place to watch leopard sharks

Hin Bida

as one of the most stunning settings in Southeast Asia. These cliffs soar over 500 meters in some areas, and beautiful green trees and bushes grow on the tops and sides of these cliffs. Swimming in a protected little cove at the base of one of these steep cliffs conjures up visions of an unearthly paradise and, no matter how popular Ko Phi Phi becomes, the stunning scenery will always create that special feeling that no one has been here before you.

Underwater, these towers shape a rugged, interesting environment for scuba divers, and over time the elements have created long caves, dramatic overhangs and swim-throughs in this soft rock. Some caves penetrate the rock as much as 100 meters or more, and provide the ingredients for exciting dives—if they are well planned and carried out under the supervision of a professional dive operator. Indeed, in other dive areas the scenery is often incidental to the flora and fauna, but here you'll find that the underwater landscape, itself, is impressive.

Other types of environments include vertical walls that plunge from the surface to over 25 meters. On these walls grow a profusion of soft corals, large orange-colored fans, black coral and long, stringy sea whips. Several types of unusual coral trees grow in the waters surrounding Ko Phi Phi, including a white coral bush that looks like a frocked Christmas tree—covered with ornament-like growth in the form of oysters and colorful crinoids.

In many places, the islands are fringed with hard-coral gardens, home to a wide assortment of resplendent tropical creatures. Most of the coral is healthy, although in the more popular shallow areas coral damage has occurred due to unscrupulous boat operators dropping anchor. However, in most areas coral growth and fish life is plentiful and most, but not all of the same, fish species that live in the Similans can be found around Ko Phi Phi as well.

Ko Bida Nok

One of the most popular dive sites in the group is located at the south-

Right: A pretty young snorkeler reaches for a sea star. A classic shot, albeit a bit shopworn. *Photo by Mike Severns.*

Below: A diver among a huge school of snappers. *Photo by Mark Strickland.*

ern tip of this tiny island. The dive normally begins in a shallow bay on the eastern side of the islet. Upon descending to about 10 meters of water, you'll find vast healthy growths of staghorn and star corals and incredible numbers of anemones and anemone fish. In fact this is one of the best places in Thailand to observe the aggressive little anemonefish *Amphiprion ephippium*, which is otherwise rare in Thailand. Watch carefully as they will make a harmless attempt to bite the unwary diver. Because of their aggressiveness, these fish are easier to photograph than their more common cousins, the clown anemonefish (*Amphiprion ocellaris*), since they are constantly trying to bite your camera.

Continuing south on your dive, you'll reach a vertical wall that is exhilarating to sail over, and continue your descent head-first. You'll come to sand at about 22 meters, but there is a gorgeous little bommie off the wall, ending at almost 27 meters, that is usually covered with thousands of glassfishes, large sea fans and pink and purple soft corals.

Swimming west along the wall, the terrain becomes less vertical, and schools of blue-striped snappers seek safety in numbers along the rocky bottom. You'll meet the usual pairs of butterflyfishes and plenty of small tropicals in the shallower depths. Octopuses are repeatedly found here if you look carefully in the numerous nooks and crannies, and large green moray eels are almost surely spotted.

Towards the end of the dive, you'll find a small cavern in the rock that makes a sharp right-turn just past the entrance. This cavern is a great place to spend a few minutes of your safety stop since the light filtering through holes close to the surface creates lovely patterns on the sandy bottom.

Just be sure to leave the shallow cavern with at least 30 bar in your tank to avoid a messy out-of-air situation and to stay near the entrance.

Getting About

The most common type of transportation available in Phi Phi Islands remains the versatile long-tail boat. For hire practically everywhere, these taxis will take you—for a modest fee—to secluded beaches, the birds' nest caves and any other scenic areas around the islands.

Many dive operators use these boats for diving trips, and they are quite comfortable to dive from if you listen carefully to the pre-dive briefing. If nothing else, it is a cultural experience to spend the day watching your friendly Thai captain (who usually does not speak much English, nor does he normally know how to swim) ply the waters of Ko Phi Phi, expertly man-handling his long-tail boat.

— *John Williams*

Day trips and overnighters from Phi Phi and Phuket

Variable, 3–30 m

Variable, often strong, good drift diving

Colorful soft corals, healthy hard corals

Coral gardens, limestone rock, walls

Excellent quantities and varieties

Leopard sharks, dramatic landscape above and below, caves, vertical walls, diveable year-round

Trang

A Newly Discovered Dive Destination South of Phuket

Located just south of the town of Krabi, Trang is the newest diving area to open up in southern Thailand. Although not as commercially developed as some of the other sites around the country— which makes it more difficult to get to—some of Trang's diving spots are decidedly world-class. Certainly, when conditions are right, the pinnacles of Hin Daeng and Hin Muang triumph over anything in the Similan Islands.

There are four principal places for diving in this area, located south of Ko Phi Phi. These are Ko Ha Yai, Ko Rok, Hin Daeng and several islands inshore from Ko Rok and just south of Ko Lanta.

Ko Ha

This is a small group of islands almost directly west of Ko Lanta. These tiny islands, separated by channels over 50 meters deep, jut straight out of the Andaman Sea. However, unlike Ko Phi Phi, the water here is ordinarily quite clear and visibility frequently exceeds 25 meters. The highlight of diving here is a series of caves, or caverns, on the largest of the islands, Ko Ha

Day trips from Ko Lanta, but only live-aboard to the best dive sites

Inshore, 5–10 m; offshore, 20–40 m

Variable, often strong

Healthy and colorful

Coral gardens, pinnacles, walls

Prolific big and small fish, sharks, rays

Deep drop-offs, lush marine life, stunning islands

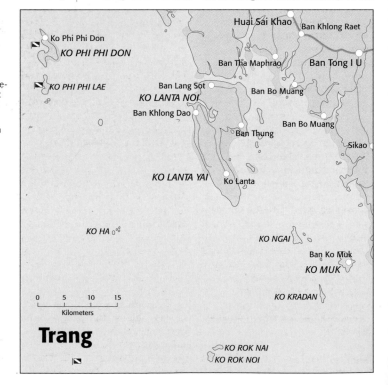

Yai. The caverns are safe to enter, even without a light, as the entrances are large and there is only one way in and one way out. The best part of entering these caverns is that you can surface inside the island to view stalactites hanging down from the ceiling over 30 meters above the surface. The quality of light filtering through the water from the entrance is truly magical.

Moving inshore to the south of Ko Lanta, the water clarity deteriorates, and the diving is quite shallow. There is one interesting place to explore called the Emerald Cave, where at high tide the diver can swim through a large cavern underwater to surface in a perfect little lagoon complete with its own white sand beach and splendid tropical jungle. Once inside, you are surrounded by tall cliffs, and the only way out is through the cavern. Therefore, an experienced guide is essential for safe exploration.

Ko Rok

About 25 km south of Ko Ha, are two sister-islands separated by a narrow channel about 15 meters deep. These islands, Ko Rok Nok and Ko Rok Nai ("Outside and Inside") have some of the prettiest beaches in Thailand and are completely devoid of inhabitants. The islands are named for a small, furry mammal called *rok* in Thai, and this animal, along with monitor lizards, can be observed onshore—with a little patience and a bit of luck.

The diving here is relatively shallow, with the best corals and fish life living above 18 meters. The bottom is composed of mostly hard corals, with small areas of soft corals at deeper depths. Blacktip sharks patrol the reef shallows and hawksbill turtles are sighted regularly. But the main reason for stopping in Ko Rok is that it is the perfect jumping-off point for trips out to Hin Daeng, and the islands make an ideal anchorage in all weather conditions.

The sole reason that diving has become popular in Trang are two pinnacles that lie approximately 25 km southwest of Ko Rok. Hin Daeng (Red Rock) and Hin Muang (Purple Rock) offer everything a

Above: The leopard shark *(Stegastoma fasciatum)* is harmless, very approachable and photogenic—a real favorite with photographers. *Photo by Mark Strickland.*

diver could want, from dramatic walls and big fish action to lush tropical underwater gardens.

Hin Daeng

This pinnacle is easily found since it protrudes about 3 meters above the surface. Although not very impressive topside, underwater the rock is huge. The southern side descends—straight down—to over 60 meters, forming the most radical vertical drop in Thailand's seas. The wall is dotted with light growths of soft corals and a few sea fans, but is otherwise devoid of life. On the eastern side, where the slope is more gentle, two long ridges descend into the blueness and if the currents are favorable, it is possible to swim along these ridges down to 40 meters or more. Here the soft coral becomes more lush and tall, and huge schools of jacks sweep past the ridge, surrounding the diver with a shimmering wall of silver.

Ascending to the shallows we see needlefishes, or long toms, skip along the surface. Barracudas stalk their prey through the clear water. Swimming between the three large rocks that form the surface view of Hin Daeng, large schools of fusiliers dart to and fro as if they were afraid of the water surging through the channels.

Hin Muang

Located just a few hundred meters from Hin Daeng, this pinnacle lies completely submerged and its position remains somewhat of a secret. What surprised us the first time we explored the rock was the incredible amount of marine life that clung to the rock. It is as if the rock were located in another ocean and not just a short distance away from the relatively barren Hin Daeng. The name derives from the thick purple growth of soft corals that are everywhere. The rock itself is approximately 200 meters long and less

than 20 meters wide, and is shaped like an immense loaf of bread with steep, vertical sides and a rounded top. The walls are decorated with large sea fans in varying hues of red, white and orange. Clouds of glassfishes, or silver sides, school around the fans and rocky out-croppings. Carpets of anemones cover the more shallow sections of the pinnacle.

One July, the water was so transparent and the sea so smooth that I could see clearly, above me, the splash of someone throwing the dregs of their coffee overboard—puffy white tropical clouds as a back-drop—from a depth of over 45 meters.

The whale shark is one animal that we see repeatedly around these pinnacles; we sighted these creatures on almost 70 percent of our trips last year. We've even given a name to one small 5-meter animal, since he is often present. Oscar doesn't seem to mind divers at all, and will swim right up to you—an impressive sight to behold. Oscar especially seems to like to make dramatic entrances with beginning divers around, and seems to know that this is an unnerving experience for most of them—nothing like a whale shark with a sense of humour.

On many occasions we swim with grey reef sharks in the deep blue water off Hin Daeng and Hin Muang. This is the only place in Thailand where I have seen more than 10 grey reef sharks together at one time. Grey reef sharks are full-bodied sharks, powerful and sleek, and are often confused with blacktips because of their similar markings. However, unlike their cousins, these sharks are true pelagic animals, and swimming with them is a stirring, emotional experience. On one occasion, I managed to hover within 2 meters of a group of these sharks who ignored me in favor of a large school of jacks—apparently they were more mouth-watering than I was.

— John Williams

Opposite: The spotted pink lobster *(Enoplometopus debelius)*. *Photo by Gary Bell.*

Ko Samui

Dive Courses and Idyllic Beaches

Ko Samui's allure to tourists began well over 15 years ago with the arrival of the traveler who came seeking a unique tropical paradise. Chasing idyllic places where locals were friendly and life was simple and cheap, they found Samui.

Today, surprisingly little has changed from those early days as the charm of Ko Samui—as well as the unhurried lifestyle—has remained largely intact. About the only noticeable changes today are the addition of an airport and the building of several top-class international resort hotels in a low rise, environmentally pleasing way.

Considering that most dive sites are situated at least 2 hours by boat from Ko Samui—and considering that the water clarity is not something the island is noted for—

scuba diving is surprisingly popular on the island. Remarkably, Ko Samui has developed into one of the main diver training centers in all Southeast Asia. Most instruction is completed in the shallow water directly off the coast at Chaweng Beach, Coral Cove or one of the other secluded little bays and beaches that make the island so lovely. Many diving centers will offer a couple of days on Ko Tao to finish up a diving course, but the waters around Samui are adequate for training.

For the advanced diver, Ko Samui has two main dive areas, each with an approximate 6-month opposite season. Hin Bai, or Sail Rock, located north of Samui and Phangan, is best from March until September. During the rest of the

Below: Ko Samui is a good place to sport dive or to further dive education. *Photo by Mark Strickland.*

year, the Ang Thong Marine National Park to the northwest is the choice spot. Both dive areas are interesting, and although most divers wouldn't take a dedicated dive holiday to Ko Samui, most divers will enjoy at least a few dives at both of these areas.

Hin Bai is the preferred day trip from Ko Samui since it offers the most exciting diving. The likelihood of seeing larger animals such as sharks is better here than in other areas. Similar in shape to the islands around Ko Phi Phi, Sail Rock juts out of the water and slopes beneath the surface, sometimes vertically, to just over 30 meters. You begin by exploring one of the deeper pinnacles away from the rock, which are covered in beautiful green trees of *Tubastraea micrantha*, and the bright yellow polyps of encrusting species of Dendrophylliid coral. Black coral trees with either lime green or reddish brown polyps also grow out of the crevices.

Up a Chimney

Towards the end of the dive, you'll be shown an underwater chimney located on the northwest side—the most impressive attribute of the dive. Two divers can enter at a depth of 19 meters where the cavern continues in for about 2 meters before bending towards the surface. At 12 meters you'll spot a hole that opens up laterally, guarded by a scorpionfish. Although a tight squeeze, it is possible to swim back into open water from here. Continuing up, the chimney opens at about 5 meters of water depth, and you'll exit the hole to find yourself surrounded by a magnificent carpet of anemones full of pink anemonefish.

People tell stories of shark sightings around Hin Bai. Although I haven't seen sharks myself, reliable sources say that some 15 animals, identified as bull sharks—an uncommon shark in Thai waters—have been spotted

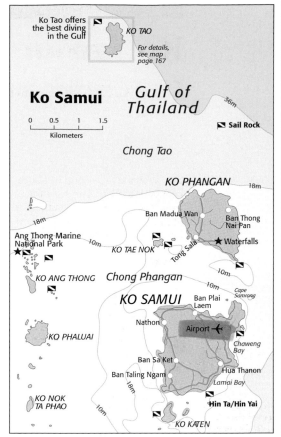

feeding from time to time at the surface. Along with the possibility of sighting a whale shark, this surely makes Hin Bai worth repeat diving.

The Ang Thong Marine National Park is a beautiful archipelago of over 40 islets, and operators offer trips to this area from December until March. While the visibility here is often poor, the snorkeling and shallow diving—as well as the striking top-side scenery—make an enjoyable outing. Ko Wao and Hin Yipoon (meaning "Japanese Rock") are the most popular areas for scuba diving and are noted for shallow caves and colorful soft corals.

Because of its laid-back charm, Samui combines many factors with diving, making it a good place to sport dive or to further dive education.

— *John Williams*

Full-day trips through dive centers; some shore diving

Variable, 2–15 m

Variable, often strong

Fair, soft and hard

Coral gardens, rocks

Excellent variety and color

Black coral, bull sharks, occasional whale shark

Ko Tao

Lazy Lifestyle and Good Diving

The sleepy little islands of Ko Tao (Turtle Island) and Ko Nang Yuan, located approximately 65 km north of Ko Samui in the Gulf of Thailand, have exploded as a diving destination over the past few years. These days there are a number of backpacker-style bungalows, one or two up-market resorts, and about 10 well-run dive centers offering scuba and snorkeling trips to the surrounding reefs and pinnacles.

An idyllic tropical paradise, Ko Tao seems to attract many divers looking for lengthy stays in Thailand—many backpackers travel to the island and end up spending months there. Some of the reasons for this are the relaxed pace of living, inexpensive accommodation, camaraderie between divers and dive centers, and of course interesting and relatively inexpensive scuba diving. All these combine to bring back visitors time and time again.

One of the best things about diving around these two small islands is the fact that the dive sites, unlike Phuket's and Samui's, are only minutes away. Including Ko Nang Yuan, which is only a short hop from Ko Tao, there are over 15 dives sites charted in the area. Sites range from deep water pinnacles to shallow coral gardens to rocky points complete with swim-throughs such as we found in the Similan Islands. Although water clarity can sometimes be limited, frequently the water becomes as transparent as the Andaman Sea, with visibility over 30 meters.

In Search of the Big Ones

One day a couple of years ago, I was visiting Ko Tao with a friend from the States. The day was perfect, the sea glassy and smooth, and the water crystalline, so we decided to take a dive or two. There had been much talk of whale sharks over beers the night before, since I had seen quite a

Full-day and half-day trips through dive centers

Variable, 3–40 m

Variable, often strong

Good to average

Coral gardens, boulders, pinnacles

Good schools of pelagic fish, nice tropicals

Whale sharks, good soft corals. Expect the unexpected

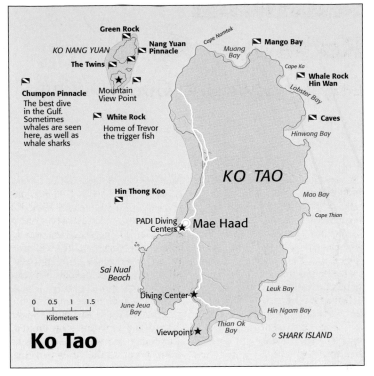

Ko Tao

Green Rock

KO NANG YUAN

Nang Yuan
Pinnacle

Cape Namtok

Mango Bay

The Twins

Muang
Bay

Cape Ka

Whale Rock
Hin Wan

Chumpon Pinnacle
The best dive
in the Gulf.
Sometimes
whales are seen
here, as well as
whale sharks

Mountain
View Point

Lobster Bay

White Rock
Home of Trevor
the trigger fish

Caves

Hinwong Bay

KO TAO

Hin Thong Koo

Mao Bay

Cape Thian

PADI Diving
Centers

Mae Haad

Sai Nual
Beach

Leuk Bay

0   0.5   1   1.5

Diving Center

Kilometers

June Jeua
Bay

Hin Ngam Bay

Viewpoint

Thian Ok
Bay

SHARK ISLAND

few on the Phuket side that year. Everyone had high hopes of today being the day that the big boys would be out to play. Well, the boys were out and then some.

As we pulled up to Chumpon Pinnacle, someone shouted "whale shark!" and sure enough, there she was next to the boat. While everyone jumped in with snorkeling gear, I hurriedly slapped on my tank so that I could follow her more easily. As the snorkelers crowded around her, she slowly moved off and only a videographer and I were able to follow. We spent the next 20 minutes swimming easily along with the shark before she swam off.

But that wasn't all. As I swam back to the boat to meet up with my buddy, a 4-meter-long sailfish (or possibly a swordfish) swam lazily below me almost the whole way back. He was a light tan colour and had a "sword" on him that extended over a meter in length.

Then, upon reaching my buddy and finally descending on the dive site proper, we descended through a spiraling school of large jacks numbering well over 1,000 individuals. We felt we were lost in some monstrous whirlpool of fish, and we were so mesmerized we completely lost sight of the rock—again.

Another long swim back to the boat with no air remaining. But it wasn't over. Some type of huge animal, surely over 12 meters, was swimming around the rock with a black back and a tiny black fin. We knew it couldn't be another whale shark with those markings, but only when we jumped in the water did we find out that two fin-back whales were frolicking with our group. Divers swam with these whales for over 1 hour. This was definitely a dive of a lifetime—even though we never found the dive site.

It is a longish trip to Ko Tao, but as it offers the best diving in the Gulf of Thailand, combined with the pleasantries of a sybaritic shore life, it is well worth a visit. You may not see whale sharks or swordfish on every dive, but you'll certainly be more than charmed by the local inhabitants of the reefs.

— *John Williams*

Opposite: The sleepy little island of Ko Tao is fast becoming a popular dive destination. *Photo by Ashley Boyd.*

Pattaya & Ko Chang

Fun Resort with Some Interesting Diving Options

Pattaya, Thailand's first resort built for foreign tourists, became infamous as a "Rest and Recuperation" destination for American soldiers during the Vietnamese War. The first dive shop opened for business during this time and as a result, many servicemen and their visiting families became some of the first foreigners to scuba dive recreationally in Thailand. Today, huge highrise hotels follow the curve of the bay and Pattaya, while still popular with international visitors, has become more attractive as a weekend get-away for residents of Bangkok.

Although Pattaya is far more densely populated than other tourist areas in Thailand, it remains popular as this city beside the sea is bustling and energetic. Even though Pattaya has received considerable negative press over the past few years—a great deal of it undeserved—it has a certain character that people return for. Pattaya is definitely an active resort and scuba diving enthusiasts will find plenty of different dive sites and courses to keep them busy.

Since Thailand's recreational diving industry was born in Pattaya, dive centers there have set valuable examples to other more recently opened diving businesses in other parts of Southeast Asia. Their main activities are teaching introductory courses and open-water certification courses to new divers. In addition, they specialize in advanced training programs for divers, offer-

Below: Highrise hotels crowd the curve of Pattaya's bay.
Photo by Ingo Jezierski.

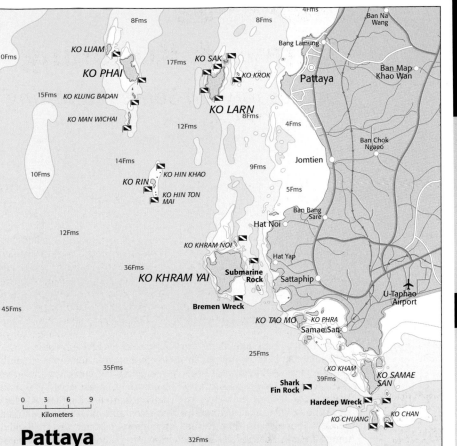

Pattaya

ing scheduling that is especially suited to residents working in Bangkok—both foreign and Thai. All dive centers in Pattaya conduct one-day diving trips, and some are now starting to delve into the live-aboard scene, offering longer trips to Ko Chang near the Thai-Cambodian border.

One problem that has frustrated dive operators is the lack of clear environmental policy. Combined with a solid population growth over the past 10 years, this has caused many dive sites to deteriorate. To side-step this, operators have been forced to go further afield for quality diving.

Visitors to the area will soon discover that some of the best wreck diving in Thailand is found here. Although there are several wrecks around, the two best sites in the area are the *Hardeep* and the *Bremen*.

The *Hardeep* is considered to be the best wreck dive and stores offer 1-day and 2-day trips to the site. Located between Ko Samaesan and Ko Chuang, the *Hardeep* is a 42-meter-long freighter that sank in 1942 and now rests on her side in 21–27 meters of water. As with all wrecks, one of the main reasons people dive on it is because of other eerie emotions they experience when the ship first becomes visible through the gloom. This aside, the best reason for diving on sunken ships is that they are a magnet for incredible amounts of marine life.

Today, the wreck is still and tranquil—except for the masses of tropical fish who have made this disaster their home. It is also home

Full-day trips through dive centers; live aboards

Variable, 2–25 m

Variable, often strong, especially on wrecks

Good in some places

Coral gardens, rock, boulders

Not bad, some unusual animals

Wreck diving

to colonies of fan corals and large barrel sponges. Although visibility is not dependably clear here—averaging about the same as in the rest of the Gulf—the prolific marine life and the possibility of a safe penetration into the wreck makes the dive one of the most inviting around.

The second popular wreck is the *Bremen,* located near the village of Sattahip, south of both Pattaya and Jomtien. Although the profile of this 100-meter steel ship is weakening each year due to its natural deterioration, the wreck attracts large schools of yellow-tail snappers and barracudas during slack tide. An excellent deep dive for an advanced course, the wreck rests at about 25 meters and visibility ranges from around 7 to 10 meters.

For those divers interested in more than ship wrecks, coral diving in Pattaya can be satisfying as well. Often dive centers will offer a coral dive during their trip to the *Hardeep,* as Ko Chuang and Ko Samaesan have healthy coral down to as deep as 30 meters. Although larger animals such as sharks and rays are occasionally seen, the big attractions here are the abundance of corals, both soft and hard, and

beautiful colorful anemones.

For a gentle coral dive especially suited to beginners, many operators offer a 1-day excursion to the nearby island of Ko Krok. As it is a private island, no jet skis are around to bother divers or snorkelers. Shallow drift dives in the coral gardens of this island are quite pleasant, and the added advantage of a short boat ride makes it a popular trip. Interestingly enough, several environmental groups from the Bangkok area have begun a project to encourage coral growth in the area. This project is funded by both the government and private donors and is an encouraging start towards a new environmental policy in the Pattaya area.

Further offshore, the island Ko Rin probably offers Pattaya's best diving. The underwater profile is more interesting here compared with other places, and water clarity can be excellent, sometimes exceeding 25 meters. Rocky canyons form swim-throughs which are not only wonderful for divers but create currents to wash around the rocks, causing great environmental conditions for the vast array of marine life that lives here. Although the day can be long due to distances involved in getting to different sites in this area, those looking for clearer water will find the longer traveling times worthwhile.

South to Ko Chang

Recently there has been much discussion of the diving possibilities southeast of Pattaya in the Ko Chang area. As of this writing, at least three dive centers are speaking seriously of expanding in the area, and one is talking about offering up to 10-day live-aboard diving trips there. Opinions vary widely on just how good the diving is. Some say it is better than the Similans—which is simply not so—and others say it is terrible—which is also incorrect. Practically speaking, the area needs further exploration, but there are definitely possibilities for some great diving.

The area itself is rich in history and culture as it is located almost right on the border with Cambodia. With the recent—and on-going—political turmoil in Cambodia, very little tourist development has occurred here. The hilly, jungle-covered islands are striking in their beauty, and many of the beaches rival those of our southern islands. The potential for tourist development is good, and once things settle down politically, the area will no doubt boom.

What excites the diving operators who express their opinions about diving around Ko Chang are the underwater pinnacles that are located offshore from Ko Chang and Ko Raet, underwater topography that hosts and attracts a wealth of flora and fauna. As with many pinnacles in Thai waters, taking divers here will require operators to have GPS navigation systems on board their boats, otherwise they will be unable to locate the site with any consistency.

The best diving spots in both the Andaman Sea and Gulf of Thailand are on pinnacles because of the rich conditions there, which

create healthy environments for marine life. Not only will the big animals such as sharks and rays be more common, but the corals and fish life on these pinnacles are far more dense. Once Pattaya's dive operators begin conducting regular live-aboard trips to the area—which will give them the time to look around more—we will all be hearing much more about this destination. When the Ko Chang area has been properly explored, it will most likely turn into a popular diving area.

As with the island of Ko Samui, to the south, Pattaya is probably not the place for a dedicated diving holiday. But for those divers looking for an active sporting life—or a busy nightlife—as well as diving, Pattaya could be the answer. For the student of scuba, Pattaya offers many opportunities on all levels. For a week or a weekend, Pattaya has the potential to keep even the most active diver happy.

— *John Williams*

Below: The eye of a parrotfish.
Photo by Mark Strickland.

DIVING AUSTRALIA

The first book of its kind, *Diving Australia* presents the continent's top dive sites in one easy-to-use book. Join our expert dive guides and world-class photographers as they take you on a fantastic underwater journey around this huge, diverse island continent. More than 200 superb photographs and lots of practical information.

ISBN 962 593 104 X

DIVING INDONESIA

This book is the result of hundreds of dives, thousands of kilometres of plane and boat travel (and weeks without a cold beer). Author and photographer Kal Muller's enthusiasm for the sport shines from every page as he invites you to explore Indonesia's dazzling underwater realm with him.

ISBN 962 593 314 X

BIRDING INDONESIA

This book is a "must" for the serious birder. Written by the world's leading authorities on Indonesian birds, it is packed with travel information and a complete checklist of Indonesian birds.

ISBN 962 593 071 X

SURFING INDONESIA

Another "first" from Periplus—the first surf guide to the world's largest archipelago. Author Leonard Lueras and his team of gonzo board-riders take you along thousands of miles of deserted shorelines, stopping at some of the best surf spots in the world. This book is very detailed, with maps, action-pumped photos and travels tips to get you there and back.

ISBN 962 593 313 1

SURFING AUSTRALIA

Capturing the adventurous spirit of Aussie beach culture, this guidebook shows the reader how to find and surf Australia's hottest beach, reef and point breaks, and get away from it all. Filled with invaluable travel tips, the book also explores Australia's surfing history, characters and the unique surf lifestyle which has inspired and entertained the world.

ISBN 962 593 322 0

Periplus Action Guides are available at bookshops, surf shops and travel stores around the world. If you cannot find them where you live, please write to us for the name of a distributor closest to you:

USA/UK/Europe:
Tuttle Publishing
RR1 Box 231-5 North Clarendon, VT 05759-9700, USA
tel: 1-802-773-8930 fax: 1-802-773-6993

Asia-Pacific:
Berkeley Books Pte. Ltd.
5 Little Road, #08-01, Singapore 536983
tel: 65-280-1330 fax: 65-280-6290

Indonesia
North Sulawesi
MANADO

Dive
ATTRACTIONS

Contents

The following sections provide background information about traveling in the various countries, including transportation options, visa regulations, health and emergency services, and information about accommodations and food. A special emphasis has been placed on dive operators and diving services.

THE PHILIPPINES

AREA LISTINGS

SINGAPORE

THAILAND

AREA LISTINGS

APPENDIX

PRACTICALITIES

CONTENTS

Indonesia Country code: 62

Indonesia, a far-flung archipelago of 17,508 islands, has radically developed its tourism infrastructure in the last few years, opening up destinations that were once the domain only of hardy travelers. It has also, at the time of this writing, become somewhat politically and economically unstable, with Suharto's stepping down from the presidency he held for more than thirty years, and the precipitous decline in the value of the country's currency, the rupiah. Bali, the cosmopolitan center of tourist services, will likely continue to be relatively unaffected by these changes, but travelers should check before planning excursions to Jakarta or some of the more remote areas.

Air travel

Indonesia is linked by air through numerous daily international flights arriving and departing not only from the capital, Jakarta, but also from Denpasar (Bali), as well as regional international airports such as Manado, Batam, Kupang, Medan and Surabaya. The national airline, Garuda, links with its sister airline, Merpati, which operates flights to all corners of the archipelago.

Garuda Head office is at the BDN Building, Jl. MH Thamrin, No. 5, Jakarta. Tel: (021) 230-0925. Fax: (021) 334430. The airline also has branch offices in the largest hotels in Jakarta and Bali.

Merpati Head office: Jl. Angkasa 2, Jakarta. Tel: (021) 424-3608, 654-8888. Fax: (021) 424-6616, 654-0609.

Land travel

Bus travel throughout the larger islands of the archipelago is frequent, quite dependable and inexpensive. However, it is not recommended for a diver with lots of gear.

Sea travel

Passenger ferries are an essential part of Indonesian travel. The country has a national passenger line, Pelni, which operates throughout the archipelago with five levels of comfort from first to economy class.

Pelni Head office: 5th floor, Jl Gajah Mada 14, Jakarta 10130. Tel: (021) 384-4342, 384-4366. Fax: (021) 385-4130. Main ticket office: Jl Angkasa 18, Kemayoran. Tel: (021) 421-1921. Open in the mornings. In Singapore: 50 Telok Blangah Road, #02-02 Citiport Centre, Singapore 0409. Tel: (65) 272-6811, 271-5159.

Visas

Most travelers (nationals of the European Union countries, SE Asian nationals and nationals of Australia, New Zealand, Japan and the United States) can obtain a visa-free entry to Indonesia for 60 days. Passports must be valid for at least 6 months. If in any doubt, check first with an Indonesian embassy.

Health

Travel to tropical Indonesia comes with some health risks for visitors from temperatre climates. It is advisable to have a tetanus and a gamma globulin shot to eliminate some strains of hepatitis. Bring suitable medication to combat stomach upsets, and drink only bottled or boiled water. And watch out for the tropical sun. The best prevention: a strong sun block and a hat.

Malaria is endemic in parts of the country, so divers intending to travel to Sulawesi, Lombok, Komodo, Flores, Kupang, Maluku, or Irian Jaya should consider options to minimize possible infection. Many forms of prophylactics exist (check with your local health center for current favorites—Maloprim and Chlorquine are usually recommended). Covering your arms and legs after sunset, burning pyrethrin-containing coils, and using repellent and a mosquito net are probably as effective against bites from the night-biting, malaria-carrying *Anopheles* mosquito.

Emergency medical assistance

Even in the big cities outside of Jakarta, emergency care leaves much to be desired. Your best bet in the event of a life-threatening emergency or accident is to get on the first plane to Jakarta or Singapore. Contact your embassy or consulate by phone for assistance (see below). Medivac airlifts are very expensive (at least $25,000) and most embassies will recommend that you buy insurance to cover the cost of this when traveling extensively in Indonesia.

Check your health insurance before coming to make sure you are covered. Travel insurance should include coverage of a medical evacuation to Singapore and a 24-hour worldwide phone number as well as some extras like luggage loss and trip cancellation.

Two good insurers are AEA International, a Singapore-based outfit that offers worldwide medical evacuation insurance, and the non-profit Divers Alert Network (DAN) which offers low-cost secondary insurance for divers.

AEA International The Americas: Tel: (206) 340-6000, Fax: (206) 340-6006; Asia: Tel: (65) 338 2311, Fax: (65) 338 7611; Europe: Tel: (33-1) 53-05-05-55, Fax: (33-1) 53-05-05-56; Australia: Tel: 61 (2) 9372–2468, Fax: 61 (2) 9372-2494.
E-mail: info@aeaintl.com
Web: www.aeaintl.com
This is a seasoned outfit that has been providing emergency services in the region for more than a decade. They combined with International SOS Assistance early in 1998. AEA offers individual and corporate insurance packages, with world-wide coverage. AEA maintains 24-hour alarm centers throughout the world, including two in Indonesia:
Bali Tel: (0361) 227-271 Frederika Nault
Jakarta Tel: (021) 750-6001 Jim Williams

Divers Alert Network (DAN) Peter B. Bennett Center, 8 West Colony Place, Durham NC 27705 USA. Membership: 800/446-2671.
Web: www.dan.ycg.org
This well-known U.S.-based non-profit has been providing medical advice in the case of diving injuries, researching diving medicine, and promoting diving safety for a long time. They are often the first organization called by local emergency personnel in the case of a diving accident. The organization publishes the bimonthly *Alert Diver*, which is distributed to members. DAN offers yearly membership for US$29, and three different insurance packages for an additional US$25 to US$35 a year. We highly recommend DAN membership and insurance. The organization maintains a medical information line for questions about diving health (919/684-2948; 9am–5pm U.S. Eastern Time) and a 24-hour-a-day hotline for dive emergencies: 919-684-8111.

DAN Southeast Asia–Pacific 49a Karnak Road, P.O. Box 384, Ashburton, Vic. 3147, Australia. Tel: 61-3/9886-9166, Fax: 61-3/9886-9155; Emergencies: 61-3/9828-2958. The Australian-based Southeast Asia branch of DAN.

Climate

Broadly speaking, Indonesia has two seasons of monsoon winds: the southeast monsoon bringing dry weather usually from May to September, and the northwest monsoons from November to March which bring rainy weather. In between, rain is sporadic and humidity very high. Maluku's weather patterns are unique to the archipelago.

What to bring

Bring at least the basics: snorkel, mask and fins; a torch and batteries, too, for night diving, and a few O-rings. Equipment for rental is not always in tip-top form, so the more you can bring with you the better.

Money exchange

Currency can be exchanged on arrival at international airports and at banks in all major cities. Bali has dozens of small money changers who offer good rates for Indonesian *rupiah*. Generally, banks and money changers prefer the US dollar, so bring some cash in dollars. Torn or blemished bank notes may not be accepted. Travelers' checks endorsed by American Express, VISA or Bank of America are acceptable at major banks and some money changers in Bali, while VISA cards are accepted at major hotels. Prices quoted in US dollars because the rupiah is currently very unstable at around $1=Rp7,500.

Manado City code: 0431

Manado—the entry point to diving North Sulawesi—is a large city and is well-connected by air to the rest of Indonesia. The Dr. Sam Ratulangi airport Airport is 7 km outside of town, and taxi coupons to just about anywhere in town cost $3–$4. If you reserve ahead with one of the dive operators, they will meet you at the airport.

In the past it was a long and expensive proposition to get to Manado, but this has now changed. There is a direct, twice a week, 3.5-hour run from/to Singapore by SilkAir, the daughter airline of Singapore Airlines. There are also rumors of flights from Taiwan, Japan, and Korea. If these come to pass, the attractions of North Sulawesi will be appreciated by many more visitors.

By Boat For information on the large passenger boats from Bitung, contact Pelni Lines, see above.

Accommodations

There are now plenty of hotels available to travelers, ranging from the luxurious 4-star properties at $300+ a day to small, simple *losmen* at $5 a day. However, if you come to Manado to dive seriously—or even as a serious snorkeler —there is no reason to stay anywhere except at one of the dive resorts.

Dive operators

For serious diving, we suggest booking a package—including accommodations and board—with one of the more established dive centers on the mainland. Three of the operators listed below—Barracuda, Murex, and NDC—have more than a decade of experience in the area. Their basic package rates are about the same, $70 to $100 a day (depending on the room) for two dives, accommodation and food. Some of the newer operators offer more upmarket accommodations.

Barracuda Molas Beach, Dusun II, Manado, Sulawesi, 9242. About 10 kms north of Manado. Tel: (0431) 854279, 854288, Fax: (0431) 864848. For reservations contact: Alfred R. Lefrandt. Barracuda, established in 1989, offers chalet-type accommodations on a small hill, the only one of the three resorts that has a view. It has a quiet charm. They also have a glass-bottom boat, on-boat dive profiles;

the larger craft are equipped with radio. They also carry oxygen onboard during their longer trips or for the shipwreck dives. Their boats are in good shape: 3 large dive boats, and 6 dive boats, each with 80 hp engines.

Indo-Pacific Divers At the Boulevard Sea-View Hotel, P.O. Box 1014, Manado 95010. Tel: (0431) 859379, Fax: (0431) 859368. E-mail: kudalaut@manado.wasantara.net.id Web: www.wp.com/kudalaut A new PADI-affiliated outfit, run by expat Europeans, specializing in PADI instruction. Two of the four dive managers are marine biologists. Their operation is 40 minutes from Bunaken. Two dives, $70. At least 15 different courses offered. Open water, $420.

Manado Diving Center (MDC) Jl. Bethesda 75. P.O. Box 11, Manado 95115. Tel: (0431) 862880, 866622, 865001, Fax: (0431) 863857. MDC has been around for several years and offers dive tours, hotel accommodations, as well as national and international package tours. They have bungalow accommodations on Bunaken Island.

Murex (Manado Underwater Explorations). About 10 km south of Manado. Jl. Sudirman 28. P.O. Box 236, Manado 95123. Tel: (0431) 866280, Tel:/Fax: 852116. European representative: DIVEX Indonesia, P.O. Box 5352, 30053 Hannover, Germany. Tel: (49 511) 647-6129, Fax: (49 511) 647-6120. Murex, which has been in operation since 1987, is the smallest, quietest and most "intimate" of the three pioneering resorts (NDC, Murex, Barracuda), with very nice landscaping featuring lotus pools. It has the best boats, and its guides all use computers and safe second stages. It is also located furthest from the dive sites. Run by Dr. Hanny Batuna, a medical doctor and dive instructor, who has been diving in the area since the '70s. Murex also runs two liveaboard dive boats, the *Serenade* and the *Arlena,* which make regular runs to the north. 8 dive guides, 5 divemasters, and 2 instructors.

Novotel Manado Jl. Sam Ratulangi No. 22. Tel: (0431) 851245 and 851174, Fax: (0431) 863545. All marine activities operate under the supervision of two Australian dive professionals with PADI Instructor ratings. Novotel operates 8 high-powered fiberglass dive boats, each with a capacity of 20 divers, plus two large passenger vessels (one for 100 passengers, the other for 200 passengers) for sightseeing cruises around the marine park. A semi-submersible viewer boat with a capacity of 40, *Aqua Scoop,* affords tours around the marine park. 5 divemasters, 30 dive guides, 2 instructors. Open water, advance, rescue, divemaster, and specialty courses offered.

Nusantara Diving Centre (NDC) Molas Beach, P.O. Box 1015, Manado 95242, Sulawesi. Tel:(0431) 860638 and 863988, Fax: (0431) 860368 and 854668.
E-mail: ndc@mdo.mega.net.id
Web: mdo.mega.net.id/ndc
This is the oldest, largest, and liveliest resort in the area. The center was started by Loky Herlambang almost 25 years ago, and some of his devoted staff have been working for NDC for 15 years. Located close to the sea, but the beach is mangrove and mud. The operation has a fun, local feel, and at night the guitars often come out. NDC has 11 boats with double 40 hp outboards, 45 guides, 350 tanks, 50 sets of rental gear, and 4 dive instructors.

Paradise Beach Hotel & Resort Desa Maen, Likupang. Tel: (0431) 868200, 868868, 868222, 868880; Fax: (0431) 862200, 864888. This operation is on the tip of Sulawesi's northern peninsula, 32 km from the airport Airport. Opened in March 1996, the Paradise Beach offers 5-star comfort near 450 hectares of tropical jungle, 2.5 kms of white sand beaches, clear seas and good reefs. The hotel runs joint ventures with Eurodivers, a PADI-affiliated dive operator (packages run about $40/dive). Two new compressors and 40 tanks, 30 regulators, 20 BCs, and several Aladdin computers for rent. This well-organized outfit has pioneered some new sites in Lembeh and around Bangka island. The resort has 320 rooms and suites, 3 restaurants, a business center, tennis courts, a golf course, watersports, the works. $130–$150 standard, $250 deluxe, $350–$550 suite.

Bali

Bali, a verdant, volcanic island with nearly three million people, is the tourist center of Indonesia. The Balinese themselves are not especially focused toward the sea, but the waters off Bali are very rich. The diving is not as immediately impressive as that in Eastern Indonesia, but it is very good, and gets more interesting the more you dive. Bali's combination of beautiful surroundings, convenient diving, plenty of tourist services and interesting culture is hard to beat.

Getting there

The best way to arrive in Bali is at the Ngurah Rai International Airport which, despite its often being referred to as "Denpasar" is actually on the isthmus connecting the Bukit Badung peninsula to Bali, much nearer to Kuta Beach than Bali's capital city. Daily Garuda flights from Jakarta, Yogyakarta, and many other Indonesian cities connect to Ngurah Rai, and a growing number of international flights—including those from Australia, Hong Kong, Japan, the Netherlands, Singapore and the United States—land here as well.

International airlines The following international airlines have offices in the Grand Bali Beach in Sanur, Tel: (0361) 288511. Direct phone lines are: Air France, Tel: 755523; Ansett Australia, Tel: 289636; Cathay Pacific, Tel: 753942; Continental-Micronesia, Tel: 287065/287774; Garuda, Tel: 288243; Japan Airlines and Japan Asia Airways, Tel: 287476/287577; Lufthansa, Tel: 286952; Malaysia Air Service, Tel: 288716 and 288511; Qantas, Tel: 288331; Singapore Airlines, Tel: 287940; Thai International, Tel: 285071 through –3. The Wisti Sabha Building at the Airport houses: Air New Zealand, Tel: 756170 and 751011 ext. 1116; China Airlines, Tel: 754856 and 757298; EVA Air, Tel: 298935; KLM, Tel: 756127; Korean Air Lines, Tel: 754856 and 757298, fax: 757275; Royal Brunei, Tel: 757292.

Local transportation

Airport taxis One-way fares from Ngurah Rai airport to the tourist centers are fixed. You pay a cashier inside, and receive a coupon which you surrender to your driver. Fares range from $3 to nearby Kuta Beach to $17 to Ubud, far inland.

Minibuses All hotels have *bemos* for hire with a driver or with an English-speaking driver/guide. Rates run $3–$5/hr, with a 2-hr minimum. Day rates run $30–$40, more for an air-conditioned vehicle.

Vehicle rental In almost all cases, it is best to leave the driving in Bali to someone who knows how to negotiate the roads and traffic. The roads are narrow, twisting, and full of hazards: unmarked construction sites, chickens, dogs, children, Vespas as wide as cars due to huge baskets of produce, and tough, unflinching truck drivers, to name just a few. You can rent a small (150cc) motorcycle for $5–$7/day if you have an international motorcycle driver's license, but you better know how to ride. Renting a car—particularly since you will be carrying diving gear—is perhaps a more practical solution. These run $25–$35/day for little Suzuki jeeps; more for larger, more comfortable Toyota Kijangs. Rent through an agency (even Avis has outlets) or from numerous local rental companies. Ask at your hotel or comb the streets where there's an agent on nearly every block. Be sure your rental includes insurance for loss and damage.

Medical

The two largest hospitals (*rumah sakit*) in Bali are in Denpasar. Both have emergency units with English-speaking doctors on duty 24 hrs:

Sanglah General Hospital RSUP Sanglah Denpasar, Diponegoro Street, Denpasar 80114. Tel: (0361) 227911–227915 (general), 223190 (ICCU), 232603 (VIP) and 224556 (director). Fax: (0361) 224206 (director), 226363 (emergency unit).

General Hospital Wangaya Jl. Kartini 109, Tel: (0361) 222141.

DCS Emergencies

There are two hyperbaric chambers in the area, one at Sanglah hospital in Denpasar, Bali, and the other in Surabaya, East Java.

Sanglah General Hospital RSUP Sanglah Denpasar, Diponegoro Street, Denpasar 80114. Tel: (0361) 227911–227915 ext. 232 for the hyperbaric medicine department. The chief doctor for the chamber is Dr. Antonius Natasamudra (home: 0361/420842), and Dr. Etty Herawati (home: 0361/223570) works the chamber as well. Both speak English and are very competent. The chamber is used regularly for beauty treatments, so it is kept in good service and the doctors and nurses are familiar with its operation. They use the United States Navy tables for their treatment regimes. The chamber was built by an American fabrication outfit in Houston, Texas, and began operation in 1996. It has capacity for six patients, and a working pressue of up to 80 psi (5.4 atmospheres).

LAKELSLA Direktorat Kesehatan TNI-AL, Lembaga Kesehatan, Keangakatan Lautan, Jl.

Gadung No. 1, Surabaya, Java. Tel: (031) 45750 and 41731. This chamber, operated by the Indonesian Navy, is run by Dr. Suharsono, who was trained in Australia and speaks English very well. The chamber has a volume of 75 cubic meters, with a capacity for five patients at a maximum working pressure of 6 atmospheres. The unit was built in 1981 by Aqualogistics International, St. Helena, UK. Other instrumentation includes spirometry, audiometery, EKG, and chromatography

Photographic supplies

P.T. Modern Foto This outfit is the local Fuji agent, with a huge showroom in Kuta just opposite the gas station and Gelael supermarket. They have the best E-6 processing in Bali and the freshest film. For prints, there are many instant mini-labs in all the larger towns and tourist centers offering while-you-wait service. You cannot buy Kodachrome film in Bali.

The biggest range of photographic equipment and supplies can be found in Denpasar at **Tati Photo**, Jl. Sumatra 72, Tel: (0361) 226912, and **Prima Photo**, Jl. Gajah Mada 14, Tel: (0361) 222505.

Accommodations

Bali has a very wide range of accommodations, from 5-star hotels to modest *losmen*. You can spend $1,200/night in a lavish suite at Nusa Dua or $3/night at a friendly little *losmen* in Candi Dasa. It's your choice. All the more up-market hotels charge 21% government tax and service on top of the listed prices.

Dive Operators

Diving tour operators in Bali are concentrated in the tourist triangle—Kuta, Nusa Dua and Sanur—and in two places close to good dive spots—Candidasa on the east coast and Lovina, between the Tulamben wreck and Menjangan Island, in the north. The bigger outfits maintain desks at the major hotels, or at least keep brochures at the desk.

Almost all the local dive guides speak some English (and/or Japanese) and dive very well. Where many fall short, however, is in dive planning—particularly tailoring a dive for your specific needs—and emergency assistance.

Prices are fairly standard. The following ranges (based on 2 divers) reflect southern-based operators, and include two full tanks, guides, transportation, and lunch:

Nusa Dua (one dive)	$30–$50
Sanur (one dive)	$30–$50
Padangbai	$50–$70
Tepekong or Mimpang	$60–$80
Amed	$60–$80
Tulamben	$60–$80
Lovina	$60–$80
Menjangan	$80–$120
Nusa Penida (near side)	$80–$110
Nusa Penida (far side)	$90–$130

Most operators offer 2-day to 5-day packages, which are more economical. Cost per dive in these runs $30–$40.

All operators have equipment for rent for casual divers. Average rental rates, per day: BC and regulator, $10–$12; mask and snorkel and fins, $3–$5; wet suit $5–$7; flashlight $5.

The area listings below work their way counter-clockwise around the island from the southern tourist triangle, which follows the diving. If you stay anywhere in Kuta and Legian, Sanur, Nusa Dua, or Tanjung Benoa there is no reason to pick an operator in that particular town, as they will all pick up clients in the southern area.

Kuta and Legian City code: 0361

A town has grown up around the beach here that has become the tourist center of Bali. Robert and Louise Koke, surfers from southern California, first built their Kuta Beach Hotel here in 1936. Still, it wasn't until the late '60s and early '70s, when a generation of hippies and other western drop-outs "discovered" Bali, that Kuta exploded.

Today, the town, which now extends north up to Legian, bustles with activity, its streets and tiny *gangs* (alleyways) lined with shops, restaurants, discos, and *losmen*. It is even an international fashion center with a distinct, colorful style falling somewhere between neon sporting wear and a Grateful Dead T-shirt. Although it is currently fashionable to malign Kuta, the place does have an irrepressible, youthful charm.

Dive operators

Bali International Diving Service Jl. Kuta Raya, Kuta 16M (in front of the Gelael Supermarket and gas station). Tel: (0361) 751342; Fax: (0361) 752956. Seven instructors, five dive masters, all CMAS-certified. Some 2–3 day dive packages available.

Baruna Water Sports Head office: Jl. Bypass Ngurah Rai 300B, Kuta (in back of gas station) Mailing address: P.O. Box 3419 Denpasar, Bali 80034. Tel: (0361) 753820, 753821; fax: (0361) 753809. Baruna, named after the Balinese water deity, is Bali's oldest and largest scuba diving operator. They operate two outriggered speedboats and a larger diesel-powered boat. Baruna organizes tours to all of Bali's dive sites, and many other sites in Indonesia. This includes obtaining airplane reservations and tickets, which can be quite difficult to do on your own for remote places. They also run special-interest diving tours, fixed program tours and can arrange yacht charters (with compressor) for groups of two to six. Baruna owns a very attractive 50-room, bungalows-style hotel, the Puri Bagus Beach, beachside, at the extreme eastern end of Candi Dasa. It is best to stay here if you are diving in the area, especially if you are on one of Baruna's package tours, as their dive operations for eastern Bali are run from here.

Pineapple Divers c/o Legian Beach Hotel, Jl. Melasti, P.O. Box 308, Kuta, Bali. Tel: (0361) 751313, Fax: (0361) 752651. A reputable outfit, specializing in Japanese clients.

Sanur City code: 0361

Sanur was Bali's first resort town and is, in a sense, the grey eminence of the tourist triangle. Compared to Kuta, it is quiet and dignified (or just dull, depending on your point of view and, inescapably, your age) and compares to Nusa Dua as old wealth does to new. The town is very quiet at night and the beach here, protected by the reef flat, is very calm. People who intend to spend a long time on Bali often stay in Sanur.

Dive Operators

Ambisi Dive Center Jl. Tukad Pakerisan 98, Sanur. Mailing address: P.O. Box 3734, Denpasar 80228. Tel: (0361) 241428; fax: (0361) 241421. Formerly Oceana. Osanu Okuno is manager-instructor and caters to Japanese-speaking divers.

Bali Marine Sports Jl. Bypass Ngurah Rai, Belanjong, Sanur. Tel:(0361) 289308, fax: (0361) 287872. Good organization, equipment and guides. Basic and advanced dive courses. A PADI International Dive Center, run by very professional westerners. They own three

12-person dive boats with radio communications to the dive center. All divers insured. Cross-certification and specialty courses offered. Various dive tours of Bali.

Dive & Dive's Jl. Bypass Ngurah Rai 198, Sanur, Denpasar, Bali. Tel: (0361) 288052, fax: (0361) 289309. Highly recommended. Dive shop with gear for sale and rent, small cafe, nice diver ambiance. Can arrange multi-day dive tour packages and trips around Bali or anywhere else in Indonesia.

ENA Dive Centre and Water Sports Jl. Tirta Ening 1, P.O. Box 3798, Sanur, Denpasar, Bali 80227. Tel: (0361) 288829, 287945, and 281751, Fax: (0361) 287945.
E-mail: enadive@denpasar.wasantara.net.id
Web: www.indo.com/diving/ena/
On a back street in Sanur, not easy to find, but like the other operators, they'll pick you up at your hotel. ENA owns the Saya Resort in Tulamben (see below). Various all-inclusive dive and accommodation packages are offered. PADI courses in English or Japanese. Also offers jetski, parasailing and other water sports.

Pro Dive Bali Jl. Sekar Waru No. 25, Sanur, Bali 80238. Tel: (0361) 286336, Tel:/fax: (0361) 288756.
    E-mail: prodivebali@bali-paradise.com
    Web: www.prodive.com.au
Australian-operated company offering PADI open water dive courses for $350 and continuing education programs in advanced open water diving, rescue diving, divemaster and specialty courses. Their 10-meter custom dive boat, *Pro Diver*, speeds you to the sites so you can spend more time in the water instead of on the water. The outfit's two- and five-day packages are popular.

Nusa Dua and Tanjung Benoa
City code: 0361

Nusa Dua offers luxury, and isolation from touts, peddlers, stray dogs, cold-water showers and other indignities. It's also quite antiseptic. Preferred by the international jet set. There are no cheap lodgings here.

Tanjung Benoa is a recently established resort just north of Nusa Dua. The beach hotels here are small and cozy, although there are some newly opened larger hotels. The nice, white-sand beach here is popular for water sports: parasailing, windsurfing, waterskiing and, of course, snorkeling and diving.

Dive Operators

Bali Hai Diving Adventures Contact Michael Cortenbach at PO Box 3548, Denpasar, Bali 80001. Tel: (0361) 720331, and Fax: (0361) 720334. Runs diving around Lembongan Island, and specializes in diving for *Mola mola* at a site dubbed "Blue Corner." Mike offers several packages, and we recommend the ten-dive package ($425) which includes the ride to Lembongan and back. While on the island, accommodation choices are two: the lovely Waka Nusa ($100/night) or the Mushroom Losmen, around $20, but much more basic. Mike will make the arrangements. The best time to see *Mola mola* is at the autumnal equinox.

Barrakuda Bali Dive At the Bali Tropic Palace Hotel, Jl. Pratama 34A, Nusa Dua. Tel: 772130, ext. 731; fax 772131. Located at the hotel. One instructor and two guides, all CMAS-certified. Also has counters in Candi Dasa and Lovina.

Wally's Special Tours Perumahan Wisma, Nusa Permai, Blok C. 35, Nusa Dua, Kampial, Bali. (0361) 772784. Cell: (087) 812-7243. Wally can also be contacted through YOS Diving in Tanjung Benoa (see below).
E-mail: walldive@denpasar.wasantara.net.id
Dive guide Wally Siagian caters to small groups whose special interests include marine life and photography. He offers custom tours to any of Bali's dive spots and can arrange yacht charters for diving further afield. He is particularly familiar with Komodo diving, which he pioneered several years back. Wally (who holds an advanced instructor ranking from SSI) can also certify divers and offer advanced courses.

His strength is his knowledge of the sites, which he has been diving longer than anyone else on the island, and particularly of the unique biology of each. He has guided, worked with, and spotted animals for Gerald R. Allen, Gary Bell, David Doubilet, Rudie Kuiter, Jack Randall, and Roger Steene, among other notables. If you are a serious about your photography, you should work with Wally, especially if you want to photograph rare animals.

We cannot recommend these tours highly enough—but give yourself plenty of time. Wally's schedule is flexible and his knowlege of the island is encyclopedic. He owns his own Bauer compressor and equipment, and his rates are no higher than the other operators.

YOS Diving Centre and Marine Sports Jalan Pratama, Tanjung Benoa, Nusa Dua, Bali, Indonesia. Tel: (0361) 773774, 752005; fax 752985. This is a very well-run operation managed by Yos W.K. Amerta. They run fast boats from the main Tanjung Benoa center to Nusa Penida, and take divers by land to any of the other sites. YOS maintains counters at the Nusa Dua hotels, and full dive centers at Lovina and at the Pondok Sari Bungalows in Pemuteran. Good compressors and new, high-quality rental gear. A professional outfit that can take divers to any site in Bali. Also fishing, parasailing, and jetskiing.

Candi Dasa City code: 0363

This town is quiet and relatively uncrowded compared to Kuta and Sanur to the south. There are at least 50 hotels, *losmen,* and homestays, and plenty of restaurants. The availability of services and its location—halfway between Nusa Penida and Tulamben—make it a reasonable place for a diver to settle.

Dive Operators

Spice Dive Balina Beach Resort. Buitan Manggis, Karangasem. Tel: (0363) 41720, Fax: (0363) 41001.
E-mail: spicedive@denpasar.wasantara.net.id
Well-known for their Lovina operation, Spice Dive now runs the concession at Balina.

Baruna Water Sports (see above under Kuta).

Sea Lion Diving Club (Stingray Dive Service) Bali Samudra Indah Hotel. Tel: (0363) 41062, 41181. Inclusive, two-dive tours: Nusa Penida ($70), Padangbai Blue Lagoon ($50), Gili Tepekong ($55), Tulamben ($55), Menjangan, minimum 4 persons ($70). Night dive at Tulamben ($40), Padangbai ($35). Two dives at any location, with accommodation ($90). Five-day course, with CMAS certification ($250). Introductory dive ($85).

Tulamben (No phones yet)

Most divers travel to Tulamben (or nearby Cemeluk) on a package tour from Kuta, Sanur, Nusa Dua, or Candi Dasa, but independent-minded divers can make their way by rented car or, if not carrying gear, motorcycle. It's about 4 hrs from Kuta or Nusa Dua, 30 min.

less from Sanur. The traffic through Candi Dasa will likely be heavy, but the last hour of the trip—from Candi Dasa onward—is very scenic. From Tulamben to Menjangan takes another 3 hrs.

Operators in Tulamben offer tanks, weights, and equipment rental, along with guides for independent divers who arrive on their own, and we highly recommend staying in Tulamben if you want to dive here or in Cemeluk. The wreck, in particular, is far less crowded in the morning before the hordes arrive from the South.

Dive Operators

Bali Dive has a branch office at the turnoff to the parking area near the entry point for the wreck. Tanks, regulators and BCs for rent.

Dive Paradise Tulamben Attached to the Paradise Palm Beach Hotel, P.O. Box 111, Amlapura 80811, Bali. No phone yet, but they can be contacted through the Friendship Shop in Candi Dasa, Tel:/Fax: (0363) 41052. This outfit, run by Emiko Shibuya, is the most experienced operator in the Tulamben area. Emiko, who has been in Bali for 11 years, keeps her compressor, tanks and equipment in fine order. There is no telephone yet (the village has unapologetically voted PDI for years) but you can get fresh Fuji Velvia at the counter. Dive Paradise's guide, Nengah Putu, holds an advanced diver rating. One wreck dive with instructor-guide ($30), two dives ($50). The dive shop also organizes dives at other spots around Bali. Prices include transportation from Tulamben, dive guide, two dives, and all equipment, are reasonable, as are the room rates at the Paradlse ($11–$16 w/fan; $35 w/AC and hot water. For snorkelers at Tulamben, the Paradise has fins, masks and snorkels, $1.50/day.

Tulamben Dive Center P.O. Box 31, Amlapura 80811. Tel: (0363) 41032. Next to the Paradise on the main road. Has a compressor, tanks and rental gear. Same prices as the Paradise. Associated with the *losmen* Tulamben Beach Pondok Wisata, 4 rooms $5–$10.

Cemeluk and Sambirenteng
City code: 0362

There is no compressor or rental gear in the immediate vicinity of this dive site. Bring your own from Tulamben, Candi Dasa or wherever, or join a group from the south for a day trip. Past Cemeluk, on the way to Karangasem, there are a few *losmen*, on the bad, but paved and spectacular road that follows the coast. One option, in Sambirenteng, is the Alam Anda.

Alam Anda Sambirenteng. Contact: Astawa Enterprises, c/o Nyumpene, Jl. Legian Tengah 436N, Legian. Tel: /fax: (0361) 752296. 9 bungalows, 4-room house. Unique, new seaside resort devoted to relaxation. Organizes trips through unspoilt landscapes, as well as sailing, snorkeling, and dive trips to Amed, Tulamben, Menjangan, and Nusa Penida. They have an experienced dive master in residence and diving equipment in top condition for rent. $24–$29 rooms, $39–$44 bungalows, w/breakfast.

Lovina City code: 0362

Lovina is the generic name for a cluster of villages spread along Bali's north coast. They are, from east to west: Tukad Munggah, Anturan, Kalibukbuk (Lovina), and Temukus. The beach is shiny black sand and the surf is calm. If you want to dive at Menjangan and if you don't stay in Pemuteran, then Lovina, about an hour's drive away, is the next closest place to stay. Operators can arrange diving (in Lovina and Menjangan) as well as local snorkeling ($3–$4), a trip to the dolphins ($5), and fishing ($5).

Dive Operators

Spice Dive On the south side of the main coastal road. P.O. Box 157, Singaraja, Bali. Tel: (0362) 41305, Fax: (0362) 41171.
E-mail: spicedive@denpasar.wasantara.net.id
A small, well-run operation. Introductory dives available. Now a PADI operation. Two dives, all-inclusive, including all gear: Tulamben ($65), Lovina ($45), Menjangan ($65). Knock off 10% if you bring your own gear. Menjangan package requires a minimum of two clients. You can also arrange dives at Nusa Penida, Padangbai and Tepekong (however, because of distance, just one dive per day).

Barrakuda At Bali Lovina Beach Cottages in Singaraja. Tel:/fax: (0362) 41385, 21836. In Sanur, Tel:/fax: (0361) 233386 and 287694. This dive operator's head office is in Sanur. Prices similar to those at Spice Dive.

Pemuteran Menjangan Area
City code: 0362

Park visitor's permit and the boat from Labuhan Lalang to Menjangan Island comes to about $15 (this fee is included in package tours).

Dive Operators

P.T. Arkipelago Selam Associated with the Taman Sari Bungalows Resort, Desa Pemuteran, Gerokgak, Singaraja 81155, Bali. Tel:(0362) 92623, Fax: (0362) 93264. Also keeps a shop at the Sol Elite Paradiso Hotel, Jl. Kartika Plaza, Kuta 80361 Bali. Tel:(0361) 761414 ext. 7153, Fax: (0361) 756944.
E-mail: tamanri@indosat.net.id
Web: baliwww.com/arkipelago/
A new outfit, which offers a Bali-wide program. The Taman Sari is the successor to the Pondok Sari with similar features. More upscale, but still very tasteful. $35 fan, $50–$65 AC, $80 suite, plus 15% tax and service.

Reef Seen Aquatics Dive Centre Desa Pemuteran, Gerokgak, Singaraja, 81155, Bali. Tel:/fax: (0362) 92339. Contact: Chris Brown. E-mail: reefseen@denpasar.wasantara.net.id
Chris Brown pioneered the Pemuteran sites, and is always continuing his explorations, including unusual dives such as at a nearby pearl farm. He can book divers at any of the local hotels. The dive boats are traditional wooden craft, customized for diving. Oxygen and a good first aid kit are kept on board. Film and 110V or 220V charging facilities, multi-system video playback, separate freshwater rinse tanks for photo and video gear. Two dives at the Pemuteran sites, just offshore, from boat, $55. Shore dives $10, with guide, $20; shore night dives $15, with guide, $25. Trips to Menjangan, including 2 dives and lunch, $75/person, minimum two divers. Equipment rental: $10/dive.

YOS Diving Centre and Marine Sports Associated with the Pondok Sari Bungalows, Desa Pemuteran, Gerokgak, Singaraja. Tel/fax: 92337. A branch of the well-run Tanjung Benoa–based operator (see above). The Pondok Sari is the original resort in the area and offers clean, comfortable bungalows in a very peaceful setting. The tasteful room furnishings and the open-air bathrooms with Japanese touches—smooth river pebbles, dripping bamboo—are very nice. The restaurant offers good western and Indonesian cuisine, plus cold beer. $18 fan, $29 AC, plus 15% tax and service.

Live-aboards

Sea Contacts Dive Voyages Jl. Mertasari no. 64A, Sidakarya Batan Kendal, Suwung, Denpasar, Bali. Tel: (0361) 725430, Fax: (0361) 725431. Cruise director: Larry Smith. E-mail: smithdiv@dps.mega.net.id
This is a brand new operation, which wouldn't mean a lot except for the name of the cruise director. Larry Smith is the most experienced live-aboard director working in Indonesia today, and any dive operation he runs is certain to be exceptional. He has selected the best of the crews that have worked with him in the last decade for this operation. We went to press too late with this edition to include details on his boat and schedule, but contact him at the numbers above—we're sure it will be worth it.

Spice Island Cruises Now run by Pro Dive Bali Jl. Sekar Waru No. 25, Sanur, Bali 80238. Tel: (0361) 286336, Tel:/fax: (0361) 288756.
E-mail: prodivebali@bali-paradise.com
Web: www.prodive.com.au
This Australian-operated company runs the *Bali Sea Dancer,* a large ship that offers diving on its three- and four-day runs to Komodo. A newer operation, called "Oceanic Odyssey" offers luxury three- and four-day cruises and charters east of Bali. Contact Richard Johnstone at the numbers of above for details.

Grand Komodo Tours & Travel (Komodo Alor Safari) This Komodo and Alor specialist offers dive trips and charters to many sites in the area. See below under "Komodo."

Komodo

There are two ways of diving this relatively unexplored region; either by live-aboard vessels based outside of the immediate Komodo area, or by shore-based diving through one of the two dive operators in Labuanbajo. Live-aboard trips are best arranged in Bali, with the best known operation being Grand Komodo Tours & Travel.

Theoretically, you can fly from Bali to Labuanbajo, via Bima (eastern Sumbawa), every day at 9:20am ($98). In practice, however, the Bima-Labuanbajo air connection is very unreliable, and you would be better off debarking in Bima ($70 one way), taking a minibus to Sape (2 hrs, $1 public bus, $18 charter), and then boarding the ferry to Komodo and Labuanbajo (9–11 hours to Labuanbajo, departs daily from Sape at 8am, $6). To make this early morning connection, one can either overnight in Sape ($5 for very basic room at one of the local *losmens*) or spend the night in Bima and catch the 5am minibus to Sape.

A much more comfortable, quicker, and less expensive alternative is to board one of the Pelni oceanliners which service Labuanbajo from Bali, Ujung Pandang or Kupang/Waingapu. 1st and 2nd class cabins on the brand-new *Tilongkabila* are as comfortable as any hotel room, the meals excellent, and divers carrying heavy gear needn't worry about overweight baggage.

Dive operators

Bajo Beach Diving Club Hotel Bajo, Jl. Yos Sudarso, Labuanbajo, Flores, NTT. Tel: (0385) 41008; fax: 41009. Owner Pak Hendrik Chandra offers dive packages (minimum 2 divers) including gear, 2 tanks, guide, and lunch, to Bidadari, Sabolan/Sebayur, and Komodo/Rinca for $50–$75/diver. This is based on local diesel boat transport, although for a slight price increase he can arrange a speed boat. The club has 2 compressors, 30 tanks and 10 full sets of dive gear. Groups of 10 persons or more receive complimentary meals and lodging at the Hotel Bajo, otherwise, AC rooms $36D. Pak Hendrik offers land-based tour packages. One includes a cave (*Batu Cermin*), a whip fight and an area where there is petrified wood. $50–$125/person depending on group size.

Grand Komodo Tours & Travel (Komodo Alor Safari) Main office: Jl. Hang Tua No. 27, Denpasar 80034, Bali. Tel: (0361) 287166, Fax: (0361) 287165. In Bima: Jl. Sukarno Hatta 45, Bima, Sumbawa, NTB, Tel: (0374) 42018, Fax: (0374) 42812. In Labuahanbajo: Jl. P.W. Papu, Labuhanbajo, Flores, NTT, Tel: (0385) 41377, Fax: (0385) 41378.
E-mail: gkomodot@indosat.net.id
Also: gkomodo@dps.mega.net.id
This experienced outfit, run by the husband and wife team of Nyoman and Reno Kirtya, takes divers to Komodo, Alor and Selayar on two newly-built live-aboards, the *Komodo Plus I* and *II,* both 20-meter hardwood boats built in the Bugis style. Accomodations on the ship

are simple, but comfortable. The *Komodo Plus I* sleeps up to 18 people in a large central cabin (non-private bunks), while the *KP II* has private cabins for 12 divers. Groups fly directly from Bali to Bima, Sumbawa, where they are met by Grand Komodo and driven overland to Sape, where the boats are docked. The southern—and best—sites were all pioneered by Grand Komodo, and this live-aboard is still the best way to dive them.

The outfit has a number of departures for Komodo, Alor and their newest site, Selayar Island south of Sulawesi. Basically, the packages offer a week of diving at each site. Some prices:

Komodo (1 week)	$750
Alor (1 week)	$750
Komodo and Alor (2 weeks)	$1,350
Selayar (1 week)	$750

These prices cover everything except airfare to Bima and drinks. Any of Grand Komodo's four Sape-based boats can also be chartered, and will meet your party in any of the diving areas:

Komodo Plus I or *II*	$800/day
Getting the boat in position	$350/day
Kembang Laut (4 divers)	$600/day
Getting the boat in position	$250/day
Kartika (capacity for 3 divers)	$400/day
Getting the boat in position	$175/day

An excellent combination for a small group is to charter one of the boats and hire Bali-based dive guide Wally Siagan—who did much of the initial pioneering for Grand Komodo, and who currently is familiar with almost 50 sites in the Komodo area—to come along as a guide. Contact Grand Komodo and Wally for details.

Grand Komodo also now offers a land-based dive operation from Labuahanbajo, which is convenient for some of the northern sites.

Komodo Kalypso Dive Center (Varanus Tours and Travel). Main office: Jl. Yos Sudarso 10, P.O. Box 3, Labuanbajo 86554 Flores NTT. Tel: (0385) 41007, fax: 41202. In Jakarta: Varanus Tours and Travel, Jl. Pulonangka Timur III C/3 Jakarta 13260. Tel:/Fax: (021) 4716360.

Owner/guide Pak Linus has been running dive tours in the Komodo area since 1992, and is very knowledgeable about diving in the area. This is a small, but safe and friendly operation, with 2 compressors, 26 tanks, 7 sets of rental gear and a twin-engined fiberglass speedboat. Day trips, including full gear, 2 dives, guide and lunch box run from $75/person for the closer reefs (Sabolan, Bididari, etc) up to $100/person for diving around Komodo and Rinca (using local wooden boats instead attracts a discount of $10/person). Flexible packages, land tours available.

Pro Dive Komodo Batu Gosok, Labuanbajo, Tel: (0361) 286336. Bali office: Jl. Sekar Waru No. 25, Sanur, Bali 80238. Tel: (0361) 286336, Tel:/fax: (0361) 288756.
　　E-mail: prodivebali@bali-paradise.com
　　Web: www.prodive.com.au

This Australian-operated company maintains a diving resort—Puribagus Komodo—on Batu Gosok Island, near Labuanbajo. They have three dive boats, and the manager is a PADI assistant instructor. Pro Dive also runs three- and four-day cruises, including diving, to Komodo on its large ship the *Bali Sea Dancer*.

Maumere City code: 0382

With the recent closing of the most famous of the Maumere dive resorts, there is currently only one land-based operation here.

Seaworld Club (Waiara Cottages) P.O. Box 3, Maumere, Flores, NTT, Tel: (0382) 21570. 38 rooms and bungalows. Lunch ($4), dinner ($5) available. $10–$25S, $15–$30D including breakfast. Daily dive rates, with accommodations, $70–$80 S, $75–$85 D; diving only, $60 for two-tank day with boat. 6 day/6 night dive packages, $420–$480S, $390–$450 D. BC/regulator rental, $15/day. Various land tours available, including Kelimutu (minimum, 4 persons) $15 per head.Kupang

Kupang Includes Roti and Alor
City code for Kupang: 0380

Kupang is a large town, the capital of the Nusa Tenggara Timur province, and has four one-star hotels and a good range of more moderately priced accommodations. English is spoken at most places. Kupang's El Tari airport is 15 km east of downtown Kupang.

Kupang receives daily Merpati flights from Jakarta ($200), Bali ($103), Ujung Pandang ($85), and Maumere ($40) among other cities in the region. Also, international flights from Darwin, Australia, land here.

Merpati Jl. Kosasih No. 2. Tel: (0380) 833833, 822884, 823111, 831949, and 832662.

Dive Operators

Dive Trek East A division of P.T. Asmara Duyung Mas watersports company. Jl. El Tari No. 19, P.O. Box 1120, Kupang, Timor, NTT. Tel: (0380) 821154, Fax: (0380) 824833. E-mail: divealor@kupang.wasantara.net.id
This outfit is run by the Australian father and son team, divemaster Graeme Whitford and PADI dive instructor Donovan Whitford, that began diving this area while managing Pitoby Watersports. Theirs is an efficient agency, and the biggest in this part of Indonesia. They offer packages for diving Kupang, Roti, and Alor. The Whitford's offer all-inclusive packages, beginning with a pick-up at Kupang airport, ranging from 4 days/3 nights to 11 days/10 nights. Here's a sample:
Kupang Bay 4 days/3 nights (5 dives), $245; 6 days/5 nights (9 dives) $345; 8 days/7 nights (11 dives) $595.
Roti 5 days/4 nights (3 dives) $375; 7 days/6 nights (7 dives) $575.
Kupang and Roti 8 days/7 nights (10 dives) $645; 11 days/10 nights (15 dives), $895.
Alor 6 days/5 nights (8 dives) $750 and 8 days/7 nights (12 dives) $1,150. Prices are twin share, and include everything—accommodation, boats, etc.—except airfare from Kupang to Kalabahi, Alor (Merpati, $80 RT). Accommodation is in new AC rooms with attached bath at a *losmen* style hotel. Non-divers 50% of divers price; single supplement, $25 day. Gear rental 15% of package price. Walk-in rates are $100/day (2 dives) including gear rental, transfers and lunch, but are subject to space available. Booking ahead is highly recommended. The Whitfords offer a full range of PADI diving courses as well, and can organize charters to other sites in Eastern Indonesia.

Grand Komodo Tours & Travel (Komodo Alor Safari This outfit offers packages and charters to Alor in its live-aboards *Komodo Plus I* and *II*. See above under "Komodo" for contact details.

Banda City code: 0910

Merpati flies one of its 18-passenger Twin Otters to Bandaneira from Ambon on Mondays, Wednesdays and Saturdays (1 hr, $50). The possibility of cancellations (weather or technical problems) is very real and should always be taken into account.
A local passenger ship makes the Banda–Ambon run on a semi-regular basis or when too many flights have been canceled or there are too many air passengers. Inter-island mixed freighters or large Pelni passenger liners also make the trip about every three weeks.

Dive Operators

Diving is available to guests at the Maulana Inn or the Laguna Inn. For reservations, contact: Hotel Maulana, P.O. Box 3193, Jakarta. Tel: (021) 360372; fax: 360308. In Banda: Tel: (0910) 21022 or 21023; fax: 21024.

Laguna Inn 12 rooms. Three meals $22. $25–$60S, $29–$70D. Some bungalows at $15 on twin-share basis. All plus 10% tax.

Maulana Inn 50 rooms. The best rooms in Bandaneira. The hotel offers a nice view of Gunung Api across the lagoon. Three meals $22/person + 10%. Cold beer, small can $2. Bottle of *arak* $3. Meals are okay, but boring. The *sashimi,* however, is great when available — order one day ahead. $60–$87S; $70–$140D, plus 10% tax.
Diving for people staying at either of these hotels (min of 4 people): To Ai, Hatta and Run, $60 (with your own gear); $75 (regulator and BC provided), $80 (all gear provided). The ride to the dive sites takes 60–70 minutes by speedboat. For other, nearby locations, the rates are: $50, $65, $70, with a two-person minimum. 5–30 minutes by speedboat. Night dives, $30.

Sangalaki and Derawan

At the time of this writing, Borneo Divers, the pioneers of Sangalaki, had not yet restarted their operations on Sangalaki, but were planning to. Currently, the only way to dive Sangalaki and Kakaban is with Derawan Resort on Derawan Island.

Borneo Divers and Sea Sports Head office: 9th Floor, Menara Jubili 88000, Kota Kinabalu, Sabah, Malaysia. Tel: 60 (88) 222226 (8 lines), Fax: (88) 221550.
E-mail: bdivers@po.jaring.my
Web: www.jaring.my/bdivers/

Derawan Resort Derawan Island. Bookings through: Benakutai Hotel OSA 202, Jl. A. Yani, Balikpapan, East Kalimantan 76113, Tel: (0542) 20258, 35997, 31896, Fax: (0542)

20293. This is a well-run operation that has been in business for three years. Two PADI-certified dive masters, both from Bali.

Around Derawan, $75 for two dives. To either Sangalaki or Kakaban, $120 for two dives plus $40 for the boat, to be split among the divers. Night dive, $35. Accommodations: 11 AC cottages with attached toilet. $30S, $50D, meals $7.50.

Jakarta City code: 021

Jakarta, with its 9.5 million people, is the center of Indonesia's government and commerce. There are many dive operators in Jakarta who take divers to Pulau Seribu and the West Java sites. Here are a few of the most reliable:

Aquasport Jl. Bangka Raya 39A, Kel. Pela, Jakarta 12720. Tel: 7199045; fax: 7198974. Contact: Vimal Lekhraj. Active PADI 5-Star IDC Center located in new premises, with a large retail area, 3 classrooms and their own 4m-deep swimming pool. A very professional, reliable full-service facility, offering snorkeling and diving equipment sales, rentals and servicing. The shop is very modern and well-stocked. Affiliate of Divemasters Indonesia.

Divemasters Indonesia Jakarta Hilton International Hotel, Indonesian Bazaar Shop 31, Jl. Jend. Gatot Subroto, Jakarta 10002 Indonesia. Tel: 5703600 ext. 9037, 9006; fax: 7198974, 4204842. Contact: Vimal Lekhraj. This outfit is the country's largest dive specialist. They are a PADI 5-Star Dive Center; a professional, reliable, full-service facility. Apart from offering a full range of PADI courses, they are Indonesia's largest equipment retailer, handling US Divers, Seaquest, Tabata, Underwater Kinetics, Bauer, Poseidon, Sea and Sea and others. Snorkeling and diving equipment sales rentals, servicing, and diving equipment repair seminars. They offer dive trips to Pulau Seribu nearly every weekend and special charters throughout the year. They can also tailor-make dive trips to your needs. They have their own custom catamaran, which is available for charter.

Jakarta Dive School and Pro Shop Jakarta Hilton International Hotel, Indonesia Bazaar Shop 32, Jl. Jend. Gatot Subroto, Jakarta 10002 Indonesia. Tel: 5703600 ext. 9008, 9010, fax: 4204842; Telex: 46673, 46698 HILTON IA. Contact: Andre Pribadi. They organize dive trips to Pulau Seribu, Bali,

Manado, Flores and Ambon. PADI 5-star training facility. Also fills, equipment sales, rentals and repairs, and u/w photography.

Laut Dive Indo Club House Cilandak Sport Centre, Jl. Tb. Simatupang Arteri Cilandak, Jakarta 12014. Tel: 7504963 ext. 109, 129; fax: 7504969. Contacts: Jono Sugiyanto or Slamet. This is a new business, and comes recommended by Jakarta expats as offering reliable service and very competitive rates. While they specialize in dive trips around the Jakarta area, especially Pelabuhan Ratu—where you really need a dive-master familiar with the currents—Laut Dive Indo also runs trips to Indonesia's top dive locations. Young, enthusiastic owner. Certification available, including PADI and SSI.

Stingray Dive Centre Gedung Mangal Wanabakti, Wisma Rimabawan 2d floor, room 4, Jl. Jend. Gatot Subroto, Jakarta Indonesia. Tel: 5703245, 5703264; Tel:/fax: 5700272. Contact: Andy or Hendro
PADI instruction, dive equipment sales and servicing and rentals. They are familiar with many dive spots throughout Indonesia, and have several scheduled departures every month to dive locations near and far. Contact them for a very extensive list of dive trips.

Pindito

The live-aboard *Pindito* is based in Ambon. Trips—around the Banda Sea and the Islands off Western Irian Jaya, depending on the season—are usually of 12 days, with all but one day for diving. Rate: $220/day, all-inclusive (even beer, liquor, equipment rental). Note: we still recommend divers bring their own, recently checked dive gear. The ship can also be chartered, for $3,000/day, with a capacity of up to 16 divers. As the *Pindito* is a busy ship, book well ahead of time (6 months or even a year) for confirmed space. Marketing is aimed at Germany and Switzerland. There are two places for booking. The *Pindito's* main office can also arrange flights, hotel bookings, and extensions to other parts of Indonesia.

Pindito Reisen Ag, Regensdorferstr. 28, Postfach CH 8108 Dällikon, Switzerland. Tel: 41 (1) 845-800. Fax: 41 (1) 845-0815. In Ambon: Pondok Permai RT 18/RW 03, Hative Kecil, Ambon, Maluku, Indonesia. Tel:/Fax: 62 (911) 51569. Contact: Ambon-based manager, Edi Frommenwiler.

Malaysia Country code: 60

Malaysia has radically developed its tourist infrastructure in the past few years, so that now a traveler has a wide choice of accommodation and travel options almost everywhere in the country. The capital, Kuala Lumpur, boasts shops as sophisticated as those in Hong Kong or Singapore, yet, happily, at grass roots level, *kampung* or village life remains much the same as ever. The Malaysians are a hospitable people, whether Malay, Chinese, Indian or mixed race in origin. The diving can be very good, particularly off the the island of Sipadan. Note: Malaysia can be dialed directly from Singapore.

Air travel

Subang International Airport, just 30 minutes from Kuala Lumpur, is the hub of air travel to, from and within the country. Apart from the national carrier, Malaysian Airlines (MAS), some 35 airlines serve the city from all continents. Other destinations within Malaysia served by busy international airports are Langkawi, Penang and Kota Kinabalu. A shuttle service exists between Kuala Lumpur and neighboring Singapore while frequent daily flights link the capital with the capitals of the East Malaysian states in Kuching and Kota Kinabalu.

Land travel

Travel by land in Malaysia is equally easy. A shared taxi service exists between many large towns; the country has a good railway system and airconditioned express buses run both intercity and interstate.

Sea travel

Ferries link the country's many islands with the mainland area. Along the East Coast regular ferry services connect the most popular islands—Tioman, Perhentian or Redang—on a daily basis, while ferries between Butterworth and Penang run every 20 minutes during the day, and those between Kuala Perlis or Kuala Kedah and Langkawi run hourly. There is also a high speed catamaran five times weekly between Penang and Langkawi.

Visas

All travelers must be in possession of a passport valid for at least 6 months. Most Commonwealth and EU countries are granted a visa-free entry for 14 days. Extensions can be made for a period up to three months at immigration offices, providing an onward ticket and sufficient funds are shown.

Health

This rarely presents a problem in Malaysia. A tropical country, it does have mosquitoes but malaria is rare. The most common complaints are usually too much sun and upset stomachs. Both can be remedied by taking preventive measure or paying a visit to a pharmacy or *klinik*—found all over the country. In emergencies, there are government-run and private specialists in all the major towns with doctors who speak English. Generally, the water throughout the country is safe, though opting for boiled water is a wise precaution.

Money exchange

Banks and money-changers will convert travelers' checks and foreign currency to the Malaysian dollar, or ringgit, as it is known, in all the major cities. Opening hours are generally 10 am–3 pm but the days vary from state to state. Credit cards are widely accepted. Carry plenty of small change and notes—invaluable for taxis and buses.

The ringgit was one of the first of the

Asian currencies to fall in the late '90s, and at the time we went to press (January 1999) it was trading at US$1=M$3.8. Since it is still fluctuating, please check before traveling.

Climate

Divers in Malaysia will enjoy tropical weather year-round. During the northeast monsoon (November to late March) the East Coast is mostly wet and the West Coast, dry. With the Westerlies, between April and October, it is the East Coast that is dry, and the west that is rainy. The same is largely true of Sabah. Temperatures at sea level rarely fall below 22°C and infrequently rise above 32°C.

Accommodations and food

There is no shortage of luxury hotels in Malaysia's capital and resort destinations! However, there is also a wealth of less expensive accommodation and simple guesthouses throughout the country. You can pay anything from M$20 (US$5) for a double room in a guesthouse to over M$400 (US$100) a double room in a 5-star resort. See the individual areas for more details.

Malaysian cuisine is varied, spicy and delicious, combining the pungent spices with local vegetables, fish and fowl. In all parts of the country, hawker stalls will serve fast food, Malaysian-style, for a few ringgit. Indian food and Chinese cuisine are also widely available, while international and western dishes can be found in restaurants in most of the more popular resorts.

What to bring

Divers should bring only the essentials. Weight restrictions apply on some of the flights served by small domestic airplanes. All resorts and dive operations will rent the basic equipment, but a suit is a recommended extra. Lycra or 3 mm will generally be fine. Bring sufficient batteries, sun cream and spares for your dive gear if you are diving off the islands.

Dive emergencies

The best advice for divers is always to dive conservatively. If an emergency arises, there are naval decompression chambers at Tanjong Gelang on the East Coast (near Kuantan) and Lumut on the West Coast of Peninsular Malaysia.

Kuala Lumpur City code: 03

Dive Operators

There are a number of operators based in Kuala Lumpur. Below are two we can recommend:

Borneo Divers and Sea Sports (KL) 127M Jalan SS21/37 Damansara Utama, 47400 Petaling Jaya, Selangor. Tel: 60-3/717-3066; Fax: 60-3/718-4303.
   E-mail: bdivers@po.jaring.my
   Web: www.jaring.my/bdivers/
Known for its excellent PADI 5-star IDC facility and diving operation in Sabah, this company runs tours to Sipadan and the islands in Tunku Abdul Rahman Marine Park. See section on Sipadan, below, for full details. In Kuala Lumpur it operates a 5-star deve center and a comprehensive underwater photo center and is a fully licensed travel reservation agency for bookings to its Sabah-based diving and beyond, as well as a well-equipped dive shop.

Scuba Point 135 Jalan SS2/24, 47300 Petaling Jaya, Selangor. Tel: 60-3/774-7288; Fax: 60-3/775-4288. This PADI 5-star IDC facility has a well-equipped dive shop offering sole distribution in Malaysia of Aqualung equipment and repair services. A number of regular dive trips are also available to the east coast islands of Redang, Tioman and Perhentian.

Sipadan

Sipadan Island is located in Sabah, East Malaysia, off the coast of northeast Borneo. Access is either via Singapore, Johor Bahru or Kuala Lumpur to Kota Kinabalu, the capital of Sabah, then by a domestic service of MAS to Tawau or Semporna on the southeast coast. From there you are taken by speedboat to Sipadan.

Three companies operate dive resorts on this island. The only way of reaching Sipadan is through their organizations.

When to visit

July through September are busiest and theoretically the best months to dive off Sipadan, with the north-east monsoon. Late November through January are the worst, with decreased visibility, colder air and water, but better possibilities to see mantas, whale sharks and hammerheads.

Diving

Sipadan is not for neophyte divers. While only basic certification is required, experience ensures a far better time. No certification courses are given on Sipadan, but Borneo Divers offer some advanced courses.

What to bring

UW flashlight, insect repellent, and a wet suit of at least 3 mm thickness.

Dive operators and resorts

Because of impending new restrictions on diver numbers to Sipadan, prices and packages were not available at the time of printing. In the past, packages at Sipadan ranged from US$125 to US$175 a day. We advise you to contact the operators directly.

Borneo Divers and Sea Sports (Sabah) 9th Floor, Menara Jubili, 53 Jalan Gaya, Kota Kinabalu, 88000 Sabah. Tel: 60-88/222-2226, Fax: 60-88/221550 and 265055.
E-mail: bdivers@po.jaring.my
Web: www.jaring.my/bdivers/
Borneo Divers runs the Sipadan Island Dive Lodge on Sipadan. Prices include airport transfers, air fares from KK to Tawau (where it has a branch office), transfers from Tawau to Sipadan, meals, twin-share accommodation and diving. Equipment is for rent on the island by prior arrangement. Specialty cavern courses are available.

Pulau Sipadan Resort (PSR) 484 Block P, Bandar, Sabindo; P.O. Box 61120, Tawau 91021, Sabah. Tel: 60-89/765-200; Fax: 60-89/763-575.
PSR offers food and accommodation packages ex-Tawau or including airport transfers, round-trip from KK. Non-divers: 20% off. Up to three boat dives per day; unlimited beach diving and night dives in front of resort, which is closest to the dropoff. PSR also has dive packages to Mabul, Kapalai and Lankayan.

Sipadan Dive Centre (SDC) 1 11-03 Wisma Merdeka, Jalan Tun Razak, Kota Kinabalu, 88000 Sabah. Tel: 60-88/240-584, Fax: 60-88/440-415.
Up to three boat dives per day; unlimited beach diving and night dives. Non-divers: 20% off.

Kota Kinabalu and Layang-Layang
City code for Kota Kinabalu: 088

Kota Kinabalu can be reached by regular daily flights from West Malaysia, Singapore and elsewhere regionally. Local buses run from the city center to the beach at Tanjung Aru and to other suburban destinations. Taxis are available at ranks in the center and are metered.

Accommodations and food

Hotel rooms vary from the expensive to the simple. Two luxury hotels offer fine accommodation, one in the heart of town and the other at Tanjung Aru. There are plenty of restaurants to suit all tastes and budgets. Kota Kinabalu excels in its seafood and has a wealth of temperate-climate vegetables from the highlands. You can pay anything from M$5 for a simple meal in an open-air market, to a US$100 for a lavish dinner in a fancy hotel.

Dive operators

Borneo Divers 9th Floor, Menara Jubili, 53 Jalan Gaya, Kota Kinabalu, 88000 Sabah. Tel: 60-88/222-2226, Fax: 60-88/221550 and 265055. operates trips to Tunku Abdul Rahman National Park (as well as Sipadan).

Coral Island Cruises 1002 10th Floor, Wisma Merdeka, Jalan Tun Razak, P.O. Box 14527, Kota Kinabalu 88851, Sabah. Tel: 60-88/223-490, Fax: 60-88/223-404. Runs day trips to Tunku Abdul Rahman National Park and arranges trips to Layang-Layang Island Resort.

Layang-Layang Island Resort Lot T028, 3rd Floor, Sungei Wang Plaza, Jalan Sultan Ismail, 55100 Kuala Lumpur. Tel: 60-3/243-3166; Fax: 60-3/243-3177. The only commercial operation on this remote oceanic atoll, Layang-Layang Island Resort has 70 guestrooms and is open for 9 months every year, from February to October. Packages include full board, twin-sharing accommodation and three boat dives.

Pulau Payar
City code for Langkawi: 04

Pulau Payar is accessible from the island of Langkawi, a popular tourist destination and a duty-free island off the west coast of Peninsular Malaysia.

Getting there

Ferries run from the mainland for M$10 one way between Kuala Perlis and Langkawi. A daily ferry operates from Penang to Langkawi for M$35 one way. The island is linked by frequent MAS flights from the capital, Kuala Lumpur, by daily flights from Singapore and seasonal flights from Penang.

The *Langkawi Coral*, a high speed catamaran, leaves from the Kuah jetty on Langkawi each morning at 10.30 am, returning at 3.30 pm. The trip takes 50 minutes and the vessel docks at a newly erected reef platform.

Accommodations and food

Langkawi's hotels and beach resorts offer a wide range of accommodation, from 5-star deluxe class to moderately low-priced hotels and chalets at budget prices. Expect to pay M$200–M$2,000 for a room in a deluxe class hotel and as little as M$15 for a budget chalet.

Seafood is the favorite in Langkawi and plenty of small restaurants in Kuah specialize in this. Breakfast or lunch in Kuah may cost as little as M$5–10 per person, while dinner starts around M$15.

Dive operators

Langkawi Coral Lot 1-21, Jetty Point Complex, Langkawi, Kedah. Tel: 60-4/966 7318, Fax: 60-4/966 7308.

Sriwani Tours & Travel The owner and operator of the Langkawi Coral offers a daily trip to Pulau Payar, for M$220 per adult, including transfers, buffet lunch, boat rides and snorkeling equipment. Diving costs are extra, rom M$70 per dive.

Terengganu

This state's coastline offers a score of delightful offshore islands and the best snorkeling and diving in Peninsular Malaysia.

Getting there

Access to the offshore islands is by boat from Kuala Terengganu, Kuala Besut, Tanjong Merang, Dungun and Marang.

All these coastal villages and towns are linked by bus or taxi from the state capital, Kuala Terengganu, and with Kuantan, south, in the state of Pahang.

If visiting a resort, the hotel boat will pick you up at the relevant port. If you want to dive or snorkel on an individual basis, you have to negotiate a fare with one of the boats that ply the route. You can get to Perhentian from Kuala Besut. It takes approximately 90 minutes and costs around M$20 per passenger. You can also get to Lang Tenggah from here. Redang is accessible from Kuala Terengganu and Tanjong Merang.

From Dungun, you can hire a boat to Tenggol. It takes some 60 minutes. Costs depend on how many share a boat. Kapas is accessible from Marang in around 30 minutes. Costs vary similarly.

Dive operators and resorts

All the companies listed above under Kuala Lumpur offer inclusive-cost dive trips to these islands. Most of the better hotels along the coast also have operational headquarters and booking offices in Kuala Lumpur.

Perhentian Island Resort Perhentian Besar. Book in Kuala Lumpur: 22nd Floor, Menara Promet, Jalan Sultan Ismail, 50250 Kuala Lumpur. Tel: 60-3/243-4984; Fax: 60-3/244-8530, 1, 2. This small hotel is accessible from Kuala Besut and offers a variety of accommodation from dormitory beds to air-conditioned chalets.

Berjaya Redang Beach Resort Book through Best Western Reservations, worldwide, or in Kuala Lumpur, Tel: 60-3/242-9611, Fax: 60-3/244-2527, or in Singapore, Tel: 65/227 3688, Fax: 65/225 4966. This 150-room international standard resort hotel on the southern shores of Redang offers good facilities for snorkeling and diving. Access takes 35 minutes by private ferry from Kuala Terengganu.

Primula Park Royal Resort On the beach at Kuala Terengganu. Reservations can be made through its Kuala Lumpur head office: Southern Pacific Hotel Corporation, Kuala Lumpur Park Royal, Jalan Sultan Ismail, 50250 Kuala Lumpur, Tel: 60-3/242-5288, Fax: 60-3/242-4877. Offers daily diving trips to Kapas Island.

Tioman and Aur

Tioman offers visitors plenty in the way of recreation and excellent beaches. There is an international-standard hotel with an 18-hole golf course, and scores of smaller, bungalow-style guesthouses and hotels can be found. Costs from M$5 for a room upwards.

Getting there

Forty-three nautical miles from Mersing on the eastern coast of Peninsular Malaysia, the daily ferry takes 90 minutes. There is also a hydrofoil service from time to time. From Singapore (122 nautical miles away) the journey by high speed catamaran takes 4.5 hours.

Tioman also has daily flight connections with Kuala Lumpur, aboard Berjaya Air, which take 70 minutes. Information through Malaysian Airlines, offices worldwide. The island is connected with Singapore, too, by daily flights on Pelangi Air, which take 40 minutes. Information through Singapore Airlines offices, worldwide.

The journey to Aur from Mersing takes around 4.5 hours, while from Singapore the journey can take between 8 and 10 hours, depending on the chartered vessel.

Accommodations

Berjaya Tioman Beach Resort P.O. Box 4, 86800 Mersing, Johor, Tel: 60-9/419-1000, Fax: 60-9/419-1718. Bookings also in Kuala Lumpur, Tel: 60-3/242-9611, Fax: 60-3/244-2527, and in Singapore, Tel: 65/227 6698, Fax: 65/225 4966. This is the smartest hotel on the island and offers international-standard rooms and suites. The hotel operates a PADI dive center and has regular departures to all the best dive sties.

Dive operators

Dive Asia operates two dive centers on Tioman, a 5-star PADI IDC facility at Kampong Salang, Tel: 60-9/419-5017, Fax: 60-9/419-5010, and another center at Kampong Tekek, Tel: 60-9/419-1337, 60-9/419-1334. It offers two dives, lunch and equipment from M$160 per day, Open Water Courses (M$795), Advanced Open Water Courses (M$550) and specialty courses. The friendly dive shop rents tanks and gear, and sells a good range of diving equipment and spares.

Tioman Island Resort (see above) operates a PADI dive center on the beach by the hotel. Tel: 60-9/419 1000 and ask for the dive center extension. Daily dives cost M$105 including equipment, Open Water Courses (M$800) and Advanced Open Water Courses. The center's dive store sells diving equipment and spares.

Live-aboards

Live-aboard possibilities can be checked out through the marinas at Tanjung Aru (KK) and Port Klang (KL).

The Reclaim II

Since 1994, when the waters to the north and east of Bintan were reopened after a 10-year ban, the *Reclaim II* has pioneered diving in the area. From April to October, she visits the Riau archipelago every weekend, and is also available for charter. Encounters with dolphins, Spanish mackerel, tuna, bumphead parrotfish, blue-spotted stingrays, batfish, several species of shark and outstanding soft and hard corals are frequent. Dive sites range from shallow pristine reefs to dramatic dropoffs (to 25m).

Built in Terengganu, Malaysia, in 1991 and owned and operated by Singapore-based Marsden Bros Dive Center, this 56-foot motor yacht has spacious teak decks, 3 airconditioned cabins sleeping 8 passengers, 2 bathrooms, a galley and dining area. Onboard diving equipment includes 2 compressors, and tanks, weights and equipment available for hire. *Reclaim II* is powered by twin 240hp diesel engines and equipped with GPS, radar, autopilot, sonar, forward-looking sounder, generator, VHF radio, CD player and inflatable dinghy with outboard motor.

The liveaboard trips are distinguished by her professional and fun crew, which includes expatriate zoologists and PADI instructors; excellent cuisine; and adventure diving in secluded waters. 3 days/2 nights package (7 dives): S$500 per person or private charter (up to 8 passengers): S$3,840. 2 days/1 night package (5 dives): S$325 per person or private charter (up to 10 passengers): S$3,250. All meals and dives included.

Marsden Bros Dive Centre 25 Faber Park, Singapore 129113. Tel: 65/778-8287; Fax: 65/773-2265. E-mail: marsbros@pacific.net.sg.

The Philippines Country code: 63

The Philippines is an island nation—7,107 of them at best count. Travel and trade between the islands has been a predominant feature of life here for centuries. Tourism is a major dollar earner and there is no shortage of domestic destinations. The traveler these days also has a wide range of transportation options, from jet planes and air-conditioned coasters to simple inter island ferries and ramshackle, crowded jeepneys. A welter of development throughout the islands is continuing to produce world class hotels and resorts, both luxury and budget in concept, in some of the most unique and intriguing corners of the country.

Eco-tourism is gaining ground too, and divers arrive in droves to discover what must be one of the best organized industries in Asia, given the tyranny of distance and poor communications which still plague some parts of the country.

In Manila and many provincial capitals, such as Cebu and Davao, giant shopping malls are becoming part of the every day scene. The Philippines is moving forward towards 2000 at a pace which amazes even the Filipinos themselves, but the outgoing, friendly character of the people remains intact anywhere you may happen to roam.

Air travel

The county's leading gateway, Ninoy Aquino International Airport (NAIA) in Pasay City, Manila, has been subject to much criticism in the local press for its lack of infrastructure from time to time. In fact, if the traveler follows a few simple rules, he will survive NAIA easily. After exiting the customs shed, one can avail of the Avis coupon taxi system, which, although costing more than a regular taxi, is a fixed price paid in full before departure. If being met by a hotel or travel agent's rep, look for the person carrying a sign identifying themselves after exiting customs. If they are not there, pass out of the main doors, cross the road and proceed down the ramp to the waiting shed adjacent to the car park where everyone is actually supposed to wait.

There is a DOT approved metered taxi rank across from the terminal. As a rough guide, expect to pay around US$1.50 to US$2 to Makati or Ermita, US$2.50 to US$4 or more to Quezon City, depending on traffic. The guard on duty is supposed to give you a slip of paper with your destination and the taxi's plate number on it in case you have any complaints. Mactan International Airport on Mactan island, Cebu, is the up-and-coming gateway, and is served by airlines flying direct from Japan, Singapore, Malaysia and elsewhere. It is a US$3.50 to US$4 taxi ride away from the center of Cebu City, US$1.75 or less to any resort on Mactan Island. Taxis in Cebu and Manila are ALWAYS supposed to use their meters: ignore any protestations to the contrary.

Both airports have tourist information centers, currency exchange facilities, and duty free shops, as well as car rental agencies and hotel hospitality desks. Inbound passengers have a duty free allowance of US$1,000 which can be used up within 48 hours of arrival at any of the huge duty free outlets in Manila (close to the airport), Subic, Angeles, Cebu, San Fernando Pampanga, and elsewhere. There is a departure tax of 500 pesos for all international flights. International flights require check-in 2 hours before departure, as immigration exit queues are often long. Reconfirm your onward flight within 72 hours of departure, and allow for the often heavy traffic, especially in Manila.

Domestic airlines

Several domestic airlines serve the provinces. Prices are very reasonable, and the coverage is extensive. Divers (and golfers) can join

Philippine Airlines' Flying Sportsman's Club to avail of increased baggage allowances. It costs 50 pesos to join. Apply at the nearest PAL office for more information. Domestic flights require a check-in one hour before departure. Unclaimed seats are usually given away to stand-by passengers 35 minutes before take off. Domestic airports around the country are mostly quite efficient, though take-off and landings can sometimes be a bit hairy. Departure tax is 50 pesos for domestic flights originating in Manila; regional airport charges vary.

Domestic airline destinations

Although domestic routes are subject to change, the following list of airlines and the destinations they fly to is accurate as this goes to press in January, 1999.

Philippine Airlines Reservations 63-2/816-6691, 815-0054, 819-1771. Destinations: Manila, Cebu, Davao, Cagayan de Oro, Zamboanga, Bacolod, Iloilo, Butuan, Kalibo (Boracay), Puerto Princesa, General Santos, Tagbilaran, Tacloban, Legaspi City.

Air Philippines Reservations: 63-2/843-7011. Destinations: Manila, Cebu, Bacolod, Cagayan de Oro, Cotabato, Davao, General Santos, Iloilo, Kalibo (Boracay), Legaspi City, Puerto Princesa, San Jose (Mindoro).

Grand Air Reservations: 63-2/833-8090; 833-8080. Destinations: Manila, Cebu, Davao, Cagayan de Oro.

Cebu Pacific Reservations: 63-2/636-4938 through –45. Destinations: Manila, Cebu, Iloilo, Cagayan de Oro, Davao, Bacolod, Tacloban, Kalibo (Boracay).

Asian Spirit Reservations: 63-2/840-3811 through –16, 840-1712 and –13, 750-1442. Destinations: Manila, Caticlan (Boracay), Cauayan, Masbate, Sandoval, Naga, Busuanga (Coron) Tablas (Romblon).

Air Ads Reservations: 63-2/833-3264. Destination: Caticlan (Boracay).

Pacific Air Reservations: 63-2/832-2731, 833-2391. Destinations: Caticlan (Boracay), Coron, Baguio.

Soriano Air Reservations: 63-2/833-3852, 831-4207. Destination: El Nido.

Land travel

Filipinos love to travel, and there is always a way to get somewhere. A wide variety of buses, from luxury air conditioned liners to diesel-spewing behemoths serve anywhere that can be reached by road. Jeepneys and motorized tricycles go where the buses can't, which can make for exciting, if uncomfortable, excursions. Carry all your valuables with you, preferably in a body belt, as bag slashings are not uncommon on some routes, especially on regular buses plying the Batangas to Manila route.

Sea travel

Visitors who have the time might prefer the option of sailing between the islands. While luxury yachts can be chartered by the affluent few, several shipping lines, such as **WG&A Superferry** and **Sulpicio Lines** have excellent services connecting Manila and Cebu with dozens of ports around the country. Accommodation ranges from deck space to first-class suites, and there are quite passable discos and restaurants on board some of the vessels.

It will almost certainly be necessary at some point to board a *banca* boat, the motorized outrigger canoe which predominates in this part of the world. Sit where the boatman tells you, and be prepared to get splashed a bit. The driest part of the boat on a smaller *banca* is usually under the bow, so stow anything that has to be kept dry there.

Visas

Most foreign nationals with valid passports and an onward ticket are given 21 days on entry. For longer trips, visa extensions up to one year can be arranged in the country at the regional bureau of immigration offices or through a local travel agent, but if planning to stay longer, you should apply for a 59-day temporary visitor's visa at any Philippine embassy or consulate. Fees are minimal, and the visa usually takes just a few hours to process.

Health

The Philippines has some excellent medical facilities, and others which are not so excellent. Dentistry is cheap and often of extremely high standard, and there are several good medical centers in Manila.

Most illnesses occur through over-indulging in any or all of the several delicacies of the islands, San Miguel beer topping the list. Overexposure to the sun is another common cause of discomfort. Proper precautions should be observed to avoid sunburn, as the local remedy of applying vinegar (or other, more pungent, liquids) on affected parts is best avoided. Tap water is heavily chlorinated in cities, and for the most part should not be consumed without prolonged boiling outside of them. Bottled water is widely available, but watch out for the ice in the soft drinks.

Climate

There are two seasons in the Philippines: the dry season (from March to May) and the rainy season (from June to February). Tropical depressions, tropical storms, and typhoons affect parts of the country from June to October, especially in the so-called "typhoon belt" from Southern Luzon to the Visayas. Between storms, the weather is often quite balmy for long periods. December through February are the coolest months. Average temperature is 22.2 degrees C; humidity averages 77 percent.

Money

Visitors can bring in any amount of currency, but you should declare any amount over US$3,000 in cash to avoid any complications when exiting. The export of more than 1,000 pesos is disallowed, and note that it is necessary to produce official central bank receipts issued by authorized currency exchange dealers to change your excess pesos back to another currency before leaving.

Banking is notoriously awkward in the Philippines. In an emergency, it is usually safer to use the Standard Chartered or the Hongkong Bank to have funds telegraphically transferred (TT) from outside the country. Most international credit cards are honored after verification. It is advisable to check first before booking into a resort or paying for services as some merchants cannot verify cards quickly. Travelers checks, although safer, are harder to cash and are exchanged at a lower rate than cash.

At the time of this writing, US$1 = P39.44, but the currency is prone to volatility.

Communications

With the advent of cellular communications and deregulated telecommunications, many resort areas in the Philippines that until recently relied on expensive, slow, extremely frustrating, and often inaccurate reservation systems are now able to transact business on the internet. This has allowed many dive resorts to make quantum leaps forward in their communications in many previously "remote" areas. Internet access can be found in most cities and in a growing number of resorts such as Puerto Galera, Boracay, the Visayas and Mindanao. There is extensive cellular coverage throughout the archipelago. International GSM roamers can utilize local Globe and Islacom cells in many areas.

Please note: to the annoyance of subscribers, telephone numbers tend to change periodically as the country's booming telecommunication providers upgrade their systems.

Photography

Serious photographers should bring their own slide film, especially Kodachrome (unavailable and no processing in the Philippines). E-6 films and processing are available, but only in Manila and on some live-aboards. Fuji Velvia is about US$7 a roll in Manila.

Although they claim to be film-safe, some x-ray machines at airports in the Philippines are not. Insist on having precious films inspected by hand and keep them in lead-lined bags if at all possible. Small lithium and even alkaline batteries are not readily available outside of major population centers, and spares for cameras and strobes, especially O-rings, seals, gaskets, etc., are almost non-existent, so be sure to pack plenty of spare parts.

Manila City code: 02

Manila Bay is not recommended as a dive spot. However, Manila is a good place to start planning and organizing your diving vacation and home to several retail stores worth a visit as well. The **Philippine Commission on Sports Scuba Diving (PCSSD)** is also headquartered in Manila, at the Department of Tourism (DOT) building at Agrafina Circle (Tel: 63-2/525-4412 or 524-3735, E-mail: pcssd@ptamisd.amanet.net). The PCSSD is the regulatory body of the local scuba industry. Registered dive operators are bound to a code of diving ethics and safety. When possible, check to see if the dive center you plan to dive with is registered with PCSSD as it can say a lot about the operator's integrity. The PCSSD operates two recompression chambers, one in Manila, one in Cebu.

There is another chamber in Subic (Tel: 63-47/252-4751 and 252-4571) operated by the Subic Bay Freeport Authorities.

The Philippine Diver is a glossy, full colour magazine filled with information, articles and complete PCSSD listings avaialble through subscription ($25 for one year, three issues a year) and at many dive centers and resorts throughout the Philippines. Tel/Fax: 63-2/525-8041.

E-mail: diver@diver.com.ph

Web: www.diver.com.ph

Dive operators

Most live-aboard vessels and many resorts around the islands have representative offices in Manila, and there are several dive tour specialists around town too. We can recommend those listed below.

Whitetip Divers Joncor ll Building, 1362 A. Mabini St, Ermita, Manila, Tel: 02/521-2751, Fax: 02/522-1165.

E-mail: whitetip@mnl.sequel.net

Web: www.umall.com/whitetip

Retails gear, including Dacor and Sherwood brands, and is an excellent source of good information wherever you may wish to visit. Whitetip Dive Tours can arrange dive travel to suit most schedules and budgets throughout the islands and overseas. They also act as agents for several budget and regular live-aboard boats. Whitetip has branches at Alabang (Tel: 63-2/842-4351, E-mail: papinc@mnl.sequel.net) and in Cebu (Tel: 63-32/254-2623, E-mail: whitetip@cebu.weblinq.net), Dumaguete (Tel: 63-35/255-2402, E-mail: whitetip@mozcom.com) and Davao (Tel/Fax: 63-82/222-1721).

Dive Buddies has two stores in Metro Manila, at Robelle Mansions, 877, J.P. Rizal St., Makati City (Tel: 02/899-7388, Fax: 02/899-7393) and at L&S Building, 1414 Roxas Boulevard, Manila (Tel: 02/521-9168 and 69, Fax: 02/521-9170).

E-mail: divephil@mnl.sequel.net

Web: www.divephil.com

This is another full-service retail store and package specialist worth visiting. Available brands include Beuchat and Ikelite. Dive courses (PADI, NAUI, SSI and CMAS) are taught using an in-house swimming pool. Technical diving training and equipment is available, and there is an in-house tank hydrotesting and inspection facility. Dive Bud-

dies also has a cozy, budget dive resort, Dinky Little Dive Camp, in Anilao.

Aquaventure Philippines 7801 Saint Paul St., San Antonio Village, Makati City. Tel: 63-2/895-3561, Fax: 63-2/813-0494.

E-mail: aqua@skyinet.net

Web: www.aquaventure.com

This is the longest and best established dive retail, training and travel operation in the country. Major brands of equipment available include Aqualung, Spiro, Sea Quest and Suunto. Technical diving courses and equipment are also offered. Aquaventure's headquarters is a custom built, three-store building featuring a dive training pool with view windows.

Other stores in Manila are at Almeda Building, 2150 Pasong Tamo St., Makati City (Tel: 63-2/844-1492, Fax: 63-2/844-1996) a PADI 5-Star IDC facility, and at Unit 10-A, Park Square 1, Ayala Center, Makati City (Tel: 63-2/813-0495, Fax: 63-2/813-0494). Other Aquaventure branches are found in Cebu (Tel: 63-32/345-1571, Fax: 63-32/346-7518) and at the Amanpulo Resort in Pamilican (Tel: 63-2/895 3561, Fax: 63-2/813-0494).

Aquaventure also have a resort in Anilao, Batangas, **Aquaventure Reef Club** (Tel: 63-2/895-3561, Mobile: 63-912/329-8214, Fax: 63-2/813-0494).

Scuba World Inc 1181 Vito Cruz Extension, corner Kakarong St. Tel: 63-2/895-3551, 890-7805 and 890-7807, Fax: 63-2/890-8982.

E-mail: swidive@compass.com.ph

Web: www.scubaworld.com.ph

A PADI 5-Star facility offering complete retail services, featuring Scubapro, Tusa, and Uwatec, and Bauer compressors. Scuba World is afiliated wtih PADI, NAUI, CMAS, BSAC and PDIC. Customlzed scuba training classrooms and a swimming pool rounds out the facitilty. Complete Technical Diving services are also avaialable. Other branches are found in San Juan at 714 Jose Abad Santos St. (Tel: 63-2/724-6501 and 724-8880) and at 90 A. Aguirre Avenue, BF Homes, Paranaque (Tel: 63-2/807-8134 and 809-4268).

Other Scuba World outlets can be found in Boracay (Tel: 63-36/288-3310) and Cebu (Tel: 63-32/412-2275, Fax: 63-32/231-6009, E-mail: swidive@cebu.pw.net.ph). The Cebu outlet is a PADI 5-Star IDC facility.

Scuba World operates several live-aboard vessels including the *MY Island Explorer, MY Ocean Explorer* and *MY Blue Planet*. Reservations for Tubataha and other remote dive sites are taken at any Scuba

World outlet.

Asia Divers 57, Gil Puyat Avenue, Villaflor Building, Unit 3, Palanan, Makati City. Tel: 63-2/845 3248.
E-mail: asiadivers@vasia.com
Web: www.asiadivers.com
This is a Puerto Galera–based PADI 5-Star IDC facility dive resort that recently opened a dive center in Manila. Retail equipment available includes Cressi-Sub, Aqualung, and Seaquest. Complete PADI training to Master Instructor is available, as is technical diving equipment and training.

Also worth checking out are:

Dive Shoppe at 71-B Constancia Building, Timog Avenue, Quezon City. Tel: 63-2/921-2020 and 413-6734, Cell: 63-917/533-1266.
E-mail: dveshop@skyinet.net
A PADI dive center with good Anilao connections. Agents for Seac Sub.

Reefs and Oceans 2nd floor Adriatico Executive Center, 1920 M. Adriatico, Malate, Manila. Tel: 63-2/526-0409 and 821-5048, Fax: 63-2/525-4644.
E-mail: rguzman@the.net.ph
Web: www.the.net.ph/~rguzman
A little hard to find, but situated very close to popular Malate hotels.

Cocktail Divers U/g 33, Citiland 8, 98 Gil Puyat Avenue, Makati City. Tel: 63-2/892-1443.
E-mail: cdiver@vasia.net
Web: www.vasia/cdiver
Operates three dive centers in Puerto Galera (Cell: 63-912/353-4177) and one in Dumaguete (Cell: 63-912/891-2066, E-mail: wet.expeditions@usa.net). Dive equipment sales, rental, PADI instruction and dive travel services. German management.

La Union Area code: 072

La Union is accessible by road from Manila. If you prefer not to rent a car, with or without a driver, there are several bus companies running regular air conditioned buses daily to La Union from Manila (**Maria De Leon, Times Transit**), about a 6 hour trip costing around US$5.

Among other private operators running scheduled trips, **Fly The Bus** has a regular schedule from Manila to La Union and Baguio, via Angeles City, every Monday,

Wednesday and Friday. Cost is about US$15 one way. Bookings can be made through **Swagman Travel** (Tel: 63-2/526-1295, Fax: 63-2/522-3663).

Dive operators

Ocean Deep Dive Centre VFW building, Kilometer 263, Marcos Hiway, Bauang, La Union. Tel/Fax: 63-72/414-440.
E-mail: oceandp@net.com.ph
Ocean Deep is home to Tim Aukshun, PADI Regional Course Director. Naturally, expert training to all levels is available here. Equipment sales, rentals, hotel and travel reservations can also be made here.

Expect to pay around US$35 for a 2 tank dive with equipment, guide and boat. Jellyfish particles are quite common in the warmer upper layers of water at some times of the year, so full coverage, such as a Lycra suit, is recommended. Trips to 100 Islands, 14 mile Reef and further north can be arranged. Diving is mainly done off 2 man *banca* boats, which can sometimes get a little hairy. They cost around US$5 per head per dive. To the north of San Fernando a few miles is a good surfing beach with cheap cottages (US$15 a night) at San Juan.

There are several smaller resorts next to each other along the coast here, all with reasonable rooms and good restaurants. Some of these are **Southern Palms Resort** (Tel: 63-72/415384), **Bali Hai Resort** (Tel: 63-72/412-504), **Cabana Resort** (Tel: 63-72/412-824), and **China Sea Resort** (Tel: 63-72/414-821), all located on Bauang Beach, La Union. Room rates vary between US$20 and US$40 a night for a double room; look for seasonal discounts.

Subic Bay Area code: 047

International flights from Taipei have now opened up the way for further development of the tourist industry in the Free Port Zone of Subic Bay. An air shuttle service from Manila is also available: unfortunately, there are no taxis to take passengers anywhere upon arrival yet. Fast ferry boats operate regular services from the PICC Ferry Terminals in Manila, close to the Manila Yacht Club, to Lamao in historical Bataan across Manila Bay. Cost is currently 140 peso. At Lamao, take a 10 peso tricycle ride to the hiway. Once there, take any Southbound bus to Dinalupan, cross the road and catch a Victory

Liner Westbound to Olongapo City, an affordable and interesting way of making the journey in two an a half hours.

A 3-hour drive from Manila, some of it over rather poor roads, Subic is visited by hordes of "duty free day trippers" from Manila, eager to spend their duty free allowance at the stores inside the Free Port Zone, formerly a US Navy Base. **Victory Liners** (Tel: 63-2/833-0293) is the easiest way to get there if travelling by bus. They run several air-conditioned trips daily to and from Olongapo. Tickets are under US$3.50. **Fly The Bus** also operates a daily service to Subic from Manila via Angeles City. Bookings can be made through **Swagman Travel** (Tel: 63-2/526-1295, Fax: 63-2/522-3663).

Accommodations

A wide variety of accommodation is available locally, from five-star hotels to small nipa huts, and bungalows at prices to suit all pockets. The beaches bordering the bay are becoming increasingly popular as weekend getaways for Manila-based families, and there is a variety of night life and dining options available. **By the Sea** (Barrio Barretto, Subic Bay Olongapo, Tel: 63-47/222-2888, Fax: 63-47/222-2718) is a popular hotel with rooms from US$10 and up. **White Rock Hotel** (Matain, Subic Bay, Olongapo, Tel: 63-47/222-5555), has just re-opened. Rooms are pricier here, starting at around US$90. There are several other places to park yourself ranging from a few dollars a night upwards.

A little further North is **Capones Beach Diving Resort** (Barrio Pundaquit, San Antonio, Zambales, Tel: 63-2/522-3650). Room rates are listed at around US$45, but PADI divers get a 10% discount, and you can usually negotiate seasonal and other discounts.

Dive operators

Subic Bay Aquasports Bldg 249 Waterfront Rd., Subic Bay Freeport Zone, SBMA, Olongapo City. Tel: 63-47/252-7343, 252-3005, Tel/Fax: 63-2/813-5677.

E-mail: sbas@potalinc.com
A duty-free scuba retail outlet and organiser of fine wreck diving aboard a variety of vessels, Aquasports also offers PADI instruction, air and equipment rentals. A two tank dive with a boat will cost around US$65, including a guide.

Nasugbu

One reaches Nasugbu in western Batangas after a two-hour drive southwest of Manila. The road takes you over the mountain at Tagaytay, where you get a breathtaking views of the volcano poking out of Taal Lake. **BLTB Bus Co** has a regular service to Nasugbu, but a rented car is a better bet.

There are several decent places to stay along the coast at Nasugbu, for instance at nearby Matabungkay Beach, but there is only a limited diving infrastructure. Aside from bringing all you own equipment from Manila and winging it, which is a viable option for those who know the area's dive sites well enough, visiting scuba divers really have three choices.

Fortune Island Resort Tel: 63-2/817-6723. Around US$70 a night with limited scuba equipment for rental (bring your own). Situated at perhaps the best dive spot in the area.

Maya Maya Reef Club Cell: 63-917/270-9544, Fax: 63-912/322-8550.
E-mail: elma@mayamaya.com
Web: www.mayamaya.com
A full-service PADI resort facility, with a resident Aussie instructor and a complete range of rental and retail equipment. A marina full of exotic yachts and speedboats sets the scene here, and the place is popular with expats and locals alike seeking to escape the grime of Manila. Single occupancy rooms start at around US$75, including breakfast. One dive with boat, tank, and weights is US$25, two dives are US$40. Book first, and ask about seasonal and other discount packages.

Philippine Divers Corporation Cell: 63-912/393-5040 and 63-917/890-0200, Fax: 63-912/392-5040.
E-mail: phildivco@aol.com
Operates a full service dive center from Matabungkay Beach Club.

There are several beach resorts along the coast from Nasugbu to Matabungkay and further south, offering varying amenities and degrees of value. These are also worth investigating. There are also many small resorts, bungalows and cottages for rent along the coast hereabouts from Balayaan to Nasugbu, for those who have their own transport.

Anilao

Most dive operators in Anilao can provide their guests with some form of transfer if they need it. Adventure lovers without their own car can take a bus to Batangas, and then a 30 minute Jeepney ride over some quite bumpy roads to Anilao. Once there, they can negotiate a *banca* boat at the town pier or take a chance on getting another jeepney along the road that winds along the brows of the lush, tropical hills overlooking the sparkling Balayaan Bay.

Anilao is all about diving. Since 1967, when Thelma Zuniga of the 70-room Aqua Tropical Resort first built two little nipa huts on the rugged coastline to accommodate visiting divers, Anilao has blossomed and grown. There is no "strip" here; in fact, it is very awkward to even visit another resort if you don't have a car. However, the diving is excellent, and most of the better established resorts serve great buffets at mealtimes, so time for beach hopping, in reality more like rock hopping, is limited for most visitors. Listed are only a few of the many resorts along the rugged Balayaan coastline offering scuba packages.

There are no landlines in Anilao; the listings quoted here are all Manila numbers (63-2) or cell phones (63-9XX).

Anilao Seasports Anilao, Mabini. Tel: 63-2/801-1850. Single rooms from US$40 up. Full diving package with meals, 2 dives and accommodation from US$120 per day.

Aqua Tropical Resort Barangay Ligaya, Anilao, Batangas. Tel: 63-2/592536 or 63-2/521-4655. The first resort to be built in Anilao, Aqua Tropical Resort now has 70 rooms set in beautifully landscaped grounds with a large swimming pool. PADI, NAUI and ADSI instruction is offered, and there are trips to all the surrounding sites going out at all hours. Japanese and Taiwanese operators have been sending groups to Aqua Tropical for decades now, and the resort's high standards reflect this. Packages start at around US$100 per person, all inclusive.

Aquaventure Reef Club Barangay Bagalangit, Mabini. Cell: 63-912/320-8214, Tel: 63-2/896-0876, Fax: 63-2/897-2547. The Anilao outlet of industry leader Aquaventure Philippines Inc., the reef resort is a cozy get-away with, as do all the resorts around here, a heavy bias towards diving. Rooms start at US$46 a

night with a 10% discount Monday to Friday. Aquaventure Club members get a good discount here!

Dive South Marina Resort Barangay Solo, Mabini. Tel 63-2/812 5888, cell 63-912/892 332 8608, Fax: 63-2/892 2465. Rooms from US$12 and up. A 10 man banca boat costs US$40 for a whole day from here: tanks rent for US$5, Regulators for US$8

Dinky Little Dive Camp Tel. 63-2/899-7388, Fax: 63-2/899-7393 for reservations.
E-mail: divephil@mnl.sequel.net
Web: www.divephil.com
Operated by Dive Buddies Philippines. Check out the Dive Buddy Directory on their web site.

Dive & Trek Resort Bauan, Batangas. Tel: 63-2/833-8031, 832-0494, and 833-8021, Fax: 63-2/833-8030. A diver-friendly resort at reasonably prices. PADI courses taught by arrangement.

Pisa Dive Resort Maricaban Island. Operated by Divepro Internationa, Manila-based dive center. TeleFax: 63-2/825-9321 or 825-8909.
E-mail: paul@divepro.com.ph
A new resort (opened December 1998) surrounded by several outstanding dive sites.

Bonito Island Resort Barangay Pisa Tingloy. Tel: 63-2/812-2292, -2294, and -2297, 818-0114, and 818-0015. An exclusive island resort catering to discriminating divers. Private, secluded and surrounded by superb diving, Bonito is a good choice for serious divers and honeymooning couples. Call for rates and other information.

Puerto Galera

Regular airconditioned BLTB and JAM Transit buses leave from Lawton Bus terminal in Manila to Batangas Pier where several ferries leave for Puerto Galera daily. The last trip is usually around 1.30 pm on the small car ferry; allow at least three hours for the bus trip. Private bancas also make the crossing from Batangas, Mayanaga and Anilao piers, charging from US$35 upwards for the one hour trip. Most resorts and dive centers in Opuerto Galera can arrange painless transfers at any time of the day or night with short notice (depending in the weather in the

Verde Island Passage).

The **Sikat Bus and Ferry** service, which leaves promptly at 9am every morning from the **Sundowner Hotel** (Tel: 63-2/521-3344, Fax: 63-2/521-5955) costs around US$15 each way and is still the best way to go for budget minded travellers.

Passengers usually take a *banca* boat from the quaint Puerto Galera pier to the beach of their choice. Rates are supposed to be posted at the pier; if in doubt, ask someone who looks like they live there. Expect to pay about US$10 for a boat to Sabang, less to Small and Big Lalaguna Beaches.

An irregular jeepney service plies between Puerto and Sabang Beach to the East and White Beach to the West, depending on the condition of the road.

Coco Beach Resort has a free bus and ferry service for its guests which picks up at several major hotels around Manila at 6 am. **The Park Hotel** and **Lalaguna Beach Club** (Tel: 63-2/521 2371, E-mail: lalaguna @llbc.com.ph) can arrange for a sea plane to drop you off right on the beach.

Diving and accommodations

There is no shortage of budget rooms on the many beaches within five kilometres of the picturesque port of Puerto Galera.

From busy Sabang Beach in the east to the quiet White Beach to the West, nipa huts and cottages, with or without catering facilities, can be rented from US$5 a day and up. Small, self contained dive resorts, such as Capt'n Greggs on Sabang, El Galleon on Small Lalaguna and Lalaguna Beach Club on Big Lalaguna go for between US$10 and US$30 and up a night and are very good value. As with all the local shops, multi-lingual PADI instructors and divemasters are readily available to teach any number of courses and specialties.

The local diving community has regulated prices so all dive centers are supposed to charge the same for all diving services. Open Water courses start at around US$275 to US$310, Advanced from US$200 to US$220. A boat and dive guide is US$25 per dive.

Many of the dive centers carry a range of equipmet for sale. Ask at any dive shop or at **Whitetip Divers** in Manila (Tel: 63-2/521-0433) for up to the minute information on dive safaris to the Sibuyan Sea, Apo Reef, Coron and other remote sites originating in Puerto Galera.

Technical diving is popular in Puerto Galera. Nitrox and IANTD Technical Diving courses and complete technical diving equipment, including rebreathers, are widely available.

Some Puerto Galera diving operators are listed below by area. There are no land lines here, all phones and faxes are cellular.

SABANG BEACH

Capt'n Greggs Cell/Fax: 63-912/306-5267, E-mail: captgreg@epic.net. A BSAC International School.

Atlantis Dive Resort Cell/Fax: 63-973/497-503. E-mail: atlantis@vasia.com. Web: www.atlantis@vasia.com. A PADI 5-Star IDC center.

Big Apple Dive Resort Cell/Fax: 63-912/308-1120. E-mail: Big-Apple@quinet.net. A PADI resort.

Octopus Divers at **Villa Sabang**, Cell/Fax: 63-912/313-4486. Has its own training pool.

These above dive centers have rooms and cottages for rent from between US$10 to US$25 and up a night. Most of the local nightlife is squeezed onto Sabang Beach.

Other dive centers on this beach include: **South Sea Divers** (Cell: 63-912/332-4286, Cell/Fax: 63-912/347-6993) and **Cocktail Divers** (Cell: 63-912/353-4177, Tel/Fax: 63-2/892-1443, E-mail: cdiver@vasia.com, Web: www.vasia/cdiver.) **Cocktail Divers** also operates a full service Dive Center and Dive Travel enter in Manila.

SMALL LAGUNA BEACH

El Galleon and **Asia Divers** Cell: 63-973/865-252, Cell/Fax: 63-912/305-0652.
    E-mail: elgaleon@mozcom.com
    Web: .www.elgalleon.com
A PADI 5-Star IDC facility owned by PADI course director Allan Nash.

Sunsplash and **Scubaplus** Cell: 63-912/388-4831.
    E-mail: martin@scubaplus
    Web: www.scubaplus.com
    A PADI facility.

Carlo's Inn (Cell: 63-912/301-0717) and **Cocktail Divers** (see listing for Sabang) are all quality resorts with dive franchises on the premises.

Other dive centers on Small Lalaguna Beach include another **Asia Divers** outlet (Cell: 63-973/782-094, Cell/Fax: 63-973/865-252, E-mail: asiadive@mozcom.com), set back a little way behind the **Full Moon Restaurant**. Small Lalaguna is also where you will find the smaller **Action Divers** (Cell: 63-973/751-968, Fax: 63-2/522-3663, E-mail: action@vasia.com, Web: www.actiondivers.com).

As with most other beaches, there are lots of cheap (US$7 and up) cottages around: try **Nick and Sonia's** first.

BIG LAGUNA BEACH

La Laguna Beach Club, or **LBC** Cell: 63-973/855-545, 63-912/363-6061, Cell/Fax: 63-973/878-409.

E-mail: lalaguna@llbc.com.ph
Web: www.lalaguna.com.ph

The premiere spot on this cozy beach. Fan rooms are US$30, aircon US$40, but check with the management for package rates, seasonal and other discounts. Good food and a private pool are among the attractions here. PADI Course Director and IANTD Instructor Frank Doyle runs the PADI 5-Star Resort facility. LBC also operates the Dive ranchise at Maya Maya in Batangas.

El Oro resort has budget rooms and a **Cocktail Divers** outlet too; there are plenty of other reasonable accommodation options to choose from.

WHITE BEACH

Not as developed as the other areas, White Beach has retained its laid-back character over the years. Cottages here are usually a bit cheaper than at other beaches. There are currently two small dive centers operating along White Beach.

Coco Beach Resort (Tel: 63-2/521-4693) with a **Philippine Divers Corporation** franchise. Cell: 63-912/392-5040 and 63-917/890-0200.

E-mail: phildivco@aol.com

A luxurious and secluded resort getaway in a very tropical setting. Double rooms US$63 and up, with seasonal and other discounts applicable. Tennis courts, a convention centre and a lovely swimming pool complement the excellent food and service here.

Encenada Beach Resort Tel: 63-912/301-2289. Cottages and rooms with fans or AC. Expect to pay up to US$40 a night for a comfortable cottage, less for a room. Encenada has its own dive center.

Boracay City code: 036

Philippines Airlines flies daily from Manila to Kalibo, a 90-minute air-conditioned bus ride from Caticlan, where a short ferry ride can usually drop you off close to your resort. If the weather doesn't permit, then you may have to cross the island, either by motorcycle taxi or on foot. For other airlines servicing Kalibo and Caticlan, Boracay's two airports, refer to the Domestic Airlines section above.

For romantics with time on their hands, it is also possible, though not recommended, to take one of several ferries from Manila or Cebu to a nearby port, such as Romblon, and negotiate the sometimes rough sea passage onward from there. In season, **WG&A Superferries** runs a service to Boracay.

Accommodations

Along the famous white beach of Boracay there are any number of accommodation options to suit all budgets. Many resorts maintain offices in Manila too, making booking a snap. There are usually plenty of options available to travellers preferring not to reserve in advance, though in peak season, January to May, especially around Easter, it is advisable to book ahead if possible.

At least 16 dive centers are doing a thriving business, and more are on the way. Windsurfing is very popular on Boracay as well. A wide range of restaurants and bars and several hot night spots complete the picture.

Many of the resorts listed here sell packages including round trip airfares and transfers; its worth calling first to compare prices and amenities.

With comfortable rooms and suites, some air conditioned, mostly starting above US$60 a night, many of the up-scale resorts are still good value for money. Check for significant seasonal and walk-in discounts.

For the less wealthy but comfort minded, **Morimar Boracay Resort** (Tel: 63-2/819-1536), **Pink Patio** (Tel: 63-2/815-3333), and **Cocomangas** (Tel: 63-2/521-9443) are good choices, priced from US$20 and up.

Budget travellers might want to try **Greenyards**, **Morning Star** or **Highland Springs**, all priced under US$20 a night in peak season.

Dive operators

Dive centers on Boracay are very competitively priced and can be booked directly or through agents in Manila, such as **Whitetip Divers** (see listing under Manila). All have multilingual PADI instruction. Dives are priced around US$20 with complete rentals, many shops have day trips including boat and lunch for US$50; a PADI Open Water course is around US$270, Advanced US$180. Due to the extreme depths sometimes attempted by the foolish few, several stores have dive computers for rent.

Calypso Divers Tel: 63-36/288-3206, Fax: 63-36/288-3478.
E-mail: georgewegmann@hotmail.com
One of the longest serving members of the local diving community, and they also retail equipment including Aqualung and Seaquest.

Scuba World Tel: 63-36/288 3310.
E-mail: swidive@compass.com.ph
Web: www.scubaworld.com.ph
A full service dive center along the beach.

Lapu Lapu Diving Safari Tel: 63-36/288-3302, Fax: 63-36/288-3015.
E-mail: lapu@pemail.net.
Lapu have been operating in Boracay for over a decade now.

Take the time to make a leisurely walk along the beach and you will find a lot more dive centers eager for your business including **Red Coral** (Tel: 63-36/288-3486, Cell: 63-918/750-0007), **Sea Gaia** (Tel: 63-2/727-0788 and 63-36/288-3661, Fax: 63-2/821-0278 and 63-36/288-3662), and **Victory Divers,** the latter Boracay Veterans who specialise in discounted *Habagat* specials (*Habagat* is the wind which blows for long periods from June to November, the off season).

Marinduque

Not much goes on around this sleepy little Island, except for the annual Moriones Festival which is frequently depicted in glossy DOT posters. The actual event is really quite tame, but the diving around Marinduque is well worth making the effort to discover.
There are a number of small resorts dotted around the island, take a jeepney or bus along the Western coastal road and pick one that seems to suit you. There are no full service dive centers, but there are a few operators with scuba gear for rent who are willing to arrange full-day dive trips if they are around. Check at any resort or hotel for more information. Most divers visit Marinduque's offshore islands to the West and South by live-aboard dive safaris originating from Puerto Galera and Boracay.

Mactan and Cebu
City code: 032

Minutes from where Cebu's first tourist, Magellan, met his untimely end while interfering in a squabble between local chiftans, Mactan's busy airport spills out planeloads of international travellers, many of them package tourists from Japan, to enjoy the resorts of Mactan and historic Cebu's cosmopolitan beat. Cebu is a hub city, a major shipping centre and the jump-off point for the rest of the Visayas.
Mactan Island is separated from Cebu City on the main island of Cebu by the Mactan Straits: a single bridge spans the gap, connecting the two.
Diving and water sports have been at the forefront of the development of tourism, a top dollar earner for the region. Cebu has several retail outlets serving the booming scuba market, among them:

Aquaventure Cebu At the Mercedes Complex, A. Cortes Avenue, Cebu. Tel: 63-32/345-1571, Fax: 63-32/346-7518.
E-mail: aqua@skyinet.net
Web: www.aquaventure.com

Scuba World Ma. Cristina cor. M. Yap sts., Cebu City.
E-mail: swidive@cebu.pw.net.ph
Web: www.scubaworld.com.ph

Whitetip Divers Unit #11, Borromeo Arcade, F. Ramos St., Cebu City. Tel: 63-32/254-2623, Fax: 63-32/254-3364.
E-mail: whitetip@cebu.weblinq.net
Web: www.whitetip.com

Liquid Assets Cebu Grand Hotel complex. Tel: 63-32/254-6359, Fax: 63-32/231-4980.

Accommodations and dving

Most resorts around Mactan have diving services on the premises; if not, you are

PRACTICALITIES THE PHILIPPINES

201

never too far away from a dive centre: there are over 100 dive operator permits issued every year by the local Lapu Lapu City Government! Most dive shops arrange one to five day dive safaris to nearby Cabilao Island and other exotic Visayan dive spots.

At the top of the range is **Shangri-La's Mactan Island Resort** Tel: 63-32/231-0288, local 8846, Fax: 63-32/231 5075. Rooms start at US$100 a night. A huge pool and outstanding landscaping complement the luxurious appointments. Scotty's Dive Center, past the pool towards the beach, has more down-to-earth prices and years of experience diving around Mactan and the Visayas. Equipment rents out for US$20 a day; dive safaris run US$89 to US$165 a day, depending on the luxury. PADI courses are available. Scotty's also operates a dive resort on Siquijor Island. **Scotty's Dive Center** E-mail: scotty@mozcom.com, Web: www.worldviews.com/scotty.

Further South, on the East coast, there are many resorts servicing divers, and most offer decent diving right off the beach. Rentals and instruction tend to be a little higher priced than the national average, PADI open water courses go for around US$350 at many dive centers.

High-end resorts on Mactan include the **Maribago Beach Club** (Tel: 63-2/597702 and 815-4819), **Mar Y Cielo Resort** (Tel: 63-2/817-4258), and the **Tambuli Beach Club** (Tel: 63-32/211-543 through –45, or 522-2308). Rooms in these places run US$80–US$100 or more a night, with facilities to match.

For the serious diver, it is hard to beat **Club Kon Tiki Resort** (Tel/Fax: 63-32/340-9935). Genuinely run by divers for divers, Kon Tiki's international instructors teach PADI, NAUI, CMAS, and SSI scuba courses in a very professional classroom with all the AVA's and up to the minute teaching aids. One of the best dives in Mactan is Kon Tiki's "House Reef," right off the beach. Rates for rentals, training, and dive trips are typically lower than other operations on the Island, more in line with Puerto Galera and Boracay. Rooms are cozy, a choice of AC or fan, and start at around US$23 a night. Seasonal and other discounts can be negotiated.

Hadsan Beach Resort is another less expensive option worth checking out, with two dive centers operating out of it: **Sazanami Marine Sports** (Tel: 63-32/254-0568, Cell: 63-912/501-2702, Fax: 63-32/254-0745) and Scubaworld (63-32/340 5938).

Sazanami caters mostly to Japanese clients, and the instructors and guides are not so adept at English.

While not really close to Cebu City, mention should be made of **Argao Beach Club** (Casay Dalagueta, Cebu, Tel: 63-32/213-532 and 812-1984), a few hours South of the city on the East coast. Rooms go for US$60 and up here, but there is some excellent diving quite close by that is otherwise hard to reach.

Moalboal

On the western side of the Island, Moalboal was one of the original scuba diving centres in the Philippines. Most of the scuba operations and accommodations are relatively humble, with prices to match. Although there were eight dive shops operating last time we visited, only one, **Seven Seas Aquanauts** (parent company of **Savedra Divers**, is registered with the PCSSD. It seems several of the operators are either too poor to register, or are unnecessarily suspicious of the program.

To get to Moalboal, one either rents a car or takes a two-hour bus trip on the rough and rugged road over mountainous central Cebu. Buses leave every half hour from the Librando bus station in Cebu. Upon arrival at Moalboal, grab a tricycle and head off to Panagsama Beach. Accommodation ranges from US$5 to US$70 a night, mostly small nipa cottages. Food is also very cheap hereabouts, with several surprisingly good options.

Visaya Divers Corp Panagsama Beach, Moalboal, Cebu. Offers diving from US$12 a dive if you have your own gear, US$17 if you don't, and teaches PADI open water courses for US$220, advanced courses for US$150 (prices about standard for the area).

Savedra Moalboal, Cebu. Cell: 63-918/770-3855, Tel/Fax: 63-32/340-9935. A professionally run PADI 5-Star IDC Center with complete nitrox and technical diving facilities (in cooperation with neighbors **Great White Diving**). Rooms for rent at US$25 for fan, US$30 for AC.

Sumisid Lodge has fan rooms for around US$10, air conditioned for about US$25 a night. Depending on season and bookings, you can often negotiate a better deal on accommodation and some diving services.

A walk along Panagsama Beach will introduce you to most of the dive operators doing business: remember, not all dive operators are created equal. **Whitetip Divers**, in Manila and Cebu, act as booking agents for several of the better Moalboal operations.

Northern Cebu

Not as well developed as the south, there are only a few places catering to scuba divers in north Cebu.

Alegre Beach Resort Calumboyan, Sogod, North of Cebu City. Tel: 63-32/254-9800, 254-9811, 254-9822, and 254-9844, Fax: 63-32/254-9833.

E-mail: abrsales@cebu.weblinq.com
Another excellent private resort. Packages here go for around US$270 per person for two nights/three days in a shared room and four dives.

Dive operators tend to come and go in the more remote locations, and unless you are planning to stay at the Alegre, you should get some current, local advice *before* planning a journey North. For more information, check with any of the dive centers listed in the Mactan/Cebu section.

Bohol City code: 038

Up and coming Bohol has an increasingly diverse choice of accommodation and dive services. Most of these originate on Panglao Island, across the causeway South of Provincial Capital Tagbilaran City.

Bohol can be reached by regular domestic flights to Tagbilaran City from Manila or Cebu, or by comfortable, fast ferry boat services from Manila and from throughout the Visayas – Mindanao region.. Once there, most divers head for Alona Beach on Panglao Island where the scuba diving business is flourishing.

Local prices are fairly standard, with dive trips running US$55 to US$80 a day. Boats rent out for about US$6 a day per person. A PADI open water course is around US$250, advanced course US$170. Equipment rents out for about US$10 a day.

Dive operators

Cebu Sea Explorers c/o **Alona Tropical Beach Resort** Panglao Island, Bohol. Cell: 63-918/740-1668.

E-mail: eldorado@mozcom.com

Web: www.cuenet.ch/seaexplorers
Cebu Sea also has branches on Cabilao Island and at El Dorado Beach Resort in Dumaguete, Negros Oriental. Owner Chris Heim, a Swiss national, is a PADI Course Director who holds several IDC's in the Visayas every year.

Bohol Divers Lodge Alona Beach, Panglao Island, Bohol. Tel: 63-38/411-4938, Cell: 63-918/770-8438. Operated by long-time resident French expatriate Jacques Trotin.

Balicasag Island Dive Resort Balicasag, Panglao, Bohol. Tel: 63-38/411-2192, 63-2/812-1984, 810-3655, 810-3703). Single rooms start at US$37, doubles at US$43. PADI open water courses US$300. Complete equipment rentals around US$28 a day; air US$10 a fill.

Alona Divers Alona Beach, Tawala, Panglao. Cell: 63-918/600-0579, Fax: 63-38/235-3007. A cozy dive resort managed by German Peter Buermann and his charming wife Maritess.

Atlantis Dive Center, Alona Beach, Panglao. One of the longest running operations on the island.

Other Panglao dive centers worth checking out include: **Genesis Divers** (Cell: 63-918/770-8434, Fax: 63-38/253 3007), **Sharky's Divers**, and **Swiss Bamboo House**.

Other dive centers around Bohol include **Polaris Dive Center** on Cabilao Island (Cell: 63-918/773-7681, Fax: 63-38/253-0265) and **Sierra Madre Divers** (at **Bohol Tropics** in Tagbilaran City, Cell: 63-912/720-1047 and 707-0669, Cell/Fax: 63-912/720-0078).

Coron

There are a few landlines in Coron: they are all difficult to reach. **Swagman Travel** (E-mail: bookings@swaggy.com) has an office in Coron and transacts bookings and other busioness thorugh a radio connection to their head office in Manila (Tel: 63-2/523-8541, Fax: 63-2/522-3663). Several of the dive operators in Coron have E-mail and/or Manila representative offices that take bookings and arrange transfers.

Refer to Domestic Airlines section for airlines flying to Coron from Manila. For the adventurous, Inter-island ferries ply the route to and from Coron and Batangas (**Viva Ship-**

ping Lines) and Manila (**Asuncion Shipping Lines**, North Harbor).

Dive operators

Philippine Divers Corporation at **Club Paradise** Dimakya Island, Busuanga, off the Northeast coast of the Island of Busuanga. Tel: 63-2/941-0047, Cell:63-917/890-0200, Fax: 63-2/948-8071.

E-mail: phidivco@aol.com
Philippine Divers calls their operation the Dugung Dive Center, and it is associated with a first class resort with rooms at US$110 and up. Reservations should be made first so that the resort can meet the plane in Coron and escort visitors on the land and sea trip to the hotel. Although too far from the "Ghost Fleet" of Coron Bay to place divers on the famous wrecks, there is plenty of excellent reef diving within easy reach of the Resort.

Around Coron itself, several small lodge type of hotels have sprung up to cater to the increasingly large number of divers visiting the area. Several outlying islands have resort developments of varying sophistication on them too.

Kalamayan Inn Coron, Busuanga island, Northern Palawan. Tel/Fax: RCPI (048) 196-2538, Tel: 63-2/633-4701 (ask for Mrs. Santos), Fax 63-2/633-4855.

E-mail: kalmayan@epic.net
Web: www.epic.net/kalamayan
Eight airconditioned rooms and a bar and restaurant called "The Tourist Trap." It is a few minutes walk from most of the dive centers in Coron.

Sangat Island Reserve on Sangat Island. TelFax: 63-2/525-8041, Cell: 63-917/320-1955.

E-mail: sangat@epic.net
Situated right in the middle of the best wreck diving in the Philippines with its own "House Wreck" a few meters off the white sand beach. Eight cottages, a restaurant, and a PADI-oriented dive center round out the facilities.

Discovery Divers Barangay 5, Coron, Busuanga. Tel: RCPI 63-2/922-3233, local 2526, Fax: 63-2/645-6616.

E-mail: ddivers@vasia.net
Web: www.vasia.com/ddivers
They have many years experience diving the wrecks and corals of Coron Bay. They also teach PADI courses (open water US$269,

advanced US$199). A dive with your own equipment costs US$16, or US$18.50 if full rental gear is required. A speed boat is available for hire at US$180 a day.

Dive Right E-mail: diving@mozcom.com.

Web: www2.mozcom.com/~diving
Arranges tours and accommodation as well as PADI courses. They also retail Zeagle and other equipment.

Lapu Lapu Diving Center (E-mail: lapu@pemail.net), one of Boracay's leading dive specialists, has a branch at the **Bayside Lodge** in Coron (Tel: 63-36/288-3302, Fax: 63-36/288-3015) conducts dive trips aboard *Busuanga Dream* and is a PADI facility.

Coron Tours and Travel (Tel: 63-2/838-4956, –64, –65, E-mail: corontur@pworld.net.ph) are agents for Asian Spirit and can be very helpful in getting seats on planes that claim to be booked out and at reserving a room at the resort of your choice.

El Nido

The most direct way to get to El Nido is by **A. Soriano Air** (Tel: 63-2/833-3852, Fax: 63-2/833-3853). It flies directly to El Nido from Manila, about US$130 one way. Alternatively, you can fly to Puerto Princessa, one way, and suffer for up to 12 hours in a jeepney from Puerto Princesa to Taytay, after that crossing the island to El Nido over often muddy roads which frequently require a shovel and a good pair of shoulders to negotiate. Or you can fly to Coron and hire a *banca* boat to take you to El Nido, a trip of several hours to a full day, depending on the waves. The price should not exceed US$100, and is usually open to negotiation. A weekly boat trip to and from Boracay sometimes runs in season.

Once in El Nido, the best hotel in town is the **Bayview Hotel**, where a single room is just over US$3 a night. When we were there, electricity was on from 5:30 pm until 11 pm. There are no private bathrooms, but the toilets flush and bathing is by bucket bath. There are also plenty of cottages for rent at around US$7 and up a night.

There are three dive shops in the town proper: the oldest is **Bacuit Diver Services**, run by German Willy Amman and his Filipina wife, Nora. It is 100 metres East of the Pier and charges US$20 for one dive, US$30 for two. Boat charges of US$30 are divided between divers. A PADI open water course costs US$200, Advanced US$250.

The town itself is very small, and you can walk from one end to the other is a couple of minutes.

Miniloc Island Resort and **Lagen Island**, both situated in El Nido bay with outstanding views and first class facilities, are operated by **10 Knots Development Corporation** (2/f, Builder's Center Building, 170 Salcedo St., Legaspi Village, Makati City, Tel: 63-2/894-5644, Fax: 63-2/810-3620). You should reserve first, as neither resort is especially welcoming of unannounced visitors. Rooms US$130 and up, which includes all diving and other activities. PADI and NAUI instruction is available, and an open water course costs US$350. **Pangalusian Island Resort**, another 10 Knots property in El Nido Bay, suffered a devastating fire in 1998, but is expected to re-open sometime in 1999.

Live-aboards

Live-aboard diving in the Philippines is an experience which, once tasted, is usually repeated. From US$65 to US$180 and more a day, a full range of vessels and destinations await divers with a yearning to discover some of the best diving in S.E. Asia.

The Sulu Sea dive sites, such as Tubbataha, Jessie Beazley and Basterra, are accessible for three or four months of the year (March to June), and only by live-aboard. Book early to ensure a slot. Other locations frequently visited by live-aboards include El Nido, Coron, Bohol and the Visayas, Apo Reef and the Sibuyan Sea. Some outfits also dive the Spratley Islands.

At the bottom end, large *bancas*, or pump boats, and sailing yachts carry six to eight people in relative comfort. Some have air conditioning, but most don't, though sleeping on the deck under a blanket of stars is quite okay for most of us. Camps are often made on deserted islands (make sure you tidy up properly before leaving please), and schedules are very much open. These budget live-aboard trips can be arranged through most dive shops in Puerto Galera and Boracay, and through **Whitetip Divers** in Manila.

For the more sophisticated diver, there is no shortage of superb, customized live-aboard dive vessels offering the absolute maximum comfort and service. Fine dining, luxurious appointments and professional expertise are very much the order of the day on these boats: some even carry E-6 film processing on board too.

Manila and Cebu are the main centres for live-aboard bookings: actual embarkation points depend on where the vessel is working. Live-aboards currently operating in the Philipines currently include:

M.Y. Island Explorer, M.Y. Blue Planet, and *M.Y. Ocean Explorer.* Operated by Scuba World.
E-mail: swidive@compass.com.ph
Web: www.scubaworld.com.ph

M.Y. Nautika. Operated by PCP Holiday Cruises, Herald Suites Building, 2168, Pasong Tamo Avenue, Makati City. Tel: 63-2/759-6270 through –75, local 2106, 759-6349, Fax: 63-2/759-6283.
E-mail: nautika@mnl.sequel.net
A stalwart, comfortable vessel with 8 double berths with ensuite shower and heads. Underwent a complete refit in late 1998.

M.Y. Jinn Sulu. Operated by Queen Anne Palawan Inc. c/o Trattoria Terrace, 353 Rizal Avenue, Puerto Princessa, Palawan. Tel 63-04821/2751, Fax: 63-04821/2894. Makes regular trips to Tubataha Reef in the Sulu Sea in season.

M.Y. Tristar. Owned and managed by Tristar Sea Ventures Corp., 2/f, Smithbell Building, 2294, Pasong Tamo Extension, Barangay Magallanes, Makati City. Tel: 63-2/816-7088, 816-7340, and 816-7851 through –55, local 16, Fax: 63-2/810-9180. One of the most luxurious live-aboards operating in the country, this ship has been cruising the "Visayan Triangle" full-time for a year or more now.

M.Y. Thor Viking. Contact: Swagman Travel. Tel: 63-45/322-5133, Fax: 63-45/322-9467.
E-mail: bookings@swaggy.com
A motor sailer that makes regular dive trips to the Sulu Sea, Apo Reef and Coron.

M.Y. Tabibuga. Diving services, including complete tek diving facilities, are provided by La Laguna Beach Club and Dive Center of Puerto Galera. Cell: 63-973/ 855-545, Cell/Fax: 63-973/878-409, Tel/Fax: 63-2/525-8041.
E-mail: lalaguna@llbc.com.ph
Web: www.lalaguna.com.ph
A 22-meter all-steel construction motor vessel with one six-berth and four two-berth cabins. A mid-priced live-aboard boat that mostly visits the Sibuyan Sea, Apo Reef and Coron.

Singapore Country code: 65

Hardly the dive mecca of Southeast Asia, Singapore is nevertheless an important center for diving concerns. Because of its location in the heart of the region, it is never far from Asia's favorite dive sites.

Singapore's Changi Airport has become the air hub of Southeast Asia. Connections are fast and efficient, and the airport is a fine place to relax between flights. Because of the competition among the republic's many travel agents, travelers have the pick of economic air fares.

All prices in Singapore dollars.

A duty-free republic

Perhaps Singapore's greatest attraction is its duty-free shopping. With the exception of cigarettes, alcohol and a few sundry items which probably would not attract the average shopper, all goods are duty-free. This does not, however, always mean they are cheap. Bargaining is still *de rigeur* in most shops and it is up to the shopper to ensure he gets a bargain.

Over the last decade, dive shops have burgeoned in Singapore as the sport has become more and more popular. Today there are over 20 dive shops selling equipment, dive courses, organizing equipment repair and servicing as well as providing a range of services for both amateur and professional diver. Most are excellent and run by knowledgeable professionals (often divemasters themselves) who will advise and help shoppers. They are also good places to talk to fellow divers, and many have their fingers on the pulse of diving out of Singapore itself. While many dive shops run Open-Water certification courses (PADI is the most popular), some offer Advanced Courses which can be done either in a Singapore swimming pool or in the rather more attractive waters of neighboring territories. Tioman is a popular destination, while some operators will even fly as far as Bali to run specialized courses.

The republic grew up on its maritime trading facilities—it was first colonized by the British in 1819 when Stamford Raffles established a trading post—and over the years developed into one of the top three busiest commercial ports worldwide. Strangely, however, it did not develop particularly as a leisure center for sailing. But with a growing middle class, and the development of tourist resorts in neighboring countries, leisure cruising began to develop. In addition, Singapore unveiled a new marine terminal for cruise ships in 1992 which underwrote its belief that it can also become the Southeast Asian hub for cruising.

Diving in Singapore

Despite variable and often low visibility caused by run-off and shipping activities, Singapore offers the observant diver unexpectedly rewarding encounters. Seahorses, turtles, cuttlefish, barracuda, eels, clownfish, copperbanded butterflyfish, angelfish and a variety of corals and sponges, not to mention several wrecks, are accessible within 10 minutes by high-speed day boat. Several small craft ranging from the slower local "bumboats" to custom-made, high-speed vessels run two-tank day trips over weekends and public holidays, from the leisure marinas around the island. Bigger boats take divers further afield into Indonesian or Malaysian waters.

Diving from Singapore

In Indonesia, there is good diving around Pulau Bintan (just 4 hours away), particularly around southern sites such as Mapor Island, accessible by live-aboard boat. Further afield, the Anambas Islands provide fine diving, and it is worth going there for a minimum of 5 days. The nearest Malaysian dive sites are around Pulau Aur (approximately 8-10 hours by boat) and slightly further afield to Tioman (11 hours away).

Boats making regular dive trips from Singapore are generally of a local design (boats that were previously designed for fishing), converted to accommodate up to 8–12 divers in cabins, and with deck space for tanks and recreational activities. The skipper or his mate will provide good basic Asian meals and handle the diving side of the operation. Few are luxurious, but most are comfortable and will leave Singapore in the evening so that by motoring overnight the diving clientele can jump into the water first thing the following day.

There are also a number of more luxurious boats for hire—either well equipped yachts or motor cruisers—that can be chartered by the day or week or which offer weekend live-aboard trips. Nowadays it is usual for a yacht or cruiser to have dive equipment on board (as well as windsurf boards and other marine toys), but they may not all have compressors which would restrict the number of possible dives. However, chartering a skippered yacht or cruiser offers well-heeled divers the opportunity of diving further afield. Apart from the East Coast of Malaysia, nearby Indonesia, both the east and western shores of Thailand are possible destinations.

General information

The island republic of Singapore is located 136 km north of the Equator. It covers a total of 639 sq km and comprises some 59 islets of which the island of Singapore covers 580 sq km. Much of the main island is urban though there are still pockets of primary and secondary tropical forests surrounding the three main water reservoirs. A recent census records some 3 million permanent residents in the republic and annual tourist arrivals of over 5 million. Of the permanent citizens and residents, 76 percent are Chinese, 14 percent are Malay and 7 percent are Indian.

Singapore has 11 public holidays annually, celebrating Hindu, Buddhist, Muslim and Christian holidays as well as its National Day on 9 August. While this means that most people are on holiday, shops and restaurants are almost always open with the exception of the two public holidays when the majority Chinese population celebrate Chinese New Year.

Shops are generally open from 10 am to 7 pm, 6 or 7 days a week while supermarkets and large department stores will stay open to 9 or 10 pm.

Climate

Singapore is a tropical island with relatively uniform temperatures year round. The average daily temperature is 26.7°C. From December to March the northwest monsoon blows, bringing slightly cooler temperatures and the heaviest precipitation. Rain generally falls in short, sharp showers. From June to September, the southwest monsoon brings lighter winds and less rainfall. The humidity is always high—averaging 84.4 percent.

Access

Most visitors arrive directly at Changi Airport, from where taxis take them directly into town (20–30 minutes). The average cost is around S$17. A public bus also operates to Orchard Road at a cost of S$1.30: it takes just over 1 hour.

Money

The Singapore dollar (S$) is the republic's currency. Banks open 9.30 am–3.30 pm, Monday to Friday and 9.30–11.30 am on Saturdays, and money changers will change international currencies, and Automatic Telling Machines (ATMs) issue currency for those carrying international credit cards. At the time of this writing US$1=S$1.65.

Getting around

Singapore has an excellent system of public buses, a relatively new and very fast mass rapid transit system (MRT) and more than 12,000 metered taxis. By international levels, fares on the public buses and the MRT are very economical, as are those by metered taxi. Currently flagfall is S$2.40.

Accommodations

Accommodation in Singapore is geared to meet the needs of most purses, but while there is some budget accommodation, much is targeted at the business traveler. Of the many hundred registered hotels in Singapore, over 50 are in the 4- and 5-star luxury category. Prices for a room vary from as little as S$60 for a basic room in a Chinese-run hotel to over

S$1,000 for a fine room in the grand old lady of Singapore, Raffles Hotel. If you select a hotel when you arrive (and that is very easy at Changi Airport), you should expect to pay in the S$150–S$200 range. However, if you secure a booking prior to leaving home through a travel agent, you will find that the real cost of the room will be much nearer the S$70–S$120 mark.

Restaurants

Singapore probably has the greatest diversity of restaurants and cafes in Southeast Asia. And more importantly, the quality of cuisine in the republic is unfailingly high. There are over 170 markets serving food from individual stalls and thousands of restaurants and cafes.

Meals in these hawker centers can cost as little as S$3.00. Singaporean food is a happy mix of Malay and Chinese, with an extra accent on spice. Seafood is its particular speciality. All cuisines from Asia are well represented as are the popular cuisines from Europe and North America. Many of the hotels have superb Asian and international restaurants. Fast-food outlets comprise numerous MacDonalds as well as Burger Kings and Pizza Huts.

Dive shops

Dive shops all over the republic offer dive gear, courses, publications, and dive tours. Listed below, in alphabetical order, are four we can recommend.

Marsden Bros Dive Centre 25 Faber Park, Singapore 129113. Tel: 778-8287, Fax: 773-2265, E-mail: marsbros@pacific.net.sg. An expatriate owned and operated PADI dive center, offering British and Australian instructors with marine biology degrees. A full range of PADI courses, including specialties such as nitrox, naturalist and wreck diving, are available. Equipment shop. The high-speed, custom-made catamaran *Typhoon* takes divers on day and night dives around Singapore, and the 60-foot motor yacht *Reclaim II* is used for live-aboard trips to Bintan Island, Indonesia, including Mapor Island. Escorted tours to dive sites such as Sipadan are available.

Pro Diving Services 32 Bali Lane, Singapore 189868. Tel: 291-2261, Fax: 291-4136, E-mail: prodiving@pacific.net.sg. Operated by William Ong, this is the only 5-star PADI IDC center in Singapore. In addition to a full range of dive courses, Pro Diving sells a comprehensive selection of gear and can also offer advice on where to dive from Singapore.

Scuba Diving Adventures 61B Pagoda Street, Singapore 059220. Tel: 227-8317, Fax: 221-2217, E-mail: enquiry@scubada.com.sg. Specializes in dive trips throughout the Asia-Pacific region and further abroad, including some South American destinations.

Sharkeys Dive & Travel 5A Pahang Street, Singapore 198606. Tel: 294-0168, Fax: 294-1832, E-mail: enquiry@sharkeys.com.sg, Web: sharkeys.com.sg. Another travel agent specialising in dive trips throughout the region including Phuket, Manado, Bali and Palawan. It has a dive cafe and plans to open an equipment shop.

Thailand Country Code: 66

You'll find Thailand an easy country to travel in as the tourism industry here is well developed and well organized. The people of Thailand are extremely friendly and polite, and crime problems are relatively rare. English is widely spoken in tourist areas, but keep your requests—and language and grammar—simple. Above all, avoid becoming frustrated and losing your temper as this will lead to doors of communication rapidly closing. The attitude of *jai yen*, or "keep your cool," will go a long way towards making time spent here pleasant and enjoyable. Unless noted, prices in US$.

Cultural considerations

Thais are very proud of their heritage—and rightly so. The country has never been colonized, but was briefly occupied by the Japanese during World War II, and Thais are happy with their freedom and their way of life. Show respect and you will be shown respect in return.

Always remove your shoes before entering a Thai house or a temple, even if your hosts insist it is not necessary. Automatically removing your shoes before boarding a dive boat will also show that you know what's going on.

The Royal Family is highly respected here, and it is in poor taste to make degrading remarks about them, even in jest. Never desecrate an image of the King or Queen of Thailand, which you will find hanging proudly in many shops or places of business. Even stepping on a rolling coin, which bears the image of the King, is considered rude and should be avoided.

The head of a Thai is considered the highest point—literally and spiritually—while the feet are considered the lowest. Therefore, never touch a Thai on the head, even children, and make an effort not to point to or touch objects or people with your feet.

The *wai* (putting your hands together with flat palms in a prayer like position) is a traditional and beautiful form of greeting here in Thailand. Rules for who *wai*s who are complicated, even for Thais, but generally paying this form of respect to children, to waiters, housekeepers or others younger than you, or of a lower social station, is not appropriate. It is appropriate, however, to *wai* persons older than you in many situations, especially older persons that are being extra kind to you. (For example, if you are invited into a Thai home, it is very polite to *wai* your hosts upon entering and leaving.) It is rare that a tourist is ever obligated to perform a *wai*, as you are a guest in this country. However, just like a handshake in Western countries, it is an important part of Thai culture and a little bit of understanding goes a long way.

Customs and habits in Thailand are different from those of other countries and can be difficult to understand. Respect them—even though they may not immediately make sense to you—and you'll find your time spent here to be enjoyable, fulfilling, and I dare say, educational.

Formalities

All travelers must have a passport valid for at least six months. For stays shorter than 30 days, visas are not required for Southeast Asian nationals or for most Europeans and North Americans. Visas are required for stays longer than 30 days, although some nationalities, such as Scandinavians, are exempt and given 90 days upon arrival. Check with a Thai Embassy in your own country before departure since entry rules do change often. Altogether, the visa process is simple, convenient and inexpensive.

Air travel

Don Muang airport in Bangkok is one of the busiest airports in the world, and hundreds of flights arrive daily from virtually every major country. Thai Airways International is the national airline, and it is consistently named one of the best airlines in the world. Singapore, whose national airline is also a world champion in passenger service, is also a great place to make your entry to Southeast Asia, as Changi Airport offers multiple connecting flights to Bangkok and Phuket everyday.

Air travel within Thailand is convenient and relatively inexpensive. The Phuket airport receives at least five flights a day (the number varies between the high and low seasons) from Bangkok year-round. Phuket's ever-expanding airport received international flights as well, from Hong Kong, Japan, Taiwan, Singapore, Malaysia, and Europe. Flights are available to and from Koh Samui and Pattaya on Bangkok Airways.

The Thai Airways office telephone number in Bangkok is 66-2/513-0121 and in Phuket, 66-76/211-195.

Land travel

Ground transportation in Thailand is very well organized, and both the trains and buses are relatively comfortable and efficient. Travel by train is probably the most comfortable and least expensive, but since the trains are often full they must be booked in advance. The state government runs the rail system, and booking trains can be less convenient than privately run buses.

Buses are common and go everywhere that's anywhere. Buses run in three different classes: *tamada* (normal), *ae* (air-conditioned), and VIP (the best). The most comfortable are the new double-decker VIP buses and their usage is common on most major routes. Be sure to bring warm clothes, however, as Thai air-conditioned buses are notorious for their extremely low temperatures!

Rot too (mini-vans) are widely available as means of transport between tourist destinations, but the majority of these drivers are extremely unprofessional, and drive as if they are in an automobile race. Caution and a strong stomach are advised when travelling this way.

Motorbike and car rental is available in most tourist areas—where there are roads, of course. If you can, buy insurance. Be careful at all times when driving, due to the duel hazards of tourists not paying attention and suicidal Thai drivers. Motorcycles are good fun and a cheap way to get around, provided you are experienced on two-wheels. Thailand is not a good place to learn. Normally a license is not required, but rental agencies will take your passport as a deposit against damage.

Local taxis and buses are widely available, and prices vary from place to place. One thing you'll notice quickly: Thais rarely walk. Thus, transportation is readily available anyplace you find people.

Sea travel

Ferries travel to Koh Phi Phi, Koh Samui, Koh Tao, etc. on a daily basis. Any travel agent can book them. Obviously, some boats are more comfortable and safer than others.

What to bring

Try to pack as lightly as possible, as the climate is very agreeable—except near the northern borders in December and January, and warm clothes are for rent there if you are planning a trek.

The diving industry is very competitive in Thailand, and equipment, usually in very good shape, is available for rent no matter where you dive. Spares are readily available in Phuket, Samui, and Koh Tao these days, but are not always convenient to purchase; it is best to bring things like extra mask and fin straps, o-rings, etc. Most centers rent wet suits.

A 3mm wet suit (even a shorty or surfing style) or a Lycra suit is adequate for diving all year-round. Keep in mind, however, that Lycra offers little or no thermal protection, and these suits are not adequate if you plan to dive three or more times per day. A full-length neoprene suit is probably best for serious diving.

Power in Thailand is 220 VAC. Although some of the more expensive dive boats offer 110 VAC, you should bring a proper adapter if you have 110V equipment. Note: Inexpensive "shaver" type adapters will not work for such devices as laptop computers and rechargers for underwater flashes. Bring the proper type. Most places stock batteries.

As of this update, many, many more dive shops are concentrating on the retail dive gear business. Prices vary, and if you are considering buying equipment while in Thailand, it's a good idea to have an idea of what it would cost at home first. In general, however, prices are competitive, and many items will be far cheaper than they would be at home. Unlike even a few years ago, selection is now excellent.

Live-aboard considerations

Keep in mind that live-aboards, no matter how large, do not have a lot of space for luggage storage. Most dive operators recommend soft-sided luggage on the boat, but will allow you to store extra bags at the dive center. Since live-aboard diving is casual, only a few T-shirts, shorts, and possibly a sweatshirt for the evening are necessary. Generally, the less you bring, the more comfortable you will be.

Underwater photography

Underwater photography services have not expanded as rapidly as other services over the past few years, and it's still difficult to rent a camera in most places. Phuket now has an underwater photography center in Kata Beach (Tel/Fax: 66-76/330-478; E-mail: phuket-photo@hotmail.com). **Phuket Photo** also does repairs and carries spares for many cameras. Film is developed everywhere in Thailand, but professional labs are only available in Bangkok. Film is widely available, but it is rarely stored cold, and is not usually very cheap. Again, batteries are rarely a problem, although batteries for the Nikonos are for some reason difficult to find. Batteries for diving computers are now easy to find in Phuket, but not in other areas. Most live-aboards have adequate power for charging strobe batteries.

Health

Since Thailand is a tropical country, certain unique health problems must be considered. Check with your health department before you leave home. Malaria and other mosquito-born diseases are only a problem in out-of-the-way places like the jungles of northern Thailand, islands near the Cambodian border, and Koh Tao north of Koh Samui. It is also a problem in Burma if you spend any time on shore. If traveling to the Mergui Archipelago, see your doctor for the latest recommendations on what medication to take. We do suggest that a good supply of mosquito repellent, sun cream, and a hat are purchased either here or at home and they should be used.

Bottled water is widely available, and you are well advised to drink only this type. Tap water is rarely—if ever—clean enough for western stomachs. All water served in hotels, guest houses, restaurants, and dive boats is bottled, usually coming from large 20-liter containers to help control the plastic waste problems. If in doubt, ask.

Health care in Thailand is widely available and inexpensive. Most first-aid supplies are easily purchased virtually everywhere. Any prescription medicines, of course, should be brought from home.

Dive emergencies

Considering the number of divers that come to Thailand, there have been very few accidents in Thailand (knock on wood!). Since this book was originally compiled, a professional recompression chamber has been installed in Phuket. This chamber is part of an international collection of chambers owned by a company called SSS Recompression Chamber Network. Run by Australian long-time resident Steve Hatchett, they have treated many patients in the past three years. Most dive shops in the south, including Phuket, Phi Phi, Samui, and Koh Tao, subscribe to the services offered by this chamber, and if you dive with them they offer insurance for free or at a nominal price. This covers hyperbaric treatment only, so it's still a good idea to have some other kind of insurance which can cover hospital bills and transportation. DAN insurance is probably the best (see page 175 for details).

There are also chambers available in Bangkok, but since most of the people dive in southern Thailand, you would probably be transported to Phuket as a first choice—unless you are diving in Pattaya. In general, you should dive conservatively, perform long safety stops, and wait a reasonable amount of time (24 hours is recommended) before flying after diving.

Money exchange

Until recently, the Thai baht remained very steady against the U.S. dollar. In 1996 the baht, along with every other Asian currency, started changing daily against most major currencies. Only time will tell if currencies stabilize again. As of this writing, at an exchange rate of US$1=Baht 36.13, Thailand represents a bargain for those traveling with U.S. or European currencies.

Changing money is easy, except in extremely remote areas (where you probably don't need much money anyway). Credit cards are widely accepted and dive centers normally do not add a service charge, though many hotels and other shops will.

Clothing

Although shorts and T-shirts are appropriate for dive boats and the beaches, Thais tend to dress more formally, and are actually offended by revealing clothing, especially when worn by women. Try to be aware of your surroundings, and avoid given offense. Topless and nude sunbathing are officially against the law, but they are widespread, especially in backpacker's hangouts. Thai people are very forgiving, but this does not mean these practices are accepted. Especially if you are on a beach with a majority of Thais, please wear a bathing suit.

Weather

Thailand has three seasons; cool, hot, and rainy. The best time to visit the west coast is between October and May; the best time to visit the east coast is February to August. The summer months of July and August are usually very pleasant, although it tends to rain in the evenings. September is not the best time on the islands, as it tends to be rainy and the seas are generally too rough for swimming or diving.

Most of the good dive sites are on islands far enough offshore to be unaffected by runoff, and rain makes no difference to the water clarity. Visibility in the Similans, for example, is actually greatest during the summer months—despite the evening rains.

Accommodations

Thailand has some of the best hotels in the world, and service is often of the highest standard. Thailand is a country with many levels of economy, and the choice of what class you want to fit into is definitely yours. Divers generally select one of the many inexpensive and comfortable guest houses or bungalows, although fancy hotels are certainly available.

On the islands, room rates range from 200–1,000 baht per night ($5–$28 at the time of this writing) for a basic bungalow with cold water and a fan to 1,500–2,500 baht ($40–$70) for a more comfortable hotel with hot water and air-conditioning. If you want to hang out

in luxury with the heavy players, figure 12,000 baht ($300) a night or more. If you are interested in the more expensive hotels, booking in advance through an agent can save you up to 50 percent.

Food

Thai cuisine is famous the world-over for its remarkable variety and often blistering flavour. Experiment as often as you can. Southern Thailand—where the diving happens—is famous for its fresh seafood. Food is usually very inexpensive, but like everywhere in the world, you can pay more for atmosphere.

Rice is the staple, and is served with almost every dish that is ordered here. Many different varieties of rice are available, depending on what kind of food you're ordering. Curries are absolutely fantastic in Thailand, and vary in degree of spicyness from mild and sweet to high-powered and fiery.

Quite often the best food available is right off the street. Thais are extremely creative in business, and it is common to see Thai families set up a portable restaurant on a street corner. Some will have a more permanent *kwait diaw* (noodle) shop on the sidewalk. This type of food is often fresher that what you will find in the more expensive restaurants because the food stalls have no refridgerators, and must buy their ingredients fresh everyday. Above all, don't be afraid to experiment, even if that means trying the fried silk-worms (astonishingly tasty with a cold Singha beer).

For those of you with more traditional tastes, in all the tourist areas most international cuisines are available, including American steak, Italian pasta, German schnitzel, and Swedish meatballs. McDonalds, if you must, is also available country wide.

Thailand is famous for its fruits, and even if you've traveled widely in the tropics, you will see fruits here that you have never encountered before. Thais have very creative ways to prepare fruit dishes, and the best season for unusual fruit is March–September. A favorite, and delicious, spring-time dish is *kao neaow matmuang,* a concoction of fresh mango slices on a bed of rice marinated in coconut milk overnight. You should also try the durian, an ugly and horrible-smelling fruit that Thais insist is the best fruit in the universe. See for yourself.

Live-aboard boats in Thailand offer some of the finest food you'll find, and often people come back time and time again not only for the diving, but for the incredible meals that are served on board.

Dive operators

Professional diving services are the norm in Thailand. The diving industry has exploded over the past five years or so and the standard of service and professionalism in Thailand is unequaled in Southeast Asia. Most dive centers are affiliated with PADI, but SSI and NAUI instruction are available in many places. Prices vary depending on what you are doing, where you are going, and how comfortable you want to be.

It is always best to contact diving centers to arrange your holiday before arriving, since at certain times of the year—especially in Phuket—dive boats are frequently full. If you are planning to join a live-aboard to the Andaman Islands, Burma Banks, or the Similan Islands, booking ahead is essential.

Most diving activities are supervised by a diving guide, either Thai or *falang* (Western foreigner, pronounced "FAH-lahng" in Thai) who speak a variety of languages. If you are a beginner, it is generally suggested that you find out as much about the dive site and the guide as possible before booking. Not all dive sites in Thailand are suitable for beginners, and like anywhere, not all guides are as competent as others; it pays to look around.

On the longer journeys—which attract more experienced divers—more freedom is usually given to the individual diver, although most outfits discourage dives past 40 meters.

All the listed dive centers offer beginning dive courses, and some offer advanced and professional-level instruction. All courses are generally of high quality, and the prices are reasonable. One advantage of learning in Thailand is that the class size is small—typically 4–6 students, or even fewer.

Environmental considerations

Protecting the environment is a fairly new concept in Thailand (and all of Southeast Asia), but fortunately more and more people are beginning be aware of the value of Thailand's unique natural environment, and more importantly, starting to do something about preserving it. Divers have long been aware of damage to coral reefs through dynamite fishing and anchoring, but only recently have dive centers starting thinking about the damage that can be done by divers themselves.

Thailand now has some of the most environmentally progressive dive shops in the world, which has helped keep our reefs healthy and beautiful.

When diving here, please try to respect the wishes of the diving community by not gathering or collecting any corals or shells, even from the beaches. Of course, never buy marine items from shell shops, as this only encourages the proprietors to order more stock.

Please do not spear fish. Although some argue that spearfishing is not damaging because it is selective, it tends to frighten fish and make them unapproachable. Also, since spearfishing is selective, the pressure is felt only on larger animals, and only on certain species. This can upset the ecological balance of the reef.

On land, you'll find that like in most countries, Thailand has its share of plastic garbage. Although this is a world-wide problem, make an effort to avoid using the stuff. Take your own bag or backpack to the store, and buy a canteen or reusable plastic container to hold drinking water during trips to the beach (your hotel will be more than happy to fill this up for you, especially if you explain why you are doing it this way). Think about where this plastic will end up. Don't take an out of sight, out of mind attitude, because you just may see that bottle washed up on your favourite beach the next day.

Finally, most islands in Thailand have a year-round fresh water shortage. Please do not waste water. You may see green tropical foliage surrounding you, but there is very little water in the ground. Shorten your showers, turn off the water while shaving, and generally be conscious of water use.

Bangkok City code: 02

Arriving by Air

Again, many connecting flights are available out of Don Muang Airport. Check with your travel agent for schedules and destinations. Reservations are recommended almost all year around.

Ground transportation

Book your taxi at one of the offices inside the airport—ignore touts. Fares to downtown run about 250–350 baht. For those who want to save this fare, walk across the overpass to the bus stop and take a bus into town for almost nothing (less than 15 baht). Be warned, however, that this takes a long time. A train is also available for around 20 baht, but you will be hard-pressed to get anyone in the airport to explain this option to you. The train station is visible from the overpass on the departure level. Free transport is available from the domestic terminal to the international, and vice versa. Do not be fooled into paying upwards of 150 baht for this short journey.

Metered taxis are available throughout Bangkok, and are extremely comfortable (air-conditioned) and convenient. Depending on the time of day, it can cost as little as 120 baht to get you back to the airport from downtown. Metered taxis are not available in the provinces, or in tourist destinations such as Phuket or Koh Samui. Make sure the meter is on before you start your journey, and if no meter is available, discuss the price before you begin your journey. Bargaining is possible in many instances, but keep smiling!

Phuket City code: 076

Some 890 km south of the capital, Phuket is accessible by land and air. Frequent daily buses ply the route from Bangkok. Fares cost as little 200 baht for the 14-hour journey in a non-airconditioned bus; 450 baht for a seat in a VIP airconditioned bus. Buses depart from the Southern Bus Terminal, Sanitwongse Road, in Bangkok and arrive in Phuket Town at the bus station on Phang-Nga Road.

Trains also connect Bangkok with Surat Thani (6 hours northeast of Phuket) and Hat Yai (8 hours southeast of Phuket) in the south of Thailand. From these points travelers can catch an inter-provincial bus to Phuket. Total cost of train and bus is about 500 baht.

At least eight flights daily connect Bangkok's Don Muang Domestic Airport with Phuket. Cost of a single ticket is 2,000 baht. Reservations in Bangkok at Tel: 66-2/280-0070; in Phuket at Tel: 66-76/211-195. In addition, Phuket's modern international airport welcomes flights from more than 12 international destinations including two daily flights from Singapore.

Accommodations and food

Phuket has probably the widest range of accommodation anywhere in Thailand, from exclusive lodging at the Aman Puri Resort for more than $1,000 per day to multiple local guest houses for often less than $4 per day— and everything in between. The most popular (and most crowded) beach is Patong, the center for entertainment, shopping and night life. To the south you'll find Kata-Karon, which is quieter and classier, and the home of Club Med. An integrated resort near the airport offers first-class international hotels and many amenities for the business traveler. These include the Sheraton, Laguna Beach Resort, and the Dusit Laguna, all of which will spoil you to your heart's content.

Food is wonderful, diverse, and readily available from noodle shops on street corners, local seafood restaurants right on the ocean, and international-style continental restaurants that will make you feel as if you've never left home. And yes, we finally have a McDonalds for those of you who insist, right in Patong Beach.

Phuket is most famous for its seafood for obvious reasons. However it is not just the availability of seafood that makes it popular. Phuket's locals have many exciting, special recipes and preparation techniques that motivate even Thais from Bangkok to make that special trip to Phuket.

Dive operators

Most of Phuket's diving centers offer one-day trips to the Racha Islands, Shark Point, King Cruiser Wreck, and Koh Phi Phi. In addition, most of the dive centers listed here can provide you with live-aboard diving to the Similan Islands and beyond, as well as Burma. Some of these centers can arrange charters to the Andaman Islands as well.

All of the dive centers here offer excellent diving instruction and many of them offer courses all the way up to the instructor level. Underwater photography courses are available, especially on the better live-aboard dive boats, some of which have on-board professional photographers.

Phuket is Thailand's center for live-aboard diving, and several of the operators offer boats that cater to a very select group of divers. These boats feature modern navigational systems, international radio communications and safety features, and the stability to travel in the open ocean. They also offer first-class service, crew, accommodation, and meals.

Prices in Phuket for a two-dive day trip are pretty much fixed at $70–$100, which includes hotel pick-up, lunch, tanks and weights, and a qualified divemaster. Two-day trips are just over double this—about $160—and include food and accommodation, a night dive, and a total of at least four day dives. Gear rental runs $20–$30 per day. Boats certainly vary in quality, so it's best to check with individual dive centers for their particular package.

Live-aboard prices vary dramatically between shops—and the services, destinations, and boats vary dramatically as well. Expect to pay a minimum of $100 per day for journeys to the Similan Islands on a basic boat, and between $180 and $350 a day for trips to the Burma Banks or Andaman Islands on a very comfortable boat. The more comfortable you want to be, the safer you want to be, and the further you want to go—the more you pay.

The following operators, listed in alphabetical order, are recommended:

Dive Asia 121/10 Mu 4 Patak Road, P.O. Box 70, Kata Beach, Phuket 83100, Thailand. Tel: 66-76/330598, Fax: 66-76/284033.
E-mail: info@diveasia.com
Web: diveasia.com
Phuket's first PADI 5 Star CDC Center. Offers live-aboard cruises, day trips, PADI courses and IDC/CDC programs..

Dive Asia-Pacific P. O. Box 244, Phuket, 83000. Tel: 66-76/263-732, Fax: 66-76/263-733.
E-mail: info@dive-asiapacific.com
Web: dive-asiapacific.com
Full service, long range live-aboard diving to the Andaman Sea, Indonesia, and elsewhere in the Asia Pacific region.

Fantasea Divers P.O. Box 20, Patong Beach, 83150, Phuket. Tel: 66-76/340-088, Fax: 66-76/340-309.
E-mail: info@fantasea.net
Web: fantasea.net
In business since 1979, and very experienced. 7 to 10 day live-aboard cruises in Thailand and to Burma.

Genesis Liveaboards PO Box 16, 83100, Phuket. Tel: 66-76/340-088, Fax: 66-76/340-309.
E-mail: info@genesis1phuket.com
Web: genesis1phuket.com
The Genesis 1 is Thailand's premier live-aboard and the outfit offers luxurious cruises to Thailand and Burma.

High Class Adventures Phuket 64/3 Bangla Square, Patong, 83150, Phuket. Tel: 66-76/344-337, Fax: 66-76/344-337.
E-mail: highclas@loxinfo.co.th
Web: phuket-traveller.com/highclass

Live-aboard diving to Burma and Thailand; two live-aboard boats, one of these for very large groups. Diving instruction.

Kontiki Diving School 66/2 Patak Road, Mu 3; Karon 83100, Phuket. Tel: 66-76/396-312; Fax: 66-76/396-313.
E-mail: kontiki@loxinfo.co.th
Web: kon-tiki-diving.com
Daytrips, live-aboards. Education from introductory to instructor.

Santana 6 Sawatderak Road, Patong 83150, Phuket. Tel: 66-76/294-220, Fax: 66-76/340-360.
E-mail: asia@santanaphuket.com
Web: santanaphuket.com
20 years experience, customer service and safety a priority, small groups, two comfortable live-aboard dive boats.

Scuba Cat Diving P.O. Box 316 83000, Phuket. Tel: 66-76/293-120, Fax: 66-76/293-122.
E-mail: info@scubacat.com
Web: scubacat.com
One of Phuket's largest PADI dive centers and dive fleets, offering quality day and live-aboard trips.

Siam Dive n' Sail 121/9 Patak Road, Mu 4, Karon 83100. Tel: 66-76/330-967, Fax: 66-76/330-990.
E-mail: info@siamdivers.com
Web: siamdivers.com
Dive center owned by the author of the Thailand section. Most complete web site on live-aboard diving in Thailand and Burma.

South East Asia Divers PO Box 15, Patong, 83150, Phuket. Tel: 66-76/344-022, Fax: 66-76/342-530. PADI 5-Star IDC offering live-aboards, day trips and courses.

South East Asia Liveaboards 225 Ratutit 200 Year Road, Patong, 83150. Tel: 66-76/340-406, Fax: 66-76/340-586.
E-mail: info@sealiveaboards.com
Web: sealiveaboards.com
Sailing and diving live-aboards to Thailand and the Mergui Archipelago; charters to the Andaman Islands; Canoeing in Mergui.

Diving the Burma Banks

Your dive operator will explain the ways and what fors of a trip to the Mergui Archipelago, as they will certainly change, but as of January, 1999, this is how it stands:

Some live-aboard trips will depart from and return to Phuket and spend at least two days diving in Thailand on the way up and back. Other trips will depart from Kawthaung (Victoria Point) in Myanmar (Burma).

There are two ways to get to Kawthaung. First, there are daily flights from Bangkok to Ranong in Thailand (7:10 am departure) via Bangkok Airways. From there the dive center will make arrangements to take you to a boat which will take you across in about 20 minutes to Victoria Point. Second, the dive shop may arrange to pick you up in Phuket for the five-hour drive by minibus or taxi to Ranong, where again, you would cross the channel into Burma.

The Burmese immigration officials require that you bring your passport (and a photocopy of it) and pay a fee—currently $85 to dive the southern area (Burma Banks, Western Rocky, and the Twins) and $130 to dive the northern areas, including Black Rock and the Torres Islands. Only U.S. cash will be accepted. These fees, not included by the operator because they are subject to change, cover a Burmese guide, national park and mooring fees, and immigration charges. For more details, please contact your operator.

Ko Phi Phi City code: 075
Some operators have mobile phones.

Regular ferries and hydrofoil services link Phi Phi with Phuket. Departures from the deep-sea harbor. Most ferries leave around 9 am and take between 90 minutes and 2 hours to reach the island.

Accommodations and food

Places to stay vary widely in Koh Phi Phi as well, though it is still dominated by bamboo-style bungalows which run less than $12 per night. On the northern shore of Phi Phi, however, four resorts offer air-conditioned rooms, first class restaurants, a feel of exclusivity, and fresh-water swimming pools. These run $80–$150 per night.

As many western foreigners have settled on the island, the food available varies from traditional Thai and seafood restaurants to hamburger joints with black and white checked floors. Authentic Italian pizza and pasta are readily available, as are steaks and seafood. You name it, they have it.

Dive operators

Some diving centres here in Koh Phi Phi now have larger boats to take you to the local sites and to areas further away like Trang and even the Similan Islands. Although the boats are not quite up to the standards of Phuket's boats, they are certainly more comfortable and safer than they were just a few years ago.

Most of the diving shops are connected with the PADI training organization and at the time of this writing there are two PADI 5-star dive centers on the island. NAUI and SSI instruction are available on the island as well. Although the majority of the dive centres are professionally run and prices do not differ much between them, as a beginner, a student, or as a serious diver who wants good information about marine life, it pays to check around before committing to a course or diving trip. Bear in mind that you generally get what you pay for, and the quality of instruction and guide service may well be more important than the price.

Day trip prices average about $40 per diving day (two dives), and equipment rental is approximately $20 per day. Tanks and weights are normally included.

The following operators, listed in alphabetical order, are recommended. Note: Since the island is so small, if you choose to write to any of these diving center just write: the name of the shop, the general location (e.g. Tonsai Bay), Krabi 81000, Thailand.

Moskito Diving Phi Phi Island, Tonsai Bay, 111 Moo 7, Krabi, 81000. Tel: 66-1/229-2802, Cell: 66-1/229-1361, Fax: 66-75/217-106.
E-mail: moskitodiving@hotmail.com
Longest running dive business on the island (1987). PADI Dive Center. Day trips, free "Discover Scuba Diving" experience in their miniature indoor pool.

Pee Pee Dragon Diving Just outside the village in Ton Sai Bay. Tel: 66-75/381-304. PADI instruction, daily dive trips. Three-day trips to the Similan Islands and two-day trips to Hin Daeng.

Pee Pee Scuba Diving Centre Ton Sai Bay. PADI instruction, daily trips. By speed boat to Koh Ha, Koh Rok and Hin Daeng.

Sea Frog Diving Ton Sai Bay; Tel: 66-75/261-6737, Fax: 66-75/259-7553. Daily diving trips. Can arrange diving in the Similan Islands and Koh Tao as well as Koh Phi Phi.

Ko Samui City code: 077

Visitors to Ko Samui have a choice of ways of reaching the island. For years they have arrived at Surat Thani by bus or train, and taken a boat from either Ban Don or nearby Donsak to Samui, and in some cases onward to Ko Pha Ngan. The cost for the 1-hour journey by express boat from Ban Don to Samui is 105 baht ($3). Alternatively travelers may fly from Bangkok to Ko Samui with Bangkok Airways. There are at least four flights a day, and the 1-hour trip costs 2,080 baht ($58). Another option is to fly Bangkok to Surat Thani with Thai Airways International and take the boat to Ko Samui. This costs around 1,815 baht ($50). Lastly, Bangkok Airways flies at least once a day between Phuket and Ko Samui. The cost of this short flight is 1,210 baht ($34).

Accommodations and food

Samui, like Phuket, has an incredible range of accommodation available. There are still many places with huts right on the beach for sometimes less than $4. And there are incredibly expensive, luxurious accommodations as well. You can probably still spend more money in Phuket if that's your style, but the difference is not much. One very delightful thing about much of the accommodation in Samui is that the hotels have tried to maintain the traditional Thai architectural style, with huge slanting roofs and lots of wood. Even the airport is built in this way, and it makes a charming first impression when you arrive. At the time of this writing, there are no high-rise Miami Beach–style hotels, and let's hope it stays that way.

As in all tourist centers in Thailand, food is available to suit any palate. Samui has great little beach-side restaurants that normally show videos in the evenings, and many little funky places run by both *falang* and Thais that serve everything from great pasta to Muslim vegetarian food to pizza. Some of the late-night food carts—restaurants on motorcycles—that hang about outside the discos after midnight offer great barbecued chicken, spring rolls, and deep fried everything. This is just the thing to eat after a few too many Singha beers.

Dive operators

All of Koh Samui's dive centers offer high-quality diving courses and are well organized and reliable. Your diving trips are always supervised by a professional divemaster or instructor.

Travel times to the different destinations such as Sail Rock and the marine park are anywhere between two and three hours. Prices do not vary significantly between the operators unless a speed boat is involved. The average two-dive day trip includes transportation, tanks and weights, and a divemaster, and costs around $70. Gear rental is about $20. Prices are sometimes lower during the low tourist season between August and January. Most operators now also arrange diving trips to Koh Tao, as well as nearby Koh Phangngan.

The following operators, listed in alphabetical order, are recommended:

Koh Samui International Diving Centre Malibu Beach resort Chaweng Beach, Koh Samui. Tel: 66-77/422-386; Fax: 66-77/231-242. PADI Five star CDC center that offers day trips and courses.

The Dive Shop PO Box 67, Koh Samui 84140. Fax: 66-77/422-114. Daily diving tours to marine park, Koh Tao, Sail Rock. PADI diving courses.

Ko Tao City code: 077

Ko Tao is easily accessible from Ko Phangngan by daily ferry, weather permitting. Cost is around 150 baht ($4) each way. A speed boat runs every morning from Chumpon and takes 2 hours—400 baht ($11) each way. Buy tickets at the travel agent just outside the train station, and take a local bus as directions to the pier are impossible for a non-Thai speaker.

Accommodations and food

Koh Tao's bungalows tend to be basic, but that, like everywhere else, is changing fast. Most of the places now have bathrooms inside the rooms, and air-conditioning is getting more common. The most up-market hotel in Koh Tao is the Koh Tao Cottages which feature such luxuries as air-conditioning and hot showers. Still, in most places electricity is not available until 6 pm and in some places not at all. When on Koh Tao, expect to rough it a little bit.

Although there are not many varieties of

restaurants on the island, most of the places serve good, if basic food. Don't expect USDA prime imported beef on any of the tables here. There is a great sandwich shop right in the village of Mae Haad. Ask the locals which is the current favorite, as places open and close all of the time. Every time I visit the island there's a new happening spot.

Dive operators

Koh Tao now has a number of PADI 5-star IDC dive centers, and all shops offer high quality instruction. The boats are becoming better and better on the island as well. Some boats are even equipped with GPS navigation systems, which enable the guides to find hidden underwater pinnacles—normally the best sites—consistently and quickly.

Trip prices hover around $40 per two-tank dive with equipment rental about $20 for the day. Tanks and weights are normally included in the price.

The following operators, listed in alphabetical order, are recommended:

Ban's Diving Centre #1 Main Street, Koh Tao, Surat Thani 84280. Tel: 66-1/725-0181 (mobile phone); Fax: 66-77/377-057. PADI 5-Star dive center. Daily diving tours, overnight trips, courses.

Big Blue Diving Centre 20/1 Moo 1 Koh Tao, Surat Thani 84280. Tel: 66-1/213-9440 (mobile phone); Fax: 66-1/213-9440.
E-mail: info@bigbluediving.com
Web: bigbluediving.com
PADI 5-star IDC center and resort. Two shops, one catering to Japanese divers. Two larger dive boats and one speed boat for 8 divers.

Koh Samui International Diving Centre Mae Haad, Koh Tao, Surat Thani 84280. Tel: 66-77/422-386; Fax: 66-77/231-242. PADI 5-star CDC center. Day trips and courses.

Koh Tao Divers 8 Mu 2, Koh Tao, Surat Thani 84280; Tel: 66-1/725-0828 (mobile phone) or 66-77/377-196. Daily diving tours, special trips to off-shore sites. Courses. Boat salvage specialists.

Master Diver 2 Main Street, Mae Haad, Koh Tao, Surat Thani 84280. Tel: 66-1/725-0828 (mobile). Day trips, underwater video, computer dives, equipment repair workshop, courses.

Pattaya
City code: 038 (Same for Jomtien)

Air-conditioned buses link Pattaya with both Don Muang International Airport and the center of Bangkok. Airconditioned and non-airconditioned buses from Bangkok depart from the Ekamai Bus Terminal, Sukhumvit Road, every half hour and take an average of just under 2 hours to make the journey.

Accommodations and food

Pattaya was the first tourist resort built in Thailand, and its got everything, including the very posh Royal Cliff Resort. For those on a budget, there are also many, many small guest houses, often run by foreigners, which are available for less than $20 per night. Since Pattaya is so big, they always have hotel rooms available and it pays to check with travel agents to find the best deals.

Although just a few years back Pattaya had acquired a bad reputation, the government has done a good job cleaning up the town, and it's again a very nice place to visit.

Like Phuket, Samui, and Bangkok, Pattaya has every kind of food available. Like Bangkok, Pattaya is a 24-hour city, and street vendors sell everything from fresh tropical fruit to Chinese noodles, and Indian curries to fried silk-worms. Eating off the carts on the streets, like everywhere in Thailand, is where you'll find the most varieties of food prepared in the most local way. You'll also find great seafood and steak houses in Pattaya along with wonderful Japanese restaurants.

And yes, there are McDonalds, Pizza Hut, Kentucky Fried Chicken, Dunkin' Donuts and all the rest of the chains. Why people eat this stuff when they are in the country with the best food in all the world I'll never know, but if you've got that homesick feeling, in Pattaya you may indulge.

Dive operators

This small city was the first place in Thailand to develop a diving industry, and most of the operators are well-established. The centers listed below all offer quality diving instruction. Most of their business comes from Bangkok, so the weekends in Pattaya can be quite crowded, and it pays to book ahead. Some of the shops offer special weekend dives or live-aboard trips which get the working diver back at work early Monday morning.

Because many of the clients of the Pattaya operators are regular divers coming in from Bangkok who own their own tanks and weights, boat prices are generally less than in other places, but equipment rental is more. If you need equipment it's about the same, around $60 to $80 for two-tank dives, but if you have all of your own equipment, diving in Pattaya can be quite inexpensive.

Pattaya's operators are just beginning to get into the live-aboard diving scene, and are now offering trips to areas that up to now were unreachable. Prices range from $60 to $90 per day and some offer unlimited diving.

The following operators, listed in alphabetical order, are recommend:

Aquanauts Diving Centre 437/17 moo 9 Soi Yodsak, Pattaya Beach Road, Pattaya City 20260, Chonburi. Tel 66-38/361724, Fax: 66-38/421-097.

E-mail: aquanaut@loxinfo.co.th
Specializes in trips to the Vertical wreck and Koh Chang National Marine park. They also have a new second shop in Pattayaland Soi 1, Pattaya Beach road.

Mermaid's Sea Sports Centre Soi White House, Jomtien Beach, Pattaya, Chonburi 20260; Tel: 66-38/232-219, Fax: 66-38/232-221.

E-mail: steve@mermaiddive.com
Web: mermaiddive.com
Specializes in technical diving and wreck exploration in the Gulf of Thailand.

Seafari Sports Centre 359/2 Soi 5, Pattaya, Chonburi; Tel: 66-38/429-253, Fax: 66-38/424-708. PADI 5-star IDC center. Day trips, wreck diving. Has a center in Chumpon as well.

Scubamoose Divecenter 224/2 Soi 12 Moo 10 Pattaya 20260 Chonburi. Tel: 66-38/424-205; Fax, 66-38/424-205.

E-mail: scubamos@loxinfo.co.th
Swedish owned, Aqualung equipment sales and service, PADI courses, wreck trips, Nitrox, technical diving.

Andaman Islands

There is one dive center in the Andaman Islands themselves. This dive shop works out of the Bay Island Resort in Port Blair, offers instruction and one day trips to the local marine park, and has been in business since 1993. Prices are relatively the same as in Thailand for both diving and instruction.

Accommodations and food

There are several hotels in the Andamans, but the only real place to stay is the Bay Island Hotel located just above Port Blair in the hills. This is also about the only place to eat on the island as well, except if you're on a live-aboard boat of course. The hotel costs anywhere from $40 up to $80 depending on the package they put together for you, the size and quality of your room, and whether or not you prefer to pay for your meals all in one go. They do have a swimming pool, the staff are very helpful and friendly (although service is only fair), and the rooms are basic, but comfortable. The restaurant and many of the rooms overlook the harbor of Port Blair, a truly beautiful view.

The food at the hotel is pretty good; I wouldn't call it gourmet, but the curries are wonderful and they usually set up a buffet in the evenings that features food from all over the world. There is not really any choice— the street carts and curry shops don't look too healthy, and there are no proper restaurants in Port Blair. This, I'm sure, will change.

Dive operators

At the time of this writing, the only way to dive the offshore areas in the Andamans are on a live-aboard boat from Thailand. Anil Chowdhary, the owner of the center in Port Blair, has plans to develop his own live-aboard program. However, the dive centers listed below in Phuket offer extended diving cruises to the best sites as of today. Prices range from about $180 to $300 per day.

Siam Diving Center 121/9 Patak Road, Mu 4, Karon 83100, Phuket. Tel: 66-76/330-936, Fax: 66-76/330-608. 6 and 12 day cruises aboard a 21-meter power yacht.

Southeast Asia Divers Patong Beach, Phuket. Tel: 66-76/340-406, Fax: 66-76/340-586. 8 and 15 day cruises aboard sailing yachts, combining diving and sailing.

The Andaman Scuba Diving Society Bay Island Hotel, Marine Hill, Port Blair, Andaman Islands 744101, India. Tel: 91-3192-21227; Fax: 91-3192-21389. Day trips, PADI instruction. Often the telephones are not clear and don't connect easily when you call from overseas. Just keep trying.

Further Reading

In addition to a good guide, a diver is probably most interested in a fish identification book, to help make some order out of the more than 2,500 species swimming around the reefs of Indonesia. Two excellent resources recently became available.

Reef Fishes

Reef Fishes of the World, by Ewald Lieske and Robert Myers (Periplus Editions, 1994), is a comprehensive guide to over 2,000 species with 2,500 color illustrations. It enables divers and snorkelers to identify the inhabitants of coral reefs wherever they are in the world.

Tropical Reef Fishes of the Western Pacific—Indonesia and Adjacent Waters, by Rudie H. Kuiter is the first extensive guide to the reef fishes of Indonesia.

This compact, handsome book is a manageable 300 pages long, and includes 1,300 excellent color photographs, illustrating 1,027 species including males, females and juveniles, where color or morphological differences exist. *Tropical Reef Fishes* covers more than 50 families of reef fishes, just about every species you are likely to see around Indonesia's reefs down to about 30 meters.

This is an indispensable work. Kuiter is one of the leading authorities on Pacific reef fishes.

Micronesian Reef Fishes

Micronesian Reef Fishes: A Practical Guide to the Identification of the Inshore Marine Fishes of the Tropical Central and Western Pacific, 2d ed., by Robert F. Myers, also belongs in the library of every diver in Indonesia. While Myers has not sought to write a book about Indonesian species, there is a great deal of overlap in the faunas of the two regions, and well over 90 percent of the species discussed can be found in Indonesia.

Myers' book is a model of accuracy and detail, with clear color photos of more than 1,000 species, complete meristics, and a dense 50–100 word description of the habitat and behavior of each species.

Other Works of Interest

The grandfather of all Indonesian fish guides is of course Bleeker's *Atlas Ichthyologique.* It is still very accurate, although not even close to being portable, or even available. Another very valuable book that became available as we were in production is Gerald R. Allen's *Damselfishes of the World.* This fine book describes and illustrates some 321 damselfish, all that are currently known, including 16 new species. Full meristics, and range and habitat descriptions of all the species are included.

The most available series of books on Indo-Pacific reef life in the United States are those put out by Tropical Fish Hobbyist publications in New Jersey. Unfortunately, however, these books are almost universally awful. They are really badly edited, with misidentified photos and poor organization.

Fishes

Allen, Gerald R. *Butterfly and Angelfishes of the World.* New York: Wiley Interscience, 1979.

——*Damselfishes of the World.* Hong Kong: Mergus, 1991. (Distributed in the United States by Aquarium Systems, 8141 Tyler Blvd., Mentor OH 44060.)

Allen, Gerald R. and Roger C. Steene. *Reef Fishes of the Indian Ocean* (Pacific Marine Fishes, Book 10). Neptune, NJ: T.F.H. Publications, 1988.

Bleeker, Pieter. *Atlas Ichthyologique des Indes Orientales Neerlandaises* (9 volumes). Amsterdam, 1877. (Dr. Bleeker's classic "Atlas." Out of print and very valuable. Look for it at a good library.)

Burgess, Warren E. *Atlas of Marine Aquarium Fishes.* Neptune, NJ: T.F.H. Publications,

1988. (Full of inaccuracies and misidentified photos; no scientific value.)

Burgess, Warren E. and Herbert R. Axelrod. *Fishes of the Great Barrier Reef* (Pacific Marine Fishes, Book 7). Neptune, NJ: T.F.H. Publications. 1975.

——*Fishes of Melanesia* (Pacific Marine Fishes Book 7). Neptune, NJ: T.F.H. Publications, 1975.

Carcasson, R. H. *A Guide to Coral Reef Fishes of the Indian and West Pacific Regions.* London: Collins, 1977. (Out of date, hard to recognize fishes from the drawings.)

Myers, Robert F. *Micronesian Reef Fishes: A Practical Guide to the Identification of the Inshore Marine Fishes of the Tropical Central and Western Pacific, 2d ed.* Guam: Coral Graphics, 1991. (Excellent, see text above. Order through Coral Graphics, P.O. Box 21153, Guam Main Facility, Barrigada, Territory of Guam 96921.)

Nelson, J.S. *Fishes of the World.* New York: John Wiley & Sons, 1984.

Piesch, Ted and D.B. Grobecker. *Frogfishes of the World.* Stanford, CA: Stanford University Press, 1987.

Randall, John E., Gerald R. Allen and Roger Steene. *Fishes of the Great Barrier Reef and the Coral Sea.* Bathhurst, Australia: Crawford House Press, University of Hawaii Press, 1990.

Sawada, T. *Fishes in Indonesia.* Japan International Cooperation Agency, 1980.

Schuster W.H. and R.R. Djajadiredja. *Local Common Names for Indonesian Fishes.* Bandung, Java: N.V. Penerbit W. Van Hoeve, 1952.

Weber, M. and de Beaufort, L.F. *The Fishes of the Indo-Australian Archipelago* (11 volumes, 404–607 pages each). Leiden, E.J. Brill. 1913–1962.

Invertebrates

Debelius, Helmut. *Armoured Nights of the Sea.* Kernan Verlag, 1984.

Ditlev, Hans A. *A Field-Guide to the Reef-Building Corals of the Indo-Pacific.* Klampenborg: Scandinavian Science Press, 1980. (Good, compact volume.)

Randall, Richard H. and Robert F. Myers. *Guide to the Coastal Resources of Guam, vol. 2: the Corals.* Guam: University of Guam Press, 1983.

Usher, G.F. "Coral Reef Invertebrates in Indonesia." IUNC/WWF Report, 1984.

Walls, Jerry G., ed. *Encyclopedia of Marine Invertebrates.* Neptune, NJ:T.F.H. Publications, 1982. (The text of this 700-page book is often good. There are the usual mistakes with photos, however, and many of the names have not kept up with recent changes. A preponderance of the illustrations are Caribbean.)

Wells, Sue, *et al,* eds. *The IUNC Invertebrate Red Data Book.* Gland, Switzerland: International Union for Conservation of Nature and Natural Resources, 1983.

Wood, Elizabeth M. *Corals of the World.* Neptune, NJ: T.F.H. Publications, 1983.

Reef Ecology

Darwin, Charles. *The Structure and Distribution of Coral Reefs.* Tucson, AZ: University of Arizona Press, 1984.

——*The Voyage of the Beagle.* New York: Mentor (Penguin), 1988.

George, G. *Marine Life.* Sydney: Rigby Ltd, 1976 (also: New York: John Wiley & Sons).

Goreau, Thomas F., Nora I. Goreau and Thomas J. Goreau. "Corals and Coral Reefs," *Scientific American* vol. 241, 1979.

Henry, L.E. *Coral Reefs of Malaysia.* Kuala Lumpur: Longman, 1980.

Randall, Richard H. and L.G. Eldredge. *A Marine Survey Of The Shoalwater Habitats of Ambon, Pulau Pombo, Pulau Kasa and Pulau Babi.* Guam: University of Guam Marine Laboratory, 1983.

Salm, R.V. and M. Halim. *Marine Conservation Data Atlas.* IUNV/WWF Project 3108, 1984.

Soegiarto, A. and N. Polunin. "The Marine Environment Of Indonesia." A Report Prepared for the Government of the Republic of Indonesia, under the sponsorship of the IUNC and WWF, 1982.

Umbgrove, J.H.F. "Coral Reefs of the East Indies," *Bulletin Of The Geological Society of America,* vol. 58, 1947.

Wallace, Alfred Russel. *The Malay Archipelago.* Singapore: Oxford University Press, 1986.

Wells, Sue, *et al. Coral Reefs of The World* (3 volumes). Gland, Switzerland: United Nations Environmental Program, 1988.

Whitten, Anthony J., Muslimin Mustafa and Gregory S. Henderson. *The Ecology of Sulawesi.* Yogyakarta, Java: Gadjah Mada University Press, 1987.

Wyrtri, K. "Physical Oceanography of the Southeast Asian Waters, Naga Report Vol. 2." La Jolla, CA: University of California, Scripps Institute of Oceanography, 1961.

Index

Map Index